Jack O'Connor

JACK O'CONNOR
The Legendary Life of America's Greatest Gunwriter

by
Robert M. Anderson

with special contributions by
Eldon "Buck" Buckner

SAFARI PRESS INC

The trademark Safari Press ® is registered with the U.S. Patent and Trademark Office and in other countries.

Anderson, R.
Buckner, E.

Second edition

Safari Press Inc.
2002, Long Beach, California

ISBN 1-57157-254-6

Library of Congress Catalog Card Number: 2001096668

10 9 8 7 6 5 4 3 2 1

Readers wishing to receive the Safari Press catalog, featuring many fine books on big-game hunting, wingshooting, and sporting firearms, should write to Safari Press Inc., P.O. Box 3095, Long Beach, CA 90803, USA. Tel: (714) 894-9080 or visit our Web site at www.safaripress.com.

DEDICATION

For Tyler

CAUTION!

This book contains data on handloading and firearms that reflect the particular experiences of the authors. The authors and Jack O'Connor used specific firearms, ammunition, and reloading equipment under conditions not necessarily reported in the book. Under NO circumstances should the reader try to copy the loads mentioned in this book. The handloading of ammunition and the discharging of a firearm should never be attempted without the supervision of an adult experienced in both handloading and firearms. The publisher cannot accept responsibility for the firearms and handloading data in this book.

TABLE OF CONTENTS

FOREWORD

Jack once said to me after we'd been friends a few years:

When I went East shortly after you joined Alfred A. Knopf and stopped off at my publishers to meet the man who had been newly assigned as my editor, I was afraid I'd meet some fancy Eastern literary guy reeking of a Brahmin accent. Instead I met this Hoosier who knew a doubletree from a singletree and could also pronounce "Coues." I was some surprised!

Of course I had one advantage over him; I had read all of his books and also had followed his columns and articles in *Outdoor Life* for years. I already liked and admired this testy Arizonan. He, knowing of me, expected a typical "high falutin" Eastern editor instead of a not-too-changed Indiana farm boy. When Jack discovered that I was also a gun nut, hunter, and fisherman and was married to a woman who shared my interests, he relaxed some. I say "relaxed some," for Jack never quite got over being just a "leetle leery" of Easterners. He'd say "Hell, to me a middle-westerner is an 'Easterner.'"

I learned over the years, both from his writing and then from a growing friendship with the man himself, that Jack had a rare quality as a shooting expert: He was absolutely honest. I noted in his shooting column that if he was sent some new item to test by one of the arms and ammunition manufacturers, he didn't look for euphemisms to describe a faulty product. If, for example, one of the ammunition companies sent him samples of a new factory load to test, he'd tell his readers just what his benchrest tests told him. If a new load wouldn't group closer than four inches at a hundred yards, Jack reported just that. He didn't look under the bed for some excuse so he would not alienate an important advertiser in *Outdoor Life*. And the curious part of it was that the arms and ammunition people came to respect this straight-from-the-shoulder expert. They soon learned that the readers of Jack's magazine columns trusted Jack O'Connor. When advertisers in the magazine produced a truly good item, they knew that Jack O'Connor's favorable report would be heeded by their market.

This rugged honesty was characteristic of all of Jack's relations with *Outdoor Life*'s advertisers. When, for example, Jack was sent a new rifle to test, it was billed to him as either "on consignment" to be returned to the factory after the test or at generous discount in case Jack decided to keep the new model for his own. Even though Jack knew that the gun manufacturers would make no mention of a failure of an expert either to return the model or pay for it at the discount, Jack meticulously either returned it or paid for it. Many of his fellow experts did not.

So, it was very good news to me to discover that Jack's voice is not yet stilled nor will his exploits be forgotten, for this book by fellow hunters will put his professional and hunting life in a formal order. This biography not only lets the reader share Jack O'Connor's rich and varied hunting life but reveals where he came from and how he came to be what one of my guide friends referred to as "that huntin' perfessor."

In his own books we can all be thankful that he was a teacher of writing and literature as well as of guns and game. Jack had much to say and said it in a legacy of notable books. Now his rich and varied professional and hunting life are forever available to his friends and admirers in this fine biography.

Angus Cameron
East Hampton, MA
April, 2000

PREFACE

When I began the writing of this book, I foresaw it as a sort of start-to-finish biography of Jack O'Connor's life. But almost immediately I began to encounter various obstacles to its development along those lines. To begin with, O'Connor gave us a superb autobiographical account of his childhood in early Arizona in his own wonderful book, *Horse and Buggy West*. There is no way I could improve on this moving and in-depth book.

Also, I had hoped that more information about certain periods in Jack O'Connor's life would be forthcoming. Among these periods were his military career, his college days, his time spent as a newspaper reporter in Chicago, and his early life as a college professor. But those times are long gone, and little such information is available. Without it, recounting those early days would require a certain subjectivity that would inevitably lead to inaccuracies. Therefore, I have refrained from writing about these periods for the most part.

I feel that O'Connor's promising early career as a novelist has never received the attention it deserved. So a chapter is included that will, I hope, give readers an insight into what he might have been had he not gone on to become America's foremost gunwriter.

Because no account of Jack O'Connor's life would be complete without addressing his big-game experiences (his sheep-hunting career in particular), this book includes chapters that address these subjects in a manner that I hope will be unprecedented and unique to readers.

No one has previously created an in-depth account of Jack's many, many firearms—their origin, time of acquisition, history, usage, and final disposition. Eldon "Buck" Buckner's wonderful contribution on Jack's firearms will be enjoyed greatly by O'Connor fans.

Various other chapters should give a better insight into the man Jack O'Connor was. However, because one learns about O'Connor where and when one can, these chapters are of a rather eclectic nature and deal with significantly different themes. Consequently, this book will appear to lack something in continuity and rhythm. For that I apologize in advance. But to help offset the book's episodic and sometimes "jagged" nature, I have included a comprehensive and chronological timeline of most of the events of O'Connor's life.

ACKNOWLEDGMENTS

I extend my sincere gratitude to Bradford O'Connor, Catherine O'Connor, and Caroline O'Connor McCullam for their trust and confidence in me during this project. I have done my best to portray their father with dignity and respect. I am also grateful to Eldon "Buck" Buckner, the most knowledgeable O'Connor scholar of all, for his indispensable contributions to this book, for flying me all over the Northwest, and for his valued support. Thanks again to both Buck and his lovely wife, Hope, for their hospitality on several occasions. I am further grateful to my good friend, Dennis Campbell, executive director of the Grand Slam Club, for making available to me the extensive personal correspondence between Mr. O'Connor and Bob Housholder, the Grand Slam Club's founder. I also thank my ever-patient publisher Ludo Wurfbain and all the wonderful people at Safari Press for their tolerance of my many derailments, alibis, and near-endless procrastinations.

To Dr. Alison Tartt of Austin, Texas, for her always helpful suggestions; Mr. and Mrs. Henry Kaufman, Al Biesen, and Arthur C. Popham; the Weatherby Foundation International; library personnel at Washington State University, Sul Ross State University, Southern Methodist University, and the University of North Texas; and to Richard Beagle for help compliling the bibliography, thanks so much!

INTRODUCTION

In the first week of December 1925, my father, who was fifteen at the time, and his three older brothers made the daunting trip from their rural family farm near Dallas to the Texas Big Bend country for a desert mule deer hunt. Their plan was a very bold move for the time and not one entered into lightly. However, in late evening, after two days of seemingly endless travel, they arrived in tiny Alpine at the northeast corner of the Big Bend, where they spent the night.

Their accommodations were in what was called in those days a "tourist camp," really nothing more than a long shed, closed on only one side, under which cars could be sheltered. Usually the ground on the closed side of the shed, in front of the parked cars, was lined with hay. Travelers simply rolled out their bedrolls or blankets and slept on the hay—not exactly a Marriott arrangement.

Early the next morning, my father and uncles made the acquaintance of a young man who had parked and slept near them during the night. They remembered him as a "tall kid with wire-rimmed glasses, the darkest tan, the yellowest hair, and the greenest eyes" they had ever seen. They further remembered his khaki trousers, a brown leather bomber jacket, and a brown fedora hat he wore. One of my uncles thought him obviously educated, well-spoken, and very intense, with places to go in life and with something of a brash air about him. They also remembered something else: the Remington Model 14-A trombone-action rifle in caliber .25-20 he had with him.

That impressive kid of so long ago was Jack O'Connor.

Not much more than ten years later—in the mid-1930s, when O'Connor's articles with an occasional photo of him began to appear in various sporting magazines, especially *Outdoor Life*—my father and uncles remembered again. It was the kid from Alpine.

What O'Connor may have been doing there at the time is a mystery, as is a great deal of Jack's life. Ironically, in less than two years he would return to Alpine with his new bride, Eleanor, and live there for almost four years while he taught school. But on that early encounter, he was apparently just passing through on his way back to Arizona from somewhere. A day or so after my father and uncles met him, Jack used his .25-20 to kill one of the last lobo wolves ever seen in Texas along the road a few miles west of Van Horn.

By the time I was twelve years old, I had heard the story from my father and uncles many times. By the time I was fourteen, in 1959, I was a hardened O'Connor reader and fan. Such were my beginnings with Jack.

As this is written, it has been more than twenty-three years since Jack passed away. But legions of fans remain who relive his adventures in conversation, pay exorbitant prices to collect his books, and even fork over as much as twenty dollars for a single cartridge personally handloaded by Jack.

Of course, Jack O'Connor is known primarily for the body of his work at *Outdoor Life*. Beginning in 1934 and flowing continuously from 1937 until his *Outdoor Life* retirement in 1972— and afterward with *Petersen's Hunting*—his hundreds of monthly columns, departmental pieces, and feature stories redefined the gunwriting trade. He wrote with unflinching candor, objectivity, and wonderful communication skills. The things he said about guns and hunting were digestible and made sense. Looking back on Jack's career, it can truly be said that he single-handedly raised the standard for gunwriting to a level that no other writer, present or future, will ever be able to attain.

But Jack is gone, and with every passing day, more and more of his old fans are gone with him. His many books were never available in really large printings, and copies of any of them are worth a small mint today. As soon as such books are purchased by O'Connor collectors, that's it. These treasures won't be back in circulation and are gone for good. A few of his works have been reprinted, but not enough. Want to read some of Jack's original stuff in old issues of *Outdoor Life*? Good luck. Collections of *Outdoor Life* don't grow on trees. And sad as it may be, there is a whole new generation of hunters and shooters out there who do not really know Jack O'Connor at all. The lamentable truth for his many fans, current or potential, is that Jack's trail grows colder by the minute. Mention the name Jack O'Connor to many hunters and shooters of today, and they'll likely say, "Oh, yeah, the .270 guy!"

But defining this enormously diverse man by his attitude toward one rifle caliber is limiting in the extreme. In fact, *any* attempt to define Jack O'Connor is limiting and prone to error. Though O'Connor was enormously well informed and well read on a huge variety of topics, he was the most private of men. I believe I can comfortably say that I have read almost every word O'Connor ever put into print—with the possible exception of one or two very early manuscripts, a few short stories, and isolated book reviews that he did for various newspapers in the early 1930s. I have been fortunate to read many hundreds of his private letters and other personal correspondence spread over his entire life. Still I am mystified. Who, really, was he? To this day, Jack remains a giant intellectual iceberg, with only a small portion exposed to view. It was my original intent in this book to reveal the "personal" Jack. In a few isolated areas I have been able to do so. But I am sad to say that the real "down inside" Jack has continued to remain, for the most part, emotionally inaccessible.

His professional writing and hunting careers are something else again. In the course of the great deal of research that has gone into the writing of this book, many new revelations have come to light regarding O'Connor's writing and hunting activities. And even these raise new questions. Still, I believe readers will find a lot of new facts to digest about Jack's writing accomplishments and hunting adventures in the pages to follow.

Much of what has been written about O'Connor's sheep-hunting adventures is inaccurate. This book will discuss that facet of his life in depth and reveal that it really involved *two* very separate careers and two distinctly different hunting periods that overlapped by only a few years.

Jack's African and Asian hunting adventures are discussed from perspectives different from those in previous works, and I have included some pertinent background information as well as some of Jack's personal thoughts.

We'll take a look at some of Jack's professional and personal relationships, his absent-mindedness, his thoughts on religion, and the sad life and death of Jerry, Jack and Eleanor's eldest son.

Until now, there has been no thorough discussion of Jack's many firearms, how and when he obtained them, how he used them, and what their final disposition may have been. Eldon "Buck" Buckner, perhaps the best of all O'Connor scholars, has done a wonderful job with this formidable task. It is a unique feature of this book and one that gun lovers and O'Connor fans are sure to enjoy.

For the most part, I have declined to retell Jack's adventures in any great depth, for two reasons: First, Jack was *there* and I wasn't. Second, any attempt on my part to pinch-hit for Jack O'Connor would be presumptuous indeed. And as scarce as Jack's books are today, they can still be had and anyone interested in reading accounts of his hunts or other activities needs to read the words of the master himself. Of course, within this book are numerous thumbnail versions of many of his hunts. But most of these are told from different perspectives and spiced with anecdotes, sidebar stories, behind-the-scenes happenings, unique twists, and new information thrown in.

As for many of Jack's hunting accounts, this book functions as a reference work of sorts, inasmuch as I have supplied the source location of many of his original stories in the pages of *Outdoor Life* or his various books. Of course, this book's coverage of certain places and certain subjects relies on Jack's own words because they are so "right-on," hilarious, or prophetic that they are essential to the proceedings. These direct O'Connor quotes range in length from a single sentence to longer accounts and have been excerpted from various O'Connor publications and sources.

There will be those who will, I'm sure, take me to task for not dismantling Jack O'Connor like a cheap watch. I see no purpose in this. Brad, Cathy, and Caroline—Jack and Eleanor's offspring—are proud, intelligent people who loved their parents and revere their memories. My commitment to them was to treat their father and mother with respect and dignity. Jack had his share of baggage. Most of us do. (Last time I checked, I had a suitcase or two myself!) But he was a proud, honorable, responsible man who was able, for the most part, to craft the life he wanted. There are many lessons to be learned from the life that Jack lived.

It is my sincere hope that O'Connor fans old and new will learn some things about him that they did not know and from which they will get a few laughs (some at Jack's expense!), and that they will emerge from this book with a newfound respect for the talents, energies, drive, and direction of this very interesting man. If so, then this book will have been successful.

Robert M. Anderson
The Eklund Hotel
Clayton, New Mexico
25 May 2001

ABOUT THE PHOTOGRAPHS

The photographs in this book are a mix of previously published and unpublished shots. Of course, many of the O'Connor's kill photos have been seen in previous publications and are the best that are available. Readers will note that many of the photographs feature inordinately long captions. This has been done because photographs offer such good focal points and provide excellent opportunities for description and other pertinent information. A great deal of research has gone into providing fresh and interesting information about each photograph.

At least one previously unpublished O'Connor book and several reprints of other O'Connor books have come out since Jack's death in January of 1978. Various photographs contained herein previously appeared in these other publications with captions that were in error. Every effort has been made to correct these errors with more detailed and accurate captions.

1

Cactus Jack: Classic Hunter of the Southwest

by Eldon "Buck" Buckner

Jack O'Connor was a genuine product of the old Southwest. At the time of his birth in the border town of Nogales, Arizona Territory, on 22 January 1902, the country was still pretty wooly around the edges. Less than two years earlier, Three-Fingered Jack Dunlap's gang had robbed the train at nearby Fairbank, and lawman Warren Earp was killed in a Willcox saloon. Just the year prior, the Arizona Rangers had been organized to help curb lawlessness. Jack's grandparents were of pioneer stock on both sides, and family members were involved in various ranching and business ventures in both Arizona and Mexico.

After Jack's parents divorced in 1907, his maternal grandfather, James Wiley Woolf of Tempe, and his Uncle Jim O'Connor became surrogate father figures and passed on their love of hunting to the youngster. It was on Jim O'Connor's Box O Ranch southeast of Florence that ten-year-old Jack bagged his first big game, a javelina, with a Model 92 Winchester Model .25-20. A couple years later, he shot his first desert mule deer buck in the same area, using an old .30-40 Krag he'd purchased for $1.50.

Jack's first experience with the dainty whitetails of the Southwest known as Coues deer occurred during the summer of 1919 in Sinaloa, Mexico, right after he graduated from high school in Tempe. By this time Jack had considerable shooting experience, having been in the Arizona National Guard since age fifteen and served in the regular army for two months until discharged due to chronic tuberculosis. One of Jack's uncles owned a sawmill in Sinaloa and hired Jack to be a truck driver. Young O'Connor proved so ill suited to this work that he was soon reassigned to a task for which he had more aptitude— shooting deer for the mill workers. For armament, Jack had his own Savage Model 99 .250-3000 and a Model 94 Winchester .30-30 salvaged from a recent Mexican Revolution battlefield. With a blond Mayo Indian boy as a companion, Jack shot lots of deer and had his first and only encounter with a jaguar. He also observed the greater effectiveness on the small deer of the higher-velocity .250-3000 bullet compared to the heavier and slower ones from the .30-30.

During the early 1920s, Jack accompanied a lion hunter on a northern Arizona scouting trip. The hunter's hounds struck a fresh lion track and soon disappeared, leaving Jack and his companion spurring their horses and popping brush to stay within hearing. When the dogs finally treed the tom lion in a scraggly juniper, Jack shot it with a .25-20 Winchester carbine. It was the only mountain lion he ever killed, for he felt, as did many others, that the real excitement of Southwest lion hunting is in the chase through spectacular country, not in the shooting of the cat.

Jack's first Arizona Coues whitetail was taken in the fall of 1923, shortly after he'd transferred to the University of Arizona at Tucson for his junior year. When deer season opened, Jack borrowed a .30-30 and talked a cute coed with a car into going with him on an afternoon hunt in the Catalina Mountain foothills a few miles north of campus. After hiking a short distance from the car, Jack dropped the buck as it ran from a brushy arroyo. He would take many more Arizona bucks, but this was one of the easiest that came his way.

After graduation from the University of Arkansas in 1925, Jack returned to Arizona. That summer he bought one of the very first Model 54 Winchesters chambered for the brand-new .270 W.C.F. cartridge. He had also received a Griffin & Howe Springfield Sporter .30-06 from an uncle as a graduation gift. That early fall, he and a friend caught up on their hunting, starting with a trip to the White Mountains in east-central Arizona's high country. Jack took his first black bear on this trip with the .30-06. They also hunted the Four Corners area on the Navajo Reservation, where Jack bagged a couple more pinyon-nut-fattened bears with his new .270.

Later still, Jack made the tortuous journey north to hunt Arizona's Kaibab Preserve, just reopened to restricted hunting the year before. Hunters were then required to stay at large camps established by the Forest Service, a fact that gave Jack an opportunity to show his new Winchester and its hot cartridge to many companions for the first time. It was used by him and others to bag several deer, and it impressed everyone with the effectiveness of its high-velocity bullet.

Jack's hunting experience in the Southwest began to broaden considerably when he moved to Alpine, Texas, in 1927 as associate professor of English at Sul Ross State Teachers College. During the next four years, he hunted the Big Bend country; the Chisos, Davis, and Glass Mountains; and made many trips into the Mexican state of Chihuahua. It was in Mexico that Jack shot his first of many pronghorn antelope. One of these was taken in 1928 with what was undoubtedly the most inappropriate rifle he owned—a Remington Model 8 autoloader in .35 Remington caliber!

Jack was newly married when he came to Texas, where he introduced his somewhat reluctant bride, Eleanor, to the sport of hunting, starting her out with a Winchester Model 57 bolt-action .22. Later, for an anniversary gift, he gave her an Ithaca Grade 2 20-gauge double with 26-inch barrels, instead of the new washing machine she'd hoped for. Eleanor went on to become a crack shot with both rifle and shotgun, the envy of many men with her skeet scores, and one of the few female hunters in the world to take record-class rams in North America, lion and elephant in Africa, and tiger in India.

Jack's love of quail hunting grew considerably in Texas after he discovered how much more deadly Eleanor's little short-barreled double was than his heavy, long-barreled, full-choked Model 12. On one occasion Jack took her gun along on a deer hunt in the Chisos Mountains and made a most unusual double with it. After seeing a great many Mearns quail during two days of hunting for the little deer that are now called Carmen Mountain whitetails, Jack decided to hunt the birds with the little Ithaca. As he worked along a high ridge of tall grama grass, scattered pinyon, and yucca, a lone quail flushed at his feet. At Jack's shot the bird fell in thick oak brush a few yards away, whereupon a buck bounded out. The deer was so close that the load of 7½ shot from the left barrel dropped it, too.

The O'Connors, including new baby Jerry, returned in 1931 to Arizona, where Jack was employed by the State Teachers College at Flagstaff. It was the midst of the Depression, and game meat was a much-appreciated supplement to the household fare. When Armistice Day vacation came that November, Jack and Eleanor headed their well-worn 1929 Chevy coupe to the Kaibab to hunt mule deer. According to old records, so did 978 other hunters from eleven states, including actor Clark Gable, whose telescope sight attracted more attention than he did himself.

Hunting on horseback from Jack Butler's Moquitch Camp, Eleanor took her first deer with a single running shot at two hundred yards from her Remington Model 30 in the now-obsolete .25 Remington caliber. The buck was old and gaunt but still weighed 197 pounds field-dressed and had impressive 6x6 antlers. Jack also bagged a buck with his G&H Springfield, but it wasn't one to brag about. As Jack said later, "Believe me, we ate those deer. I skinned and quartered them in the Kaibab; and when we got home, we hung the quarters in a screen porch on the north side of our house. When we wanted a hunk of venison, we whacked it off. Eleanor's buck went mostly into stews. As broke as we were, we ate him right down to the toenails."

Jack took his first big mule deer buck the next fall on the Kaibab, a 4x5 with 29¾-inch main beams, but the spread was not very wide. The following year, 1933, he again returned to the Kaibab and took his prettiest deer—a 6x7 with 28-inch beams and 33-inch spread. It is listed in the 1939 Boone and Crockett record book with an erroneous kill date of 1934. In truth, Jack took another large buck in 1934, one with the widest spread of any he ever shot—37½ inches! During the three years he and Eleanor spent at Flagstaff, they also hunted wild turkeys, ducks at Horse Lake, and Gambel quail in the Verde Valley. Despite being hard-pressed financially, Jack did manage to buy his first varmint rifle, a Winchester 54 chambered for the new .22 Hornet. He and Eleanor worked over the local prairie-dog population with it.

In the fall of 1934 Jack moved his family, which now included a yearling, Bradford, to Tucson, where he taught English and journalism at the University of Arizona. He had begun writing outdoor articles for *Sports Afield* and *Field & Stream* the year he'd moved to Flagstaff and by now had a growing reputation. His first article for *Outdoor Life*, "Arizona's Antelope Problem," had just appeared in the spring of 1934.

Jack's Tucson years, from 1934 to 1948, spawned numerous hunting tales of Arizona and Sonora, many written under pen names. Bill Ryan, Joe Ryan, Jim Ryan, Barry Williams, Ralph Williams, Henry E. Peters, and Carlos Ryan II were all old Cactus Jack himself, and their articles appeared from 1939 to 1950 in *Outdoor Life* and from 1951 to 1971 in *Gun*

Digest. Jack took advantage of Tucson's proximity to the Mexican border and the liberal hunting seasons in Mexico, where the limit on deer was three per person per trip, and where, with his connections, he could hunt desert bighorn sheep twice a year. Then, too, his occupation allowed lengthy Thanksgiving and Christmas vacations and summers free of teaching duties. Hunting from horseback was much more common in those peaceful and uncrowded days before the advent of noisy ATVs, and much of Jack's writing pertained to the proper use of saddle scabbards and advice on rifles suitable for such sport.

Arthur C. Popham Jr. of Kansas City was an early O'Connor fan and a pre-law student in Jack's journalism class in the fall of 1934. He accompanied Jack on his Kaibab deer hunt during Thanksgiving break and also on a Coues deer sortie into Sonora about thirty-five miles east of Imuris, where Jack shot a buck that later appeared in *North American Big Game* (Boone and Crockett, 1939). Following Jack's first, unsuccessful sheep hunt that December, Art and Jack hunted desert bighorns the next summer on the Sonora coast with Charlie Ren, a well-known guide. This trip, nearly disastrous due to water shortage, was detailed by Art nearly fifty years later as a chapter in his anthology *Stalking Game from Desert to Tundra* (Amwell Press, 1985). A couple months later, Jack took his first desert ram, as related in another chapter in this book, and began his illustrious sheep-hunting career. Art Popham, now a retired attorney in Kansas City, still fondly remembers his many hunting trips with Jack and Eleanor.

The Coues deer was Jack's favorite game animal, next to sheep. He rated a trophy Coues buck as being generally more difficult to bag than an old desert ram. It is not surprising that he wrote more than twenty stories about Coues deer, starting with "Elves of the Brush Country" in the October 1935 issue of *Field & Stream* and ending with "Southwestern

Whitetail: That Magnificent Midget" in the March 1975 *Petersen's Hunting*. Few modern-day Coues hunters are aware that a chapter in the 1939 Boone and Crockett record book titled "Hunting the Coues Deer," authored by Jack O'Connor, was the first major piece to bring widespread attention to the little whitetail.

A favorite spot for O'Connor family whitetail hunts was Arizona's Canelo Hills, where they hunted out of a ranch near Patagonia owned by Frank Siebold and his two sisters. One of the girls, Doris, had met Jack through her teaching profession and, through his influence, started hunting. She and Eleanor teamed up to shoot an atypical buck with eighteen antler points that had eluded local hunters for years. Doris, the last of the Siebolds, still lived at the ranch when she died in 1995, and when Jack's daughter Caroline accompanied Bob Anderson and me there in early 1999, things hadn't much changed since she'd last visited as a little girl in 1948.

Although Jack is rightly credited with helping create what has become almost a cult of Coues deer hunters, his methods were greatly different from the high-tech strategies used by serious trophy hunters today. Jack shot his last Coues deer—a 118-pound giant—in the mule-deer country of the Tortolita Mountains in 1946, a few years before the Boone and Crockett Club published its first modern-day record book in 1952. Because his hunting was primarily for sport and meat, not record heads, Jack loved to ride the oak and grama-grass hills until he jumped a buck, then leap from his horse, jerk his .270 or .30-06 from the scabbard, and try to connect before the deer disappeared. Toward the end of a lifetime of hunting, he still considered this the most enjoyable way to hunt.

Most trophy Coues deer hunters today spend endless hours behind high-powered, tripod-mounted binocular glassing for a shootable buck. After a stalk, a laser range finder is used to determine the distance, and a long-barreled magnum rifle equipped with a bipod and high-powered telescopic sight is used to make the shot.

As one who has done his share of prolonged glassing for Coues deer and has witnessed the high-tech method in action, but who still enjoys horseback hunting in interesting country, my vote goes to the O'Connor style.

In Mexico the O'Connors hunted Coues deer, desert mule deer, javelina, and occasionally antelope, exploring the length and breadth of Sonora. Many of these hunts served as family vacations after the two boys were old enough to go along. The story of one such family trip, entitled "We Shot the Tamales," is classic O'Connor. Although the piece did not appear until 1955, it tells how venison from the O'Connors' six-deer limit was used to brighten the spirits of the starving inhabitants of a tiny Mexican village at Christmastime in the 1940s.

Jack's best desert mule deer, the only one he still had at his death, was taken the last day of 1941 while hunting with Eleanor in the Sonora Desert about twenty miles from the Gulf of California. This heavy-bodied buck was somewhat atypical; its impressive antlers may still be seen in the O'Connor collection today.

Many O'Connor fans are unaware that Jack collected numerous specimens for the Arizona State Museum and thus frequently had special museum permits that allowed him to hunt outside the usual regulations. The museum, established in 1893, was then and is now located on the University of Arizona campus. It once housed a sizable natural-history collection, including several life-size mounts of big game, some taken by Jack, but is today known as the oldest and largest anthropological museum in the Southwest. When I recently visited there to see if any of Jack's specimens were still around, I learned that all the natural-history collection had been transferred to other departments or sold, and I was not able to locate any of them.

As a student at the university in the early 1960s, I remembered seeing a pair of antelope collected by Jack. Some of his other specimens hadn't survived that long. In a letter to me dated 17 June 1970, Jack wrote, "The best desert bighorn I ever shot was hung one year in the Arizona Museum there on the university campus. The director wasn't particularly interested in game heads; and when a tourist came along and offered to buy it, he sold it to him. This had a 38¼-inch curl and as I remember it, a 16-inch base."

Many of Jack's hunts on which specimens were collected for the Arizona State Museum or for Professor A. A. Nichol, a University of Arizona biologist of great renown, are documented in *Outdoor Life* issues of the 1930s and 1940s. They include quests in Sonora for javelina, Coues deer (and a smaller version of the Coues that the Mexicans called *cabritos*, which Nichol identified as the Sinaloa whitetail), Mearns quail, and the rarer Benson quail.

In Arizona Jack wrote of collecting a pair of antelope on Anderson Mesa for the museum in 1936. The buck is listed in the 1939 record book as having 15⅛-inch horns. At the time, Arizona antelope had been protected since the turn of the century. Due in large part to Jack's efforts, the season was first opened in 1941. Later in the 1940s, when Jack hunted thinhorn sheep in Canada, a museum permit allowed him to take an extra ram or two there.

The native Merriams elk was exterminated in Arizona by the turn of the century, and elk from Montana were reintroduced in 1913. When the season was reopened in 1935, the O'Connors and their young friend, Arthur Popham, had permits. On a snowy, cold hunt on the Mogollon Rim, related years later in *Outdoor Life* by both O'Connor and Popham, Jack took his first of twenty-one elk, using his .30-06.

Late in 1936, Jack negotiated a contract with *Outdoor Life*'s editor, Ray Brown, that allowed him to take the 1937–38 academic year off to write and hunt. An excerpt from Brown's letter of 7 December 1936 reads:

Would $150 apiece for eighteen articles a year, part under your name and part ghosted, interest you? Of course, if the articles were so darned good that they doubled the circulation and in consequence increased the revenue of the magazine, the rate would go up.

Thanks to the Depression, Jack's University of Arizona salary was then down to $2,000 per year. During his sabbatical, the O'Connors lived in Tempe. In addition to writing the *Outdoor Life* articles agreed upon, Jack finished a novel, *Boomtown*, and *Game in the Desert*, a Derrydale limited edition now in great demand. He and Eleanor also did a lot of hunting for Gambel quail near Granite Reef Dam on the Lower Verde River, mule deer on the Kaibab, Coues and mule deer in Sonora at Rancho El Datil, and desert sheep on the Sonora coast.

In January 1938, Jack drove to Houserock Valley to observe the culling shoot of Arizona's buffalo herd. He left with a low opinion of it due to the lack of sport involved.

The O'Connors summered in 1938 at Oak Creek Canyon, where Eleanor indulged her passion of fly fishing for trout while awaiting the birth of their first daughter, Catherine, which occurred in August. The next fall, Caroline, last of the O'Connor children, was born in Tucson.

Energetic and exceptionally intelligent, Jack was very much involved in conservation issues of the day. He was a frequent speaker at sportsmen's groups, did a sportsmen's radio broadcast on a regular basis, and appeared at game commission meetings to campaign for a restricted open season on antelope and desert sheep to focus hunters' attention on these neglected species. His letters to the editor and articles on these and many more subjects appeared frequently in the local newspapers as well as in *Arizona Wildlife & Sportsman*, official organ of the Arizona Game Protective Association, which he edited for a time.

Outdoor Life chose Jack to be its new gun columnist in 1939, replacing Captain E. C. Crossman, who committed suicide. Jack's column, "Getting the Range," appeared for the first time that November. A couple years later, in 1941, Ray Brown chose Jack to replace aged Major Charles Askins as arms and ammunition editor. The major, a noted shotgun expert and old-time cavalryman, had held the position since the 1920s and ended up moving on to *Sports Afield*. His son, the late Colonel Charles Askins, past national pistol champion and gunwriter, never forgave O'Connor for taking his father's job.

In 1941, at long last, Arizona reopened antelope hunting with a limited hunt on Anderson Mesa south of Flagstaff. Jack and Eleanor camped with fellow Tucsonans Al and Marion Ronstadt and Carroll Lemon at Chavez Pass the afternoon before the season opened. At daybreak the next morning, Eleanor killed the first buck of the new season with her .257 Roberts. It had heavy horns nearly 16 inches long with large prongs and was the largest of the five bucks taken by the party that day.

Pearl Harbor was bombed in December 1941, drawing the United States into World War II. The single outdoor magazine chosen for publication and free distribution to servicemen, and printed on special lightweight paper, was *Outdoor Life*. This helped the magazine become the leader in its field in later years, but at the time it created a problem with reader mail. Jack's popular question-and-answer section received up to 3,500 letters per month, requiring an assistant and three secretaries for response.

Few Tucson hunters were reloaders and shooters to the extent that Jack and Carroll Lemon were. Fewer still had the desire to burn up expensive deer-rifle ammo on jack rabbits and coyotes as they did. Typical of the others was my great-uncle, Greeley Tyler, a fellow Tucson educator who had known Jack since their days at Flagstaff together. Greeley loved to hunt and took me along on my first deer hunts before I was a teenager, but when I would ask about my idol, O'Connor, he would always include a remark about the amount of money that Jack wasted on varmint shooting.

Wasted money or not, Jack enjoyed a reputation as a superior running-game shot, and he told me many times he owed it to his frequent practice on jacks and coyotes. In fact, Jack wrote frequent stories about these off-season hunts in which Eleanor and the two boys, and frequently Carroll Lemon, would participate. As Jack's son Brad said:

> Carroll Lemon must have been a tolerant sort because he never objected to my tagging along with him and Dad on jack rabbit hunts, most often near hills north of Oracle Junction. I'd ride in the back seat of his Plymouth coupe. I enjoyed the adventure because Carroll always had a cooler of crushed ice and Coke in the trunk of his car to break out at the end of the hunt.

Although Jack was born in desert country, he preferred cooler weather than Tucson's summers. Slade Ranch in Arizona's White Mountains high country, elevation 9,000 feet, provided the perfect retreat for O'Connor summer vacations in the 1940s. Jack and the boys got plenty of rifle practice at the numerous crows and prairie dogs, and Eleanor found plenty of trout in the West Fork of the Little Colorado at nearby Sheeps Crossing. The rustic cabin was situated at the edge of a spruce, fir, and aspen forest and faced great green meadows used by elk, deer, and turkeys.

Because the cabin was within my old ranger district on the Apache National Forest, I sent some photos of it to Brad and his sister Cathy years ago. Cathy wrote:

> I was eight or nine the last time I was there. Earlier, my brother, father, and I were once chased into the woods by an angry bull, and as we made our hasty escape we found ourselves facing a black bear. The bear promptly turned and ran away—but for a four year old (me) it was one of the most terrifying experiences in a young life.

Brad had these recollections:

> I have lots of vivid memories of Slade Ranch. I remember the thick forests of blue spruce and the stands of aspen where many of the trunks bore carved graffiti of initials and love notes from a century earlier. I recall the old weathered log barn in which someone had written on a wall 'snow is ass deep to an elephant' or something similar, and the faint sweet smell of mold and mice droppings on the floor. Dad, Jerry, and I shot prairie dogs on the prairie just east of the cabin, shot crows perched on tree branches at the edge of the forest and plinked tin cans in front of the cabin with Dad's .38 Special. I dug worms for bait and fished with Mother for pan-sized rainbows with a fly rod on the Little Colorado at Sheeps Crossing and on the Apache Indian Reservation in a narrow but deep meadow creek where the air was sweet with the scent of mint.

When I accompanied Brad and his wife Anne back to the Slade Ranch cabin in August 1997, he was heartened to see everything just as he remembered it fifty years earlier. Even the wood range in the cabin was the same. Only the log barn had finally collapsed.

Jack became such a popular writer for *Outdoor Life* that the magazine sent him on a month-long pack trip to hunt the game of the Alberta Rockies in 1943. It was Jack's first hunt in Canada and provided lots of story material about many species new to him. He loved the crisp cold of the sheep mountains, the freedom of traveling with a packtrain in remote country, and the uncertainty of what kind of game might be encountered next. That trip marked the beginning of the end of Jack's days in the Southwest.

In 1944 Jack made a successful mixed-bag hunt in Wyoming and in 1945 resigned his professorship at the University of Arizona. He made an extensive hunt in the Yukon that year, described elsewhere in this book, and followed up with another trip to northern British Columbia the next year. When he returned home, he had completed three Grand Slams of wild sheep, though that term had not yet been introduced.

That fall of 1946, Jack took Brad deer hunting on Major Healey's ranch in the Huachuca Mountains, where the thirteen-year-old collected his first Coues deer with his mother's .257 Roberts. Late in the season his brother Jerry connected on a mule deer.

In November Jack took his last desert ram in the Los Mochos Range in Sonora, and in December he returned with the boys for another successful deer hunt.

Jack shot his last javelina and Brad his first and only during a hunt the two made in the spring of 1947 along the Sasabe road south of Robles Junction. By this time, Tucson and Arizona in general were experiencing a population boom brought on by servicemen who had discovered the state during the war and then returned with their families afterward. Tucson's population of 40,000 was too much for Jack, so in July of 1948 he moved his family to Lewiston, Idaho, where he spent the remainder of his life.

Jack went on to become the best-known and highest-paid outdoor writer of his time, receiving prestigious awards such as the Weatherby Trophy in 1957 and the Winchester Outdoorsman of the Year in 1972. He was known as an authority on sheep hunting and authored over a dozen books on hunting and firearms. He seldom returned to Arizona but stayed in touch with relatives and old friends like Carroll Lemon, Roy Dunlap, George Parker, and a few others.

In the winter of 1966, Jack and Eleanor hunted Mearns quail near Patagonia with Wendell Swank, former director of the Arizona Game and Fish Department, and Commissioner Jack Mantle. Jack returned in 1970 and 1971 for Winchester's promotional dove shoot near Phoenix—his last hunt in his native state.

As one who left Arizona for many of the same reasons Jack did, I understood how he felt when he wrote the following lines in 1977 shortly before his death:

> The state still produces some fine mule deer, desert bighorn and antelope trophies. There is still pretty good quail shooting. But on the whole a visit to Arizona leaves me depressed and unhappy. Seeing Arizona as it is today is a bit like encountering an old sweetheart in a bordello.

2

Novelist Young, Novelist Old

"O'Reilly would always come up out of the mine during a rainstorm. He'd stand watching the bombardment of the raindrops, listening to the cannonading of the thunder, and watching the lightning play over distant peaks. He'd inhale deeply, driving out of his lungs the smell of dynamite and sweaty human hides. He could smell the earth washed clean by rain and catch the odor of pines and fir way back in the mountains. Storms always made him hungry and horny and put him on his feet."

Boom Town, 1938

It will never be known exactly when young Jack O'Connor first began to consider a career as a writer. He had obtained a bachelor's degree from the University of Arkansas in the spring of 1925. This degree was in banking and finance, of all things! But by the time he received his master's degree in journalism from the University of Missouri in June of 1927, he was obviously beginning to think about writing as a vocation. However, Jack had wanted to try his hand at a novel for several years before this.

In midsummer of 1927, O'Connor accepted a job teaching English and journalism at Sul Ross State Teachers College in Alpine, Texas. His choice of Sul Ross was something more than accidental. He had been through Alpine by train during his undergraduate days as he went back and forth between Arizona and Fayetteville, Arkansas, where the University of

Arkansas was located. Tiny Alpine had a crispness and a freshness that appealed to Jack after a young lifetime of Arizona's heat. There was an unusual mix of characters: old frontiersmen and college professors, Texas Rangers and the occasional Mexican bandit, lungers and a few socialites from the East. O'Connor didn't want to go back to Arizona. Alpine had rail service with crack passenger trains every day and seemed a likely jumping-off point for destinations to the east and north on which the young about-to-be writer had his eye. It was also somewhere in between Arizona and St. Louis, Missouri, the home of nineteen-year-old Eleanor Bradford Barry, with whom Jack was thoroughly smitten and to whom he was engaged. More than that, the teaching post was a job, and about-to-be-married Jack needed work.

In late July of 1927, Jack sent a to-the-point telegram to Eleanor, who was vacationing at a guest ranch near Creede, Colorado. It read: "Got job Alpine, Texas. Thirty-six hundred a year. Why wait? Love, J.O'C." The "why wait" referred to Jack and Eleanor's plans to elope. So, at two o'clock in the afternoon 10 September 1927, the young couple was married in Columbia, Missouri, and set off on a short honeymoon trip by train, which really amounted to nothing more than the journey to their new digs in Alpine.

There the newlyweds settled into a little clapboard bungalow on Holland Avenue, and Jack assumed his duties as associate professor of English. He also worked as an Associated Press correspondent on the side. The young couple took picnics out in the hills and hiked about. Jack hunted some quail and javelina and began teaching Eleanor how to shoot. Otherwise, there wasn't enough to do. Because his teaching duties and Associated Press work didn't really keep him all that busy either, the energetic Jack found himself with time on his hands. He had been wanting to write a novel, if only for fun. So one Sunday afternoon in the winter of 1928, he simply sat down, rolled a sheet of paper into the bail of his old black Underwood, and began typing. As quickly as that, the novelist career of Jack O'Connor was born.

A few words are perhaps in order at this point regarding young Jack's special qualifications for the novelist's trade. Even as a small boy, he had always been a keen observer of people and personalities and had a memory like an elephant. He had also heard astute observations about human nature by his beloved grandfather, James Wiley Woolf, and his equally loved uncle, Jim O'Connor. From these two gentlemen young Jack had learned that people were not all good or bad and that things were not always what they seemed. The Arizona Territory of his youth had been a harsh place in which to grow up, a land of tough, hard people. He'd been more or less fatherless since boyhood and was always a loner to some degree, traits that were reflected even in his early writing, which had a certain edge and anger to it that seemed to mark him for great things in the future.

There were other reasons O'Connor, even before he had ever produced any significant work, seemed well suited for the writing craft. He was highly educated, loved the English language, and was a talented wordsmith. More importantly, he was a curious mix of disciplined pragmatist and incurable romantic. The disciplined side of him was capable of remaining harnessed to his typewriter for long periods while he hammered out literally thousands of words. Moreover, even as a young writer he was very careful and needed little editing. From the romantic standpoint, O'Connor had already packed about two lifetimes of living experiences into his twenty-six years. By 1927 he had already served an underage hitch in the army and another, longer one in the navy. He had attended four different colleges and had two degrees. He had traveled extensively for the day and for his age. Besides his military experiences, he had been at various times a fraternity man, newspaper reporter, press correspondent, prospector, meat hunter, movie extra, and general hell-raiser.

So Jack worked on his novel, which he decided early on to call *Conquest*, throughout the first half of 1928. At this time, Eleanor still had not met Jack's family, so in July of that year, the young O'Connors took a trip to Arizona for that reason and for Eleanor to see Jack's native state. Later, in the fall, Eleanor was diagnosed with tuberculosis and spent much of the winter of 1928–29 in Homan Sanatorium in El Paso, Texas, where she eventually made a complete recovery. Jack continued with his teaching duties at Alpine, journeying back and forth by train on weekends to visit Eleanor in El Paso, a distance of some 250 miles. He actually finished his final draft of *Conquest* while living part-time in a boarding house at 1314 Montana Avenue in El Paso during her illness.

The writing of *Conquest* had not been part of any master plan. O'Connor had not consulted a single publisher prior to beginning the work. Further, he sought no advice from anyone in the literary trade. By the time he completed the manuscript in mid-1929, he had narrowed his list of potential publishers to just two. One was Harper and Brothers, and the other was Alfred E. Knopf. He solved the publisher question by the simple expedient of tossing a coin. Harper and Brothers won. Jack bundled up his manuscript, mailed it to Harpers, and sat back to wait.

He didn't have to wait long. In rather short order Harpers agreed to publish *Conquest*. Just how many copies were printed and what the royalty arrangements may have been are not known. *Conquest* went on to sell only modestly, and what money O'Connor made from it was eventually lost in a Depression-related bank failure. However, I'm getting ahead of myself.

First, let's take a look at *Conquest* itself. On the surface, *Conquest* is a western, a shoot-'em-up, wild-and-wooly tale of Indian battles, holdups, and massacres in the American Southwest during the second half of the nineteenth century. In describing the book, Jack himself once said: "I thought it started off with a bang. In the opening chapter, Apache Indians ambush a group of Americans and kill all except one of them. In every page the blood is ankle deep and bullets fly around like hail." Beyond the action, however, the plot itself is pretty straightforward and unremarkable.

The central character of the book is something else again. *Conquest* centers on the struggles of Jard Pendleton, a young brute of a man with only the vaguest sense of right and wrong. He is descended from "Southern poor white trash" and lands in Arizona Territory in the 1850s by way of San Francisco. He is a man of unbridled will, raw physical strength, and enormous appetites. He is also deadly, ruthless, and unscrupulous. Initially he hunts down and murders Apache Indians, scalping them and bringing in their scalps for bounty. Along the way he learns that the scalps of innocent Mexicans do just as well. But the bulk of the story deals with Pendleton's struggle against the Apaches. In time he takes a wife, who soon deserts him. Later he fathers a passel of kids by a Mexican woman and subsequently runs them all off. But for all his savagery and greed, Pendleton is somehow farsighted. Besides conquering the Apaches, he plows the desert, builds roads, brings in stage and rail lines, and even creates a city. He serves all of his own hedonistic desires and, more by accident than design, the purposes of civilization as well. In the end, though, Pendleton outlives his own purpose. He is rich, heavy-footed, bored. Longing for the battles and blood of his youth, he sits, waiting to die, in a world made oddly more civilized by his own brutality.

No one will ever know whether or not O'Connor's development of the complex character of Jard Pendleton was truly planned or simply occurred as the book developed. But it would catch the eye of some pretty important people in the literary world. More about that a little later. However, O'Connor added other twists to *Conquest* that would stir up several hornets' nests.

Perhaps Jack remembered the generally cynical attitudes toward people of his grandfather and his uncle. By this time, Jack was developing his own rather low opinion of humankind as a whole. For these reasons, and perhaps because he harbored some resentment toward the Arizona of his youth, O'Connor peopled *Conquest* with hard-bitten, shady characters. One reviewer would later say, "Mr. O'Connor has given us a set of unprincipled, lustful adventurers who finally expelled the Apaches because they themselves were very much nearer to being absolute savages."

Also, prior to and during the writing of *Conquest*, O'Connor read many of the fiction works of various eastern European authors. Many of these writers were pretty salty and wrote with none of the naiveté of American fiction writers of the day. A classic example concerned the handling of profanity. In the innocent American literary style of those far-gone days, curse words or other profanity often appeared in print as a series of dashes that replaced the actual words. For example, the words "son of a bitch" would generally appear as "— of a ——" or something similar. Perhaps Jack was influenced by European writers of the time. Anyway, in what was a daring move for the day, young novelist O'Connor unilaterally decided to let the chips fall where they would. No dots or dashes for him. If his characters said it, O'Connor put it down in plain English (though, oddly enough, profane language appears in *Conquest* in only two or three isolated instances). His publisher, Harper, decided to ride along with the kid author from Alpine.

Conquest, with its rough characters and five or six words of profanity intact, was released 16 September 1930, and it didn't take long for public indignation to reach fever pitch. Perhaps word leaked out that the new book by the young punk writer from Arizona via the Texas Big Bend had some steam in it, because it was pounced upon by newspaper reviewers all over the United States and western Europe. Many applauded Jack for his unglamorized, raw look at the development of the Southwest, his unflinching characterizations, and the book's sordid, gutsy style. Others heaped abuse on O'Connor's head for exactly the same reasons. The profane language brought howls of indignation from an unexpected source when numerous public libraries in the Southwest banned *Conquest* from their shelves. Most notable among these was the El Paso City Library, the very town in which Jack had completed the book.

Also, many native Arizonans pompously accused O'Connor of using some ancestor of theirs as the basis for a character in *Conquest*. There were veiled threats of tarring and feathering and riding Jack's flat butt out of town on a rail should he ever be so bold as to show his face at an Arizona Pioneers Society meeting. In Alpine, Jack began to hear rumors of a petition being circulated demanding his dismissal from Sul Ross. Dr. H. W. Morelock, president of the college, called O'Connor in and showed him the petition. Jack quietly asked Dr. Morelock what he intended to do about the situation. Dr. Morelock laughed and said, "I told them all to go to hell! I also told them that you were a credit to the college and I wasn't about to fire you just because you had more ambition than anybody else around here!"

To his last days, Jack had a soft place in his heart for Dr. Morelock.

Morelock's squelching of the furor over *Conquest* ended all talk of Jack's getting the gate. The incident blew over in time, and Jack continued his teaching duties there until the spring of 1931, although he was probably emotionally done with the place for the last year he was there.

But the whole process hurt and angered O'Connor. It also galvanized his belief that the public was generally stupid and unsophisticated. The reaction to *Conquest* almost certainly hastened O'Connor down the road toward what eventually became a hardened, bitter, and low opinion of mankind in general.

Prior to the book's release, O'Connor had stated publicly that he planned it as the first of a trilogy of novels about the Southwest. Despite the mixed reaction to *Conquest*, Harper was enthusiastic about the opportunity to publish the next two novels in the planned trilogy. Poet and writer Carl Sandburg, perhaps the foremost figure in American literature of the day, had read *Conquest* and recognized O'Connor's promising talent. He fired off a telegram to his publisher, Harcourt, Brace and Company, encouraging the firm to get young O'Connor into its stable of writers. This was pretty heady stuff. Sandburg and O'Connor later became friends and kept up a lively correspondence until Sandburg's death in 1967.

But all the adverse hoopla over *Conquest* put O'Connor into a funk. In the spring of 1931, judging by all his outward appearances and announcements, it seemed that Jack had tabled his plans for subsequent novels.

Many years later, in 1977, writing in *The Best of Jack O'Connor*, Jack had this to say about his first novel: "I wrote *Conquest* very easily. I simply started at the beginning, ended at the end. When I couldn't think of anything else, I'd have a fight with the Apaches. I had few characters and they were simple." On the surface, Jack's remarks were self-deprecating—for one thing, Jard Pendleton was anything but simple. Looking at the book in retrospect, we are left to wonder: Just how important had *Conquest* been to Jack O'Connor?

I found the answer one cold, rainy day in Seattle, Washington, more than seventy years after *Conquest* was written. In doing general research for this book, I had occasion to spend several dreary but utterly delightful days there interviewing Jack and Eleanor's daughters, Cathy and Caroline, their son Bradford, and Brad's wife Anne. One wintry afternoon I pored through an old scrapbook compiled by Jack in the late 1920s and early 1930s. The scrapbook's pages were of very fragile, black paper. Clippings and photographs had been carefully pasted in and labeled with white ink in Jack's distinctive handwriting. There in those old pages I saw all the proof anyone would ever need to realize just how important his career as an emerging novelist had been to Jack O'Connor. *Conquest* was released 16 September 1930. As mentioned before, for several weeks afterward it was widely reviewed by newspapers throughout the country and in Europe. Whether his publishers had sent the reviews to him or O'Connor had gathered them himself will never be known. But there they were. Not five. Not ten or twenty. I counted sixty-three detailed reviews that Jack had meticulously clipped out and pasted into his old scrapbook. They came from papers as near as Tucson's *Arizona Republic*, from the *Chicago Tribune*, from the East Coast's *New York Times*, and from as far away as the *London Times*. Each review was labeled and dated. In personal interviews regarding the book soon after its release, O'Connor himself had run the gamut of behavior, depending upon the latest review he had read. He had been everything from warm and receptive to a cad and a whiner and a complete boor. But despite his defensiveness and sometimes devil-may-care attitude when questioned about it, he had obviously poured his heart and soul into *Conquest* and wanted very much for it to succeed. The old scrapbook told it all.

The old adage that "the world is full of people who could make a million dollars if they didn't have to worry about making a living" was never more applicable than to young Jack O'Connor in the spring of 1931. Had he been a single man, he might have been able to survive while he gathered material and wrote other novels subsequent to *Conquest*. Given the glowing recommendations he had received from Carl Sandburg and others, great success as a novelist may have been only a matter of time for O'Connor had he remained with his craft.

Twenty-nine-year-old Jack, the married man with a baby son and another child on the way, had no such luxury. After a while the smoke and fury generated in Arizona from *Conquest* had cleared away. So, in the fall of 1931, Jack and Eleanor, with their one-year-old son, Gerald Barry O'Connor, presented themselves in Flagstaff, where Jack had accepted a job teaching English and doing public-relations work at Arizona State Teachers College. By then, another novel seemingly was the farthest thing from O'Connor's mind. Of that, more a little later. But at the time, the Depression was on, and he had mouths to feed.

In Flagstaff, Jack rather quickly found that his salary from the new teaching duties and public-relations work did not quite keep the wolf away from the door. To help out, Jack began writing the occasional short story (JOC's short stories are discussed in another part of this book) for various popular magazines and some of his first pieces for outdoor magazines. The immediate, if minimal, income provided by these short pieces helped to put beans in the pot. Actually, not much has ever been made of the reason for O'Connor's change of direction from novel writing to short stories and sporting articles. The reason was very simple. Publishers generally paid novel royalties twice a year. Short-story and sporting-article money was "now." Young Jack needed the dough. For the rest of his life, O'Connor referred to the hard times at Flagstaff between 1931 and 1934 as the "cruel pinch of want."

Between graduation from the University of Missouri with his master's degree in May of 1927 and the summer of 1934, Jack O'Connor had been a very busy young man. Marriage, fatherhood, a reasonably demanding job at Sul Ross, the writing of *Conquest*, two very demanding jobs at Arizona State Teachers College in Flagstaff, his short-story writing, and the beginnings of his freelance outdoor writings kept his back to the wall.

Therefore, it would seem that O'Connor would have had no time or energy for anything beyond sheer economic survival during those harrowing and busy years. Think again. Want to hear what else Jack did during those seven years? It is one of the mysteries of his life. It provides a crystalline look into the boundless energies, the drive, the privacy, and indeed the very mystique that characterized and surrounded O'Connor.

In existence today among the O'Connor family records and papers are *two* complete, unpublished novels written between 1931 and 1934. The first of these is a complete thirty-two-chapter manuscript centered on the Mexican Revolution of 1916. The hero is Tiger Ordunio, a Pancho Villa-type who leads the revolt. His cause takes him all the way to the presidency of Mexico before he is finally assassinated. Along the way there are bloodbaths, a torrid love affair, and much other action. The manuscript looks today as if it is ready to go to press.

The second complete manuscript has the working title "Shadows on a Screen" and is a story dealing with the Hollywood movie set of the 1920s and 1930s. Much of the plot takes place on movie locations in the Southwest. This would have been a natural plot for O'Connor, given his fascination with the movie industry in his youth. "Shadows on a Screen" is a thirty-seven-chapter affair that, again, looks to be ready for publication.

Then there is a 171-page manuscript that was obviously intended to be the sequel to *Conquest*. It deals with a young man's courageous attempts to build a life in pioneer Arizona and the loss of his wife, child, ranch, and cattle.

There is also the three-chapter beginning of a novel that Jack had tentatively titled "Forever This Memory." It would appear to focus on Jack's own early childhood in Arizona and is, in fact, eerily reminiscent of portions of his *Horse and Buggy West*, which was written and published in 1968, almost forty years later.

Then there is a portion of a novel entitled "The Kid with the High IQ," a tightly autobiographical account of an unusually bright boy growing up in old Arizona.

Finally, there are several chapters of a novel entitled "The Year of the Rat," an account of a year in the life of a young man following his mustering out of the navy right after World War I. The hero, Ryan, is obviously Jack himself. This work's opening chapter would be included in *The Last Book*, published in 1984 after Jack's death. And that's not all.

There are indications that Jack may have written the manuscript for still another novel during this period. He confirmed as much many years later in a 5 December 1961 letter to his great friend and Knopf editor, Angus Cameron, when he commented:

> Sometime when you are ready for a good cry, I'll tell you about a novel that I had 99%/10 percent finished between the time of *Conquest* and *Boom Town* which was thrown out with the rest of the garbage by a half-wit.

If this manuscript were indeed accidentally thrown away, it would not be among those manuscripts in the possession of the O'Connor family today.

Two more intriguing stories: In October 1930, O'Connor told a reporter from a Spokane, Washington, newspaper that "The year I left college (1927) I wrote a 100,000 word novel, read it over, and put it in my trunk—where it still lies, thank God!"

In another scenario, he had cranked out a 75,000-word manuscript and gave it to Eleanor to read. She allegedly turned up her nose at the work, and Jack, in a fit of petulance, threw the manuscript away. Given O'Connor's practical nature and the hard work that would have gone into such a manuscript, this seems unlikely. But what happened to these two works and whether or not they are the same as some of the later manuscripts is anybody's guess. Could they still be stuck away somewhere else?

The above-mentioned manuscripts represent an awesome amount of thought, planning, and hard work, especially when one considers that they were created during a time frame when Jack apparently did not have a spare moment. Anyone who doesn't think this work was demanding needs only to sit down and peck out a few words on an old manual typewriter (if you can find one). In those days there was no leapfrogging of one whole paragraph over another, no cut and paste, no delete or insert button to hit. You just pecked away at the keys. Hard.

Perhaps more than anything, the manuscripts are a testament to Jack's work ethic and incredible energy.

No one knows what Jack eventually planned to do with the various manuscripts. Given the hard work that had gone into them, he certainly had in mind their publication at some point in time. Perhaps the best explanation for why that didn't happen is that his career soon took a different direction.

In the summer of 1934, O'Connor accepted a position as the head of the brand-new journalism department at the University of Arizona in Tucson. He began there in the fall semester of 1934. These new responsibilities and the growing success of his freelance outdoor writing kept him very busy.

Jack's responsible and conscientious nature soon had him immersed in all manner of university-related projects and committees, and once again he found himself working very, very hard, as he had at Flagstaff. Even so, quietly in the spring of 1937 he yielded to his passion for novel writing and began working on yet another manuscript. At that time, he sought and was granted a year's leave from the university to work on various writing projects. Besides the new novel, these projects included eighteen new stories for *Outdoor Life*, which by this time had contracted to publish Jack's hunting and shooting stuff exclusively. But also included were five short stories for *Esquire* and the assembly of a group of previously written hunting stories into a new book to be called *Game in the Desert*. O'Connor decided to call the new novel *Boom Town*.

During 1937, O'Connor endured great personal heartache, the details of which do not need to be mentioned in these pages. But this experience left him with a sense of fatalism and further sapped his faith in mankind, traits that would be with him until the end of his days. Many of these feelings of fatigued spirit and futility come through in the pages of *Boom Town*. The book's characters are more complex and sophisticated than those of *Conquest,* and O'Connor develops their personalities to a much greater degree. But from page one there is a sadness to the book that is inescapable, and even in its early stages, a reader of *Boom Town* gets a morbid feeling that all is not going to work out in the end.

Boom Town is the story of Smiling Frank O'Reilly, a down-on-his-luck prospector who dreams of making a big gold or silver strike. O'Reilly is a knowledgeable miner, but for five years he shuns good-paying jobs in big mines for the lure of desert and mountain and the hope of the big find. As the story opens, Frank is out of grub and embarks on a meat hunt for, of all things, a desert ram. He kills a big one right at nightfall on the third day and practically stumbles over a mega-rich silver lode as he is dressing out the sheep. He files on his claim and grows rich. A boomtown soon springs up at the site. Much of the rest of the book deals with the sordid nature of O'Connor's assemblage of characters. One by one they come, lured by greed and the promise of quick and easy riches. One by one they are consumed. As for the character of Frank O'Reilly, although he is capable of the same ruthlessness as *Conquest*'s Jard Pendleton, he is far more intelligent and humanistic. In the craze of the silver boom, O'Reilly is about the only one who maintains any objectivity. But a black aura surrounds Frank early in the book, and we are aware of his inevitable doom long before it comes to pass.

The sad demise of Frank O'Reilly finally occurs when he is trapped far below the surface in a huge mine cave-in. He lies fully conscious but with his back broken as floodwaters from below begin to cover his paralyzed body. He mutters to himself, "Well, this is the last of Frank O'Reilly." Upon digesting these lines, readers familiar with the author are left with the feeling that O'Reilly's pronouncement was perhaps eerily reminiscent of Jack's own feelings about the novelist career that he had wanted so much but was destined never to be. *Boom Town* simply runs out of energy and limps to a close as though its author's focus had already turned elsewhere. By 1938, the cloth was cut for O'Connor. He was on his way to being *Outdoor Life*'s golden boy for the next thirty-five years. At the time, though, *Outdoor Life* may well have been the choice of necessity and not O'Connor's Holy Grail.

Boom Town was published by Alfred E. Knopf and released in mid-1938. It got good critical reviews and was particularly well written-up in *Time* magazine. The novel sold relatively well in the United States and very well in Great Britain. Sooner or later it made O'Connor some nice royalty money, although the income was strung out over about twenty years.

A curious thing happened after *Boom Town*'s release. Within six months MGM made it into a major motion picture starring Clark Gable and Spencer Tracey. Very shortly after the novel hit the market, MGM had contacted O'Connor in hopes of hiring him to rework it into a screenplay. For whatever reason, Jack did not agree to this. An MGM writer then created a screenplay based rather loosely on the novel. Possibly Knopf Publishing failed to properly protect the rights to *Boom Town*. It may have been Jack's responsibility to copyright his works. More likely perhaps is that the movie version so loosely resembled Jack's book that no copyright violation existed. At any rate, *Boom Town*, the movie, was fairly successful, but Cactus Jack never got a nickel from it. It would not be the last time that Jack's innocence and general naiveté regarding the contractual aspects of his writings would cost him good money.

As mentioned earlier, Jack had collected and saved dozens of reviews of *Conquest*, living and dying over each one. But interestingly, in all of the O'Connor family papers, correspondence, and other memorabilia, there is no indication that O'Connor saved or even paid much attention to the reviews of *Boom Town*. This strongly indicates that reality was upon him and that his novelist aspirations had been laid to rest. By 1938, his life had turned a major corner and he was on his way to other destinations.

After *Boom Town*, O'Connor's responsibilities as head of the journalism department of the University of Arizona and his growing role at *Outdoor Life* kept him so busy that he certainly had no time to consider another novel. He resigned from the university in 1945, but by then he was firmly entrenched as America's foremost gunwriter. Between 1947 and 1967 he produced numerous books, but all dealt with guns and hunting. In truth, his experiences with *Conquest* and *Boom Town* were, on the whole, disheartening and probably left him somewhat disenchanted, at least at the time.

Thirty-one years were to pass before O'Connor would return seriously to fiction writing, though here and there he dabbled with it, once completing three chapters on a new novel, but nothing was ever published. In 1961, Knopf publisher Angus Cameron encouraged Jack to do another and more expanded western novel, but nothing ever came of it. *Outdoor Life* and the writing of gun and hunting books consumed him until 1968. Then he wrote the wonderful *Horse and Buggy West*, an autobiography of his boyhood up until the age of about fifteen. *Horse and Buggy West* was basically factual, but through fictional names and some cover-up, O'Connor gained enough leeway to really bring his storytelling skills and raunchy sense of humor into play. Many O'Connor fans will agree that the book may have been Jack at his very best. It is full of Boy Jack's antics, pranks, adventures, and observations about human nature in general. In places it is highly introspective, in other places wildly funny. And anyone who reads *Horse and Buggy West* quickly becomes aware of one simple fact: As a boy and an adolescent growing up in Old Tempe, Arizona, young Jack was a prickly miscreant.

O'Connor loved doing *Horse and Buggy West*, largely because of the writing freedom it gave him. It received wonderful critical reviews and sold very well. A copy in good condition today is a minor treasure. It is this author's belief that the enjoyment and writing freedom he got from doing *Horse and Buggy West* may have started him thinking about retiring from *Outdoor Life* and possibly writing more fiction.

O'Connor's final book, appropriately entitled *The Last Book*, was published in 1984, more than six years after his death. Written in the last two years of his life at the encouragement of his friend Jim Rikhoff, the book's subtitle is "Confessions of a Gun Writer." Again, this is O'Connor unleashed. This book, too, is an autobiography of sorts, dealing mainly with Jack's professional career. In it he sounds off about everything from overzealous copyreaders to the new breed of egomaniac trophy hunters. It is full of O'Connor joys and grievances accumulated over more than forty years of writing about guns and hunting. By not naming names and using some subterfuge, O'Connor really swings the bat in print in *The Last Book*.

The novelist in O'Connor never died. This fact was never more evident than in the early 1970s, when Jim Rikhoff encouraged Jack to return to his first literary love and take a whirl at another novel. O'Connor was reluctant at first, allowing as how the world had probably passed him by and would have no interest in what he would have to say in fiction. However, Rikhoff's encouragement secretly must have been music to O'Connor's ears. He repaired to his Lewiston, Idaho, lair and dug up the forty-four-year-old manuscript of "The Year of the Rat." He then did some reworking of the first chapter and sent it to Rikhoff for his thoughts. For reasons unknown, "The Year of the Rat" progressed no farther, and the last of Jack's novel efforts came to an end.

But JOC reserved for his very last days a couple of parting shots about his novelist passions. The first remark showed just how much enthusiasm he had retained for novel writing (western novels in particular). In *The Last Book*, he made this hilarious but only half-kidding remark:

> I'd like to write a novel about a heroic cowboy named Creesap McCracken who went about rescuing beautiful school teachers with lily-white tits and golden hair from bad men and Indians!

We are left to wonder whether one last novel, particularly an autobiographical one, might have shown us more of the man himself than the world had ever seen. At seventy-five years of age, would this immensely philosophical man, of whom the world really knew so little, have been able to dig down in his own guts and let us know what really made him tick? Had he been able to do so, we would all have been the better for it.

In his entire *Outdoor Life* career, O'Connor was absolutely honest with his readers. He felt that such honesty was his primary responsibility to them. Perhaps even more than his writing skills, his candor and truthfulness are his greatest legacies. But his adherence to the truth created a literary "prison" that at times chafed and frustrated him. His early novels and short stories had given him a freedom and a flexibility that he never felt he had at *Outdoor Life*. Subsequent novels would almost certainly have taken the bridle off his rich imagination and his keen knowledge of human nature to an even greater degree. Novels would have permitted him a free range to use his passion, energy, edge, cynicism, and biting wit. A reader of either of his two novels or many short stories quickly finds that O'Connor's fiction moves along with energy and vitality. Sure, the plots are rather simplistic by today's standards. But make no mistake about it: It is his fiction writing that gives readers the deepest and most revealing look at the man inside O'Connor.

In his second and final reference to his what-might-have-been career as a novelist and the fame it might have brought, the ever-realistic Jack himself perhaps said it best. In a personal letter of 5 January 1970 to a close friend who had broached the novelist question to him, Jack replied:

> Various other friends of mine have told me that I have wasted my talents by working for *Outdoor Life*. However, I have enjoyed it. I have been all over the world. I have met a hell of a lot of interesting people and I have done a lot of interesting things. Maybe it is better to have been a good gun writer than a second-rate novelist.

3

How Many Desert Sheep?

*I came down fascinated by the country and
the game and resolved to get myself a desert ram
if I had to wear my legs down to the knees to do it."*

Jack O'Connor, reflecting on his frustrations
with early desert sheep hunting in 1934–1935

The voice from the tape player seemed to come from the very bowels of the earth. It was the voice of Jack O'Connor, recorded 15 November 1977, two months and five days before his death. Virtually all American adults of that time remember the great voice of the late Orson Welles and his advertisements for Eastern Airlines, in which he dramatically intoned: "Eastern Airlines, the wings of Man." And we have all heard the death-knell voice of Darth Vader in the *Star Wars* movies, as spoken by the powerful actor James Earl Jones. Although the voice of Jack O'Connor never had the great exposure of the two gentlemen mentioned above, it was every bit as distinctive. Gravelly and mock-gruff (and sometimes just gruff), it carried the tenor and power of many years of tough living and the loudness of a man who was near deaf from the thunderclap reports of too many high-powered rifles. This occasion was part of a series of taped interviews made by Jack's friend, Dr. David Heusinkveld of Lewiston, Idaho. Dr. Heusinkveld correctly realized that there were few, if any, recordings of Jack's authoritative and often booming voice and wanted to preserve a bit of it for posterity. The idea was a good one, and O'Connor apparently enjoyed the whole process. The taping sessions took place at the Pheasant Valley Shooting Preserve in eastern Washington in the late summer and fall of 1977 and were generally conducted over lunch and a few scotches after a morning of pheasant shooting.

On this day, during the course of what would be the last of these taping sessions, O'Connor elected to talk about one of his favorite subjects, desert sheep hunting. He began by saying: "In my day, I have done quite a bit of desert sheep hunting and have killed quite a number of rams." Here there was a long pause, after which he dramatically added:

"Just how many is a state secret!"

Following this comment, the grand old man chuckled deeply as if saying to one and all: "You didn't really think I was going to tell all of you the whole truth about that, did you?"

And to this day the mystery has ever remained, known by only one man who may not have chosen to remember and who certainly isn't talking.

On another occasion, when he was asked the "how many desert sheep" question by his friend Jim Rikhoff, O'Connor responded tiredly, "You don't want to know, and I don't want to remember."

But for the sheep-hunting nuts of the world who cut their teeth on the writing of JOC, this is the most intriguing O'Connor question of all. The careful observer can figure out a chronology and ram count of his other sheep hunting, but this is not so for his desert-sheep experiences.

In the forty years that I have been a Jack O'Connor fan, I have heard more horror stories, half-truths, misconceptions, and windy tales regarding Jack's desert-sheep hunting exploits than I could count. On many occasions I heard comments such as: "Old Jack killed all those big rams in Arizona!" or

"Once when Jack was huntin' down in Baja. . . ." I especially liked the one an overzealous Jack fan told me several years ago, and I quote: "Old Jack really shot the crap out of them desert sheep. Killed over forty of 'em!" And of course, in addition to all such hoopla, there have been the inevitable remarks accusing him of poaching many of his desert rams.

As is usually the case, the facts are less wild and somewhat more to the middle of the road than the fiction.

For the record, O'Connor *never* hunted desert rams in his native Arizona. In fact, he never saw many rams in Arizona, spotting only an odd ram here and there during his years of whitetail and desert mule deer hunting. Such sightings were far from routine. And again for the record, O'Connor never hunted sheep in Baja, although he was issued permits to do so in 1951 and again in 1958–59.

But it *will* come as a surprise to many O'Connor fans that in the years from 1934 until 1947, which encompassed his entire desert-sheep-hunting career, there was *never* an official open season on desert sheep in the Mexican state of Sonora, where O'Connor collected all of his rams. At first, this may leave you with the impression that O'Connor *must* have poached these sheep. But this is just not true. What is true is that O'Connor had numerous influential friends south of the border, even as far south as Mexico City, who could and did provide him with special permits or at least some documentation allowing him to hunt, collect, and possess rams. It is also true that in some cases the documentation was so flimsy as to be almost invisible. But at least Jack made an effort to comply with the law, however nonexistent the laws and law enforcement may have been. O'Connor also became rather adept at wrangling museum and institutional permits from various sources on the American side that allowed him to take rams south of the border. Many years later, in a letter to Grand Slam honcho Bob Housholder dated 25 October

1961, O'Connor had this to say regarding his early-day Mexican "permits":

> As you can well understand, when I was doing my sheep hunting in Sonora, law enforcement was on the sketchy side and the whole game regulation business was pretty informal. At various times I had special permits for sheep, and of course, if you had a permit in your pocket, you couldn't get in too much trouble. Sometimes my *permiso* was current. At other times I had only a letter from a "general" instructing everybody who came in contact with me to aid me and abet me in every way possible because I was a great *amigo* of his. That's the way things were done in the old days. Actually I believe my special permit on the first desert bighorn I ever shot was a bottle of American whiskey and a 20-peso bill.

For a number of reasons, the mapping-out of O'Connor's desert-sheep-hunting career is very difficult. One of the most significant is the simple fact that this period in Jack's hunting life is so far back in the past. Before he began hunting desert rams in 1934, O'Connor doubtlessly knew that such experiences would produce material for the hunting stories that he was already beginning to write for *Outdoor Life*, *Field & Stream*, and other sporting magazines. However, he apparently kept no in-depth notes, journals, or diaries of these hunts, instead relying on his excellent memory to recount them. But most of these accounts were not written until as much as twenty years later. Dates and what would have been fascinating details of such hunts were never recorded except in Jack's head and are simply gone with the man himself. Also, despite the fact that Jack was a photography buff from an early age, for some reason he took relatively few photographs during the course of his desert-sheep hunts. He used two different 35mm miniature cameras during those days, one a Contax and the other a Welti. The Contax was equipped with a self-timer. So, photographs of O'Connor with rams taken while he was hunting alone would have been at least feasible, assuming the Contax's self-timer wasn't on the fritz. Then, too, hunting in the desert was a tiring and draining business and left little time or energy for a full photographic record of a hunt's events.

Also, O'Connor often did not identify hunting companions by name—particularly during his desert-sheep period. With only one exception, these individuals are gone from the earth forever. But if these identities had been known, certain information might have been available from their families that would have allowed a better timeline of JOC's sheep career in this book.

The hunts themselves were so physically demanding that they often became exercises in survival. Camps were primitive and uncomfortable. There was never enough water. All water for camps had to be carried in cans from neighboring ranches or wells, often as far away as thirty miles. All of the actual hunting was done on foot, much of it in scorching heat. In many cases the hunters had to walk as long as two hours to get to the base of a mountain before the day's hunting could really begin. This obviously meant a similar hike back to camp at the end of the day (and often after nightfall). In later years, O'Connor would recount hunting days that began at four o'clock in the morning and ended with him getting back to camp, more dead than alive, by starlight and long after midnight.

In the entirety of his writings, O'Connor provided his readers with only five in-depth accounts of his taking of *different* desert rams. Here and there, he also mentioned the killing of other rams that for various reasons can be determined to be different from the ones he described in detail. But we'll save that for later. The five accounts cited above were told so masterfully by O'Connor himself that I'm damned if I'll insult Jack's memory by attempting to retell them in any depth in these pages. Instead, as I have done elsewhere in this book, I'll tell them in encapsulated form and reference where these various accounts can be located in Jack's books. Further, I will try to arrange the main five accounts in some sort of chronological order, and I will relate some otherwise unknown details about each hunt, some sidebar information, and in a few cases O'Connor's private thoughts.

To begin: Before O'Connor was successful in taking his first ram, he made a series of three Sonoran hunts between late 1934 and August of 1935 that were "learning experiences" of a most harsh nature.

But Jack was a pretty quick study, and he remembered from boyhood the big desert ram taken by his maternal grandfather Woolf and another taken by someone he described as his "lawless sheep-poaching uncle John Woolf." These heads functioned as doorstops in his grandfather's house for years, and Jack remembered their great weight and mass. He also remembered the big set of sheep horns he had found in a cave near Hole-in-the-Rock and lugged ecstatically home. Before he ever saw a desert sheep in the field, he instinctively knew that a big ram head was the trophy of trophies.

O'Connor climbed his first serious desert-sheep rockpile in late December of 1934. He planned the hunt for the days between Christmas and New Year when he was off from his teaching duties at the University of Arizona and because Eleanor had taken their sons Jerry and Bradford by train back to St. Louis to visit her family. Jack and three unnamed companions crossed the border at Nogales and traveled more than two hundred miles southwest over roads that were mere tracks through the desert to the rugged Sierra del Viejo Mountains, where they spent a fruitless week in pursuit of sheep. But it was this hunt that galvanized O'Connor's desire and spawned the quote that appears on the title page of this chapter.

On Jack's second hunt, in the spring of 1935, he could scrounge only a few days off from his teaching duties. For this reason, he crossed the border at Sonoyta and hunted in the Sierra San Franciscos, a range farther north and therefore more accessible. But the results were similarly grim. He saw few sheep. The "Friscos" were drying up, and the observant Jack began to realize that sheep migrated from dry areas to areas that had experienced recent rainfall.

For his third hunt he headed south to the coast near Kino Bay with his desert-sheep mentor, Charley Ren; Mexican sheep hunter José Del Rosario; a young man named Arthur C. Popham; and a deputy sheriff from Ajo, Arizona. Popham, a student of Jack's at the University of Arizona, was an early O'Connor fan and a keen sportsman and became a lifelong friend. O'Connor orchestrated the hunt to take place in August of 1935 for the simple reason that his teaching duties would begin in September and he didn't know when he would get another chance. The heat was so terrific that O'Connor described it as a "furnace." The party got rams, but Jack wasn't one of the lucky hunters, although he may have co-killed a ram with Ren. This is not known for sure. An old photo from the hunt that appears in several O'Connor books shows Jack, in sweaty and stained khaki pants, and Charley Ren standing behind several ram heads on the ground. Although the inference is that one of these heads was taken by O'Connor, this is not the case.

When he began this three-hunt pledgeship, O'Connor had a notion that he could hunt desert rams like Coues deer—jumping them out of the heads of canyons and blasting them on the run. But after a while of never being able to get the drop on a ram, he began to realize that sheep had to be spotted at long range and then carefully stalked. He also learned quite a bit about the right equipment for sheep. He found that his 10½-pound .30-06 with its 26-inch barrel and heavy stovepipe German 4X scope used on his first hunt weighed about as much as a bank safe at the end of the day. His heavy hob-nailed boots were about as appropriate for Sonora rock as in-line roller skates, and what he described as his "funny little French binocular" made his eyeballs feel as though they were in the wrong sockets. But gradually he worked through all these obstacles, making rifle, boot, and binocular changes. And after three hunts, he felt he deserved a ram.

His experience in the inferno of the Sonoran coast in August of 1935 left O'Connor more determined than ever to get a ram. Somehow he arranged the time off and was back for another try within a month. With him again was the seasoned Mexican hunter, José Del Rosario. And this time things were finally different. The two men hunted on Tepopah Mountain, a big, triangular peak just across the straits from Tiburon Island. One morning they trailed a big ram and two ewes into a steep-walled canyon with heavy cover in its bottom. Each man took one side of the ridge and began carefully working up toward the head of the canyon a half-mile away. Three-fourths of the way to the top, O'Connor heard rocks rolling just above and ahead of him. He scrambled up to some higher ground just in time to get a short running shot at the big ram as it boiled over a ridge. He hung the bead of his rifle on the ram's butt and tripped one off just before it went out of sight. Silence. But after rushing to the edge of the cliff, Jack saw the great ram down and out a short distance below. The jinx was finally broken.

Several things about that first ram are significant. First, in Jack's hands that day was a slender little Minar-stocked 7x57mm Mauser with a 22-inch barrel, equipped with a Lyman 1-A peep sight mounted on the cocking piece of the rifle's bolt. He killed the ram with a Western Cartridge Company factory load that pushed a 139-grain hollowpoint bullet at a velocity of 2,800 fps. The day's events marked the real beginning of Jack's lifelong love affair with the 7x57 cartridge. If Jack's Sukalle-Minar 7mm is in existence today and could be located and positively identified, it would command a fortune among O'Connor memorabilia collectors.

Secondly, although the ram was O'Connor's first, it also had the best head of any desert ram he ever killed and may well have been his best overall sheep trophy. O'Connor had the ram measured for inclusion in the 1939 Boone and Crockett record book entitled *North American Big Game*. At that time sheep heads were ranked according to length only, although base circumferences were printed in the book. The big ram "green"— measured 36½ x 37½ inches with bases of 16½ inches. Bases were sometimes measured in a rather careless and cavalier manner in those days, but assuming these were accurately measured and further assuming that the horns carried their great mass throughout their length, it seems reasonable to believe that the head would have scored 180 under the current B&C system and may well have neared 185. What happened to O'Connor's big ram, coming after so long and at the expense of so much boot leather, sweat, and strain? The answer will break your heart.

O'Connor supplied the answer in a letter to Bob Housholder dated 18 October 1961.

> The best (desert) ram I ever shot was a very good ram indeed. I have forgotten the measurements but I believe it was 37½" or 38" on one side, very heavily broomed and very massive. When I was teaching at the University of Arizona I took a year off (1937–38), and since we were going to live around in rented places I left this head with a guy who had scant interest in heads. He had a chance to sell it, and did sell it. Such is life in the Far West. That head was not recorded, sad to say.

By "not recorded" O'Connor meant that the head was never measured for inclusion in modern Boone and Crockett record books, the first of which appeared in 1952. By the time the current B&C measurement system came into being in 1950, Jack's big 1935 head had been gone for thirteen years.

O'Connor's own best account of the taking of that first ram appears on page 106 of a chapter appropriately entitled "Hunting the Desert Bighorns" in his 1974 book *Sheep and Sheep Hunting*.

For the rest of his life, O'Connor always said and wrote that he felt his first ram was a sort of "fluke." He felt that the whole process had been more of a "still-hunt" than a stalk and that the kill itself had a sort of "quail-flush" feel to it.

But that all changed with the taking of his second ram. Flushed with his first success, Jack was back in action in the late winter of 1936. This time he hunted alone in Sonora's Sierra San Francisco range with only a Mexican helper, Ramon, along to tend camp and help him pack out a ram if he got lucky. And get lucky he did.

One morning, O'Connor spotted three rams high on a ridge about a mile away. By this time he had an excellent 8X30 Baush and Lomb binocular, and he stated in his account of the hunt that without the aid of his glass he would have never seen the rams. He watched them feed until they bedded down for what he hoped would be the remainder of the morning. He began his stalk around 7:00 A.M. by making a long circle around the rams and climbing the mountain behind them, having marked them down by an unusual rock formation. At five minutes before eleven o'clock, he peeped over the ridge. The two largest rams were still bedded, with the other feeding a short distance away. The two best rams were both old. One had heavy, close-curled horns broomed two or three inches wide at the ends. The other ram had equal mass with perfect points, but the horns drooped down in lazy circles. In an uncharacteristic decision, Jack, who usually preferred heavy, broomed, close-curled horns, decided to take the ram with the perfect points. The two rams were bedded facing away at around two hundred yards and somewhat below him. Jack was again carrying his little iron-sighted 7mm Mauser. Two hundred yards was no cinch shot with receiver sights. Peering through the Lyman peep, he centered the gold bead on the big ram's tailbone and cut one loose. His bullet broke the ram down in the rear end, and it required a finishing shot. Hurrying to the ram, he sat down to drink in the moment.

With a little imagination, one can almost imagine the thirty-four-year-old O'Connor as he sat nursing a cigarette, alone in his exultation. There by him lay the old ram, the little Mauser leaning against its slate-gray body. O'Connor alternately gazed at the ram and then off into the distance. Finally he had seen a ram before it had seen him, had made a well-executed stalk, and had taken the ram cleanly in its bed. O'Connor, all by himself on a mountain a very long way from anyone or anywhere, certainly felt that he had finally arrived. He was a real sheep hunter at last!

The story appeared in print only one time—on pages 137–38 in the chapter "The Art of Sheep Hunting" in Jack's 1967 book *The Art of Hunting Big Game in North America*. He had the head mounted, and it is still owned by the O'Connor family. The old head can be seen in a photograph of Jack's trophy room that appears on page 186 of the book *Great Hunters, Their Trophy Rooms and Collections,* Volume 2. By today's taxidermy standards the mount is a poor one. The old papier-mâché form has a skinny neck and no shoulders. But the big-based horns tapering in lazy circles to their long, thin tips are interesting and certainly most unusual for a desert ram. Recently, upon touching this strange head, I had the feeling of going back in time a very long way.

Jack took his next ram in December of 1937. His one written account of this hunt appeared in his book *The Complete Book of Rifles and Shotguns* (1961, 1965), on page 326–27 of a chapter appropriately titled "The Problem of Wind Allowance." It happened this way.

He was hunting alone on a gray and very windy day just inland from the Gulf of California. From a high ridge he spotted a good ram bedded just below the left end of a flat mesa and across a wide flat from his position. The ram was about a half-mile away. O'Connor backed down off the ridge and made a big circle to his right. He planned to cross the wide, brushy flat and climb up the right end of the mesa on which the ram was bedded. From there he would cross the mesa and have the ram below him. But as he hurried across the flat, the ram got up, crossed back over the ridge, and saw O'Connor. Jack, pinned down, knew he had only seconds to do something. He got into a prone position and took a quick look at the ram through the 4X Noske scope he now had on his 7mm. A twenty-five-mile-per-hour wind howled from right to left. The ram was around three hundred yards away and looking directly at him. To allow for the bullet's wind drift, O'Connor decided to hold a foot and a half to the right. It was a strange feeling holding the old Noske's post reticle out in thin air to the right of the ram's chest. But with the post rock-steady, Jack eased one off. The 139-grain hollowpoint blew the ram's heart to pieces.

As for the quality of the ram's head, Jack mentioned only the "broomed and massive horns" (what a surprise!). Sadly, it was just one more O'Connor desert sheep head that he either gave away or that just got lost over the passage of the years.

O'Connor always maintained that his favorite time to hunt desert sheep was in the spring. The desert was fresh and green with new vegetation. Weatherwise, mornings were deliciously cool and sunshine warmed the afternoons. The rams had recovered from the rut and were back in good, tender flesh. Eating desert sheep meat was one of the things that Jack always claimed he "did best." Indeed, there were numerous reasons to plan a ram hunt for the Sonora spring.

Such a hunt in the Sierra San Francisco range in the spring of 1938 was the subject of what is, for my money, the single best piece of hunting writing O'Connor ever did. To my knowledge, Jack wrote no real account of the hunt until more than twenty years after it took place. But when he did, it was a classic. The first, best, and most poignant version of the story appeared on pages 48–49 of O'Connor's beautiful *The Big Game Animals of North America* (1960), a book, incidentally, that is difficult for collectors to find. A similar version of the story appears on pages 111–113 in *Sheep and Sheep Hunting*.

I will not sully O'Connor's tale other than to say that right after dawn one morning he found the fresh trail of two rams, one very big. They were feeding their way through a desert flat with some low, rocky mountains on the left. At first O'Connor trailed along quietly, expecting at any moment to see them feeding ahead. But gradually he became convinced that the rams would turn into a left-hand canyon just ahead and climb higher to a morning bedding ground. Jack turned into another side canyon, made a fast climb to the top, and crossed over into the head of the next canyon, where he expected the rams to bed. There he waited quietly for the animals to appear below him. And they did.

This hunt was Jack's last with Charley Ren. The old outfitter and desert rat had been O'Connor's companion on several early sheep hunts, and Jack had learned much of his sheep-hunting skills from Ren. Ren died a few months after the hunt described above.

There's an interesting sidelight to the taking of this ram: It is not generally known that O'Connor was without a .270 in his arsenal in the years from 1931 or 1932 until late 1938. But late in 1934, he took delivery of his first truly custom rifle, a beautiful Minar-stocked .30-06 Springfield. The new Minar began its sheep-hunting career that spring day in 1938 when JOC killed the ram mentioned above. Jack would use the Minar seven years later in 1945 to take a pair of big Dalls in a howling snowstorm in the peaks high above the Yukon's St. Clair River.

The story of that hunt, entitled "Rams in the Snow," appeared many times over the years and is arguably O'Connor's other top sheep-hunting yarn. We'll take an in-depth look at the Minar Springfield in another chapter of this book.

O'Connor gives us no other substantive account of a desert-ram kill until the taking of his last desert sheep in 1946. By the beginning of World War II, Jack and Eleanor had four children under the age of eleven, and Jack's family demands were increasing. During the war, gasoline and rubber rationing curtailed his desert sheep hunting to a certain degree. It was nearly three hundred miles from his Tucson home to many of his favorite sheep haunts, and the rocky Sonoran desert took its toll on the paper-thin tires of Jack's old Ford station wagon. By this time, O'Connor was *Outdoor Life*'s full-time shooting editor, and the magazine demanded more and more of his attention. If that wasn't enough, it must be remembered that O'Connor was also still a full-time journalism professor at the University of Arizona. So, although he continued to hunt desert sheep during the war, for a variety of reasons these hunts were less frequent than they had been during the decade of the 1930s.

Jack O'Connor collected his last-ever desert ram in November of 1946, and the story of how he did it is the last of his five most significant desert sheep accounts. The hunt took place in Sonora's Sierra Los Mochos Mountains some six weeks after Jack had returned from a fantastically successful Stone sheep hunt in British Columbia. During a complicated stalk, a band of rams moved somewhat closer to him and bedded down along the rim of a small mesa, with the result that O'Connor crept right into the band before realizing it. The animals got his wind and bolted. Jack opened up with his beloved Minar .30-06 on the largest at a range of thirty-five yards and dropped the ram with a single running shot. The Minar's report sounded oddly flat that day in the wind up on the little mesa top, and although JOC couldn't know it at the time, the dying echoes of the '06's report heralded the end of a personal era. He had killed his last desert ram.

An excellent account of the action, along with a detailed artist's illustration of the stalk, appeared on pages 148–153 in *The Art of Hunting Big Game in North America*. The ram was old and in poor condition. O'Connor commented in a 10 September 1958 letter to Housholder:

> The last desert ram I shot was down in the Sierra Los Mochos, not far from La Cienega, Sonora. This ram was as skinny as hell without an ounce of fat on him and he was one of the few mountain sheep I have ever eaten that wasn't good. About the only good meat he had on him was the backstraps.

Although Jack had taken the ram on a permit issued by the Arizona State Museum in Tucson, he apparently did not have to turn the ram over to the museum. The head officially scored 168⁶/₈, appeared in the 1952 Boone and Crockett record book (the first one that utilized the new scoring system), and has been in every one since. O'Connor had the head mounted by the old master, Colomon Jonas. After Jack's death, it was among the collection of his trophies donated to the University of Idaho at Moscow, where it is on display. The old mount is an excellent one and in perfect condition. The head itself is a typical O'Connor favorite with its massive, close-curled, and heavily broomed horns.

OTHER DESERT RAMS

The previous stories have been thumbnail versions of the five major accounts of desert sheep kills by O'Connor. One other fragmented story by Jack told of the taking of another ram in the late 1930s. He was out of sight behind a ridge and in the last stages of a stalk on a ram. He related how a " . . . cruising crow came by, saw me, let out a startled squawk, and started flapping for other parts. I heard rocks roll as the ram took off, and presently I saw him bounding up the other side of the canyon."

This little tale ended with a cryptic quote regarding the ram's fate: "But his luck ended right there." At the time he killed this ram, O'Connor had years of shooting running jack rabbits under his belt. He just deposited his flat butt on the sun-baked, rocky ground and mowed the running ram down with one shot from his little 7x57. O'Connor may have been hunting with old Charley when he got this ram. Nothing is known about how good the head was or what became of it.

In 1938 O'Connor acquired his first custom .270 rifle. The rifle began its life when Jack acquired an old Mauser Model 98 sporter for the 8x57 cartridge. An interesting feature of the rifle's Mauser action was its curiously flat bolt handle, which was shaped somewhat like a butter knife. After being rebarreled by Bill Sukalle and restocked by Alvin Linden, this rifle became O'Connor's front-line big-game rifle for several years thereafter. As with the Minar Springfield, this rifle is discussed at much greater length in the chapter dealing with Jack's firearms.

It is known that O'Connor killed at least one desert ram with his Linden-stocked flat-bolt Mauser. Jack said as much in *Sheep and Sheep Hunting* (page 273) with this quote in reference to the flat-bolt:

> It was still on the heavy side and the barrel was too long, but I carried it in rough country in Sonora, Wyoming, Alberta, British Columbia, and the Yukon, shot it well, and with it had collected good specimens of most North American game animals as well as all varieties of North American sheep by 1946.

Little is known about the ram (or rams) taken with this rifle in terms of horn quality, exact kill location, whether the head(s) were mounted, or what finally became of the horns.

There is no account of the taking of such ram or rams anywhere in O'Connor's writings. Obviously the ram(s) were killed after 1938, since that was the year when the flat-bolt was built, but beyond that the trail disappears.

In various writings, O'Connor also mentioned that in addition to the .270, the .30-06, and the 7x57, he had also collected rams with a .348 Winchester and a .257 Roberts. Since it is well known that he never shot any northern sheep with such calibers, these rams must have been desert sheep. O'Connor's .348 was a lever-action Model 71 Deluxe Winchester that he bought shortly after this rifle first came out in 1936. By that time he owned a very accurate, scope-sighted custom .30-06 and a similar scoped custom 7x57 Mauser. Just what may have possessed him to latch onto the big .348 when he already owned two such tack-drivers is anybody's guess. Perhaps, like many westerners, he yielded for a time to the romance of the lever-action. Closer to the truth, probably, is that O'Connor simply liked fine guns for their own sake and never really needed an excuse to acquire another one. At any rate, many years later, in his December 1968 *Outdoor Life* column, he had this short comment regarding his .348: "I had one around for a while, shot a sheep and a couple of deer with it."

The entire .348 business above is related only to establish the fact that Jack collected a desert ram with such a rifle. Again, there is no photo or written account of the taking of this ram, its quality, or the final disposition of the head. He almost certainly killed it in the years between 1937 and 1940, and that is about all that will probably ever be known.

The same holds true for a ram he killed with the .257 Roberts. For this one he may have used a custom, scoped Remington Model 30 that he'd had made for Eleanor. He also might have used one of a couple of custom .257s that he had built in the very early 1940s. This ram was more than likely taken in the years between 1938 and 1943. Here, too, sadly there is no known account or photo.

After he killed his last desert sheep in 1946, O'Connor did make one last foray after Sonora rams, although how much personal hunting he may have done is uncertain. This was in 1947. O'Connor had touted desert sheep hunting to his 1945 Yukon hunting companion Myles Brown and agreed to do all that he could to help Myles get a Sonora ram. O'Connor worked his "permit magic" and secured one for Brown from Mexico City friends. The hunt took place in the Sierra Del Chino (Mountains of the Chinaman), where O'Connor had done much of his own early desert hunting. Jack himself had never had much luck in this area, but he was able to find several rams for Brown early in the hunt. Brown was getting along in years, was very heavy, and his health was deteriorating. For whatever reason, he did not connect on any of the rams that Jack the Guide located for him. O'Connor did not have much time to spend with his old compadre and after a few days returned to Tucson. A local Mexican rancher and outfitter, Epifanio Aguirre, took over Jack's guiding duties, and Brown was able to get a nice ram a day or two later, completing his Grand Slam and making him the fifth man to pull off the feat.

That fall of 1947, when he crossed the border back into Arizona, O'Connor could never have guessed that he had seen his last Sonora desert ram. For the record, he did secure one last Sonora sheep permit, dated 28 November 1951 and good until 28 February 1952, but Jack never used the permit. Indeed, it remains unknown whether he ever again visited Sonora, where he had enjoyed so many fine hunts and had so many adventures.

It was mentioned earlier in this chapter that Jack never hunted desert sheep in Baja. Though this is correct, through his Mexico City contacts he did secure not one but two Baja permits, which he figured to use in April 1959. He planned to hunt with his new hunting pal Elgin Gates, with whom he had made an African safari to the Chad Republic in January of 1958. O'Connor had been much impressed with the hunting skills, perseverance, and resourcefulness of the young Gates and looked forward to his Baja hunt. He discussed the upcoming hunt in several letters to Bob Housholder in the fall of 1958 and late winter of 1959. However, because of some O'Connor family obligations, the hunt never came off.

At one time or another, O'Connor hunted in every Sonora range that held sheep. From 1934 until 1947, he made twenty to twenty-five sheep hunts in Sonora. Hunting and camping conditions ranged from primitive to almost unbearable. He once spent ten tough days in rugged country near Puerto Libertad with his Mexican sheep-hunting buddy, Felipe Wells, never seeing a sheep, and made other, shorter hunts without seeing rams. He hunted desert sheep whenever he could get the time and rake up the few dollars that these trips cost. He loved it. Of this there can be no doubt. And one thing became clearly apparent to me after I'd done a great deal of research for this chapter: Jack O'Connor was one tough cookie.

What happened to all those great desert ram heads? For those taken on museum permits, O'Connor may well have had to donate the heads to the institutions involved. At least one and possibly two heads were stolen. Another desert ram taken by Jack is listed in the 1952 and 1958 Boone and Crockett record books with a kill date of 1939 and a score of 156 (before minimum scores were raised). However, no details are known of the ram, the hunt, or the head's whereabouts. One head is still owned by the O'Connor family and another by the University of Idaho.

The marked absence of kill photographs of O'Connor with desert rams should cast absolutely no shadow on the credibility of his desert-sheep-hunting career. There was no fakery in O'Connor. If he said he killed 'em, you could take it to the bank.

But back to the question that forms the title of this chapter: How many desert rams did O'Connor take? I hope the answer is at least a little clearer than it was before you read this chapter. Jack certainly killed no fewer than nine desert rams but probably no more than twelve. In fact, he himself may have provided the answer, albeit in a left-handed way. Writing in *The Big Game Rifle* (1951), he had this to say regarding his ram count: "As this is written, I have shot eighteen rams of all North American species—desert bighorn, bighorn, Stone, and Dall." At that time it was definitely known that he had taken three bighorns, three Stones, and four Dalls. Subtracting these ten from his stated total of eighteen leaves us with a total of eight desert rams, a figure that all true JOC fans (myself included) want to think is conservative. But Jack's statement above would also seem to be contradicted in a 1975 personal letter to a friend wherein Jack commented: "I have always really soft-pedaled the number of desert rams I have taken."

And when all is said and done, the "how many" question is one to which all O'Connor fans probably really *don't* want to know the real answer. Better that it continue to be largely unanswered. Better still for it to remain a part of the much larger and more complex mystery that was Jack O'Connor.

4

A Chronology of Bighorns, Dalls, and Stones

A few days before beginning this chapter, I had separate, interesting conversations with two of the most dedicated O'Connor fans I know. Each of these guys is a hard-core sheep hunter. Each has read, reread, and digested just about everything O'Connor ever put into print. Not surprisingly, each of these conversations turned in time to Jack's sheep-hunting career. On the subject of Jack's Grand Slams, one of these guys, who knew Jack perhaps as well as anyone ever did, stoutly maintained that O'Connor had taken only one Grand Slam. The other commented, "Hell, Jack killed seven or eight slams. Nobody really knows for sure."

Of course, as is so often the case, the real truth almost surely remains somewhere in the middle. The man who said Jack had seven or eight slams was probably misled by the fact that O'Connor told his sheep-kill stories over and over, with different twists and for different reasons. O'Connor wanted his readers to learn from his own hunting experiences in addition to being entertained by them. In some cases, these different recountings of sheep-hunting experiences make it seem that they were more numerous than was actually the case. Conversely, the man with the one-Grand-Slam theory undoubtedly based his opinion on the fact that O'Connor did relatively little bighorn hunting, collecting all of his three lifetime bighorn rams during 1943 and 1944.

Throughout his career, O'Connor was the most truthful of writers. He almost never embellished his accounts. He "told it like it was." Readers could rest assured that he was telling them the truth insofar as he knew it. His accounts of sheep hunting were no different. He wrote his sheep stories with the greatest of joy and verve, and they are among his very best writings. Yet for all his life he remained curiously silent on the taking of a certain few rams. There are at least four of these minor mysteries. When he talked at all in print about the killing of these "mystery rams," it was only to demonstrate some point about stalking, animal behavior, shooting technique, bullet placement, etc. There can be no doubt that all these rams were legally taken under totally fair-chase circumstances. Two of the four rams were absolutely first-class trophies. But again, the accounts of those hunts are mostly brief and obscure. Just why O'Connor chose to share so little of these hunting moments we can only wonder.

From the perspectives of geographical locations and time periods, Jack O'Connor's sheep hunting really involved two distinctly different careers. As described in the previous chapter, he did all his desert-sheep hunting between December of 1934 and December of 1947. All of it took place in the Mexican state of Sonora. He began hunting bighorns, Dalls, and Stones—or "northern sheep" as he sometimes referred to them—with an Alberta bighorn hunt in the fall of 1943. Timewise, therefore, these two significantly different sheep-hunting passions overlapped each other by a short four years. The second part of this rather in-depth and, I hope, unique look at Jack's sheep-hunting adventures will take a further look at his thirty-year love affair with the wild sheep of North America.

During this thirty-year period, O'Connor made fifteen hunts for bighorns, Dalls, and Stones. Although he hunted other game to at least some degree on almost all of these hunts, rams were always his main focus. These expeditions produced at least fifteen rams for O'Connor, perhaps as many as eighteen. It is during this "second" sheep-hunting career that a few inconsistencies appear.

Almost every ram O'Connor collected in this long period is a story in itself. I'll not embarrass myself by attempting to retell any of these stories already told so masterfully by O'Connor. As mentioned before, Jack related these accounts over the years from different perspectives and with different purposes. O'Connor saw every hunting situation as a learning experience and was ever anxious to share these with his readers. Therefore he "killed" his rams over and over in print.

Rather that just retelling Jack's sheep stories, I'll try, where possible, to bring out an occasional "behind the scenes" happening, curiosity, or Jack "nuance" that may never have come to light in the past. Most are merely curiosities, and some are sort of funny. Along the way, we'll explore Jack's "mystery rams" and why, in some cases and for no apparent reason, he was almost evasive about them. And just maybe we'll flesh out this talented and complex man a bit more.

By 1943 O'Connor was firmly entrenched as *Outdoor Life*'s shooting editor. The war was raging in North Africa, Europe, and the South Pacific, and the tide had not yet really begun to turn in favor of the Allies. *Outdoor Life* was distributed monthly to U.S. armed services personnel serving in all theaters of operations. Jack's departmental columns and hunting features earned him growing popularity with each new issue. But O'Connor was beginning to be impaled on the horns of a dilemma. Prior to 1943 (and all his life, for that matter), O'Connor basically confined his writing to areas with which he had personal experience. Before 1943, besides his substantial desert-sheep hunting, he had hunted Coues deer, desert mule deer, javelina, antelope, and black bear. He had hunted elk on a very limited basis. He was also an avid dove and quail hunter. But if he was to go forward as a writer at

Outdoor Life, he needed to expand his hunting horizons. In short, Jack needed new material.

No one will ever know whether this subject was first broached by O'Connor or Ray Brown, his editor at *Outdoor Life* and Jack's longtime friend. But sometime in the late winter or early spring of 1943, Brown pulled the bridle off O'Connor, telling him in a letter that *Outdoor Life* would spring for any reasonable North American mixed-bag hunt that O'Connor wanted to book. The "mixed-bag" part was important because Brown wanted as much story mileage as possible from Jack. O'Connor didn't let his beloved editor down. His accounts about adventures with rams, grizzlies, caribou, goats, and moose made it sound as if he had been on several different hunting trips, a useful skill that O'Connor employed effortlessly.

O'Connor's 1943 hunt proved to be a wonderful experience even before it began. Early on a morning in the first week of September, Jack flew from Phoenix to Vancouver, British Columbia. This was one of O'Connor's first experiences (if not his very first) with air travel, which was to become almost a way of life with him in later years. Leaving Arizona's withering heat behind, he arrived in Vancouver, one of the most refreshing climates on earth. After a good night's rest in a hotel, he was off by train in early afternoon to Mount Robson on the British Columbia-Alberta border. Train travel was one of O'Connor's lifelong passions, and he thought it relaxing and romantic. He had a fine dinner in the dining car and a sound night's sleep in his berth as the train rumbled on into the night over the Canadian National rails. So it was a keen and well-rested JOC, who alighted from the train into the coolness of a Mount Robson late morning and shook hands with Roy Hargreaves, one of the great professionals of the early-day Canadian outfitting business. As he waited around for the arrival of his hunting companion, Jack Holliday, from Hammond, Indiana, Jack breathed the tangy air and drank in the rugged mountains, purple timber, and glittering snowfields in the distance. This was going to be great!

O'Connor and Holliday had met in Tucson, where Holliday had a winter home. Both men were rifle nuts and reloaders and had run into each other in Tucson gunshops or shooting ranges. Holliday made a fine hunting partner.

Writing in *The Last Book*, published in 1984 after his death, O'Connor went into great depth about all aspects of the 1943 trip in a chapter entitled "Pack Trips I." From this and other writings, it is rather obvious that the 1943 trip remained in O'Connor's mind as perhaps the favorite hunting experience of his entire life.

O'Connor killed his first bighorn ram on opening day of the 1943 Alberta sheep season (15 September, I believe). The ram was a massive 39-incher. But it was to be eight more years before the horns would finally feel the cold steel of the official measuring tape. In fact, the twin gurus of the Boone and Crockett Club, Grancel Fitz and Dr. James L. Clark, did not even devise the current B&C measuring system until 1950, and the first record book reflecting the new system was not published until 1952. O'Connor's ram, with its official B&C score of 178 points, appeared in the 1952, 1958, and 1964 books. After this the bighorn minimum score was raised from 175 to 180, and Jack's ram got washed. Ironically, had the new measuring system been in place in 1943, and had O'Connor's ram been measured soon after the required sixty-day drying period, it would probably still be in the book as the score would almost assuredly have been over 180 at that time. The passage of eight years allowed for a lot of horn shrinkage.

It is worth mentioning here that it is almost eerie how closely Fitz's and Clark's system matched O'Connor's own notions about what constituted a true sheep trophy. Previous B&C record books had evaluated sheep heads solely on the basis of horn length. O'Connor had long contended that age

61

and horn mass were the prerequisites for a real trophy sheep head. Jack knew Clark slightly and Fitz well during this time and, inadvertently or not, undoubtedly had their ears and some input in the devising of the ram scoring system.

The best account of the taking of the bighorn ram appears in *Jack O'Connor's Big Game Hunts* under a chapter entitled "Tale of the Jinxed Ram."

I mentioned at the beginning of this chapter that O'Connor killed four or possibly five northern rams, about which very little is known. It was later in the 1943 hunt that O'Connor collected the first of these "mystery" rams.

Since so little is known about the taking of this ram, perhaps a little scene setting is in order. To begin with, O'Connor's 1943 hunt unfolded along the Albert-British Columbia border. Its early stages were conducted on the western edge of Alberta. But he had bought licenses and tags for British Columbia as well, and Roy Hargreaves had an outfitter's license for each province. The second half of the trip took place in British Columbia, and very few O'Connor fans know that Old Jack collected a bighorn there in addition to the Alberta ram taken earlier in the hunt. Besides his original feature story in the June 1945 issue of *Outdoor Life*, O'Connor gave us only one other brief account of the event. I'll let him tell us in his own words as they appeared on page 42 of *Sheep and Sheep Hunting*:

> One time in the Canadian Rockies I was traveling with a packtrain when I saw an excellent billy goat all alone at a salt lick in a timberline basin. I told the outfitter that I would stalk the goat and, if I got it, I would take off the head and cape, put the meat where it would cool, and follow the trail of the packstring to camp. I tied my horse to a handy rock, and started crawling through the stunted arctic willow in a timberline basin toward the billy. The billy was still about 300 yards away, licking busily at some clay below

a big black cliff to my left, when I heard rocks roll about 200 yards away and to my right. I looked up to see a band of seven bighorn rams coming over a ridge. Possibly they were heading for the lick. They saw the billy and stopped. I was planning to take a ram on this hunt and here was a good bunch to pick from practically in my lap. I got into a good prone position, switched off the safety of the Winchester .270 I was carrying, and put a 130-grain Silvertip through the largest ram's lungs. He dropped at the shot, dead instantly.

With the ram down, O'Connor found himself alone on a broad mountainside. He managed a couple of mediocre self-timed photos, a tedious business without a tripod. Then he faced a tricky caping-out job in the very late evening. Of course, this was no real chore to O'Connor, who had done it many times. The fact that he had stalked and taken the ram all by himself meant nothing in particular to him, since by this time in his life he had probably killed ten or more desert rams when he was utterly alone. So O'Connor caped out the ram, got the backstraps, loaded up, and trudged wearily down the mountain to his anxious, lonely horse. He then groaned into the saddle, put the ram's head in front of him, and rode off down the trail a couple more miles in the chilly gloom to where his outfit had made camp for the night.

It is interesting to note O'Connor's statement that he "was planning take a ram on this hunt." This was misleading. It would have been more correct to say that he was planning to take a ram on this "segment" of the hunt, inasmuch as he had already taken a ram earlier. This was classic O'Connor, leaving the impression that each animal taken represented a hunt all its own. Why his apparent lack of regard for this ram? Perhaps much of the "bighorn itch" had gone out of his trigger finger when he had taken his big ram earlier in the trip. Or maybe the fact that he had gotten the ram through a sort of fluke, as a byproduct of stalking a goat (of all things—O'Connor was not a goat man!), lessened this ram's importance in his mind. In fact, the ram had been pretty much a gift—so much so that his original account of the event in the June 1945 issue of *Outdoor Life* was titled "Ram on a Silver Platter."

Another indication of how apparently ho-hum the taking of the ram had been for Jack was the fact that he waited almost two years after the kill to pass the news along to his readers. Then, too, he never really liked the head. Though it was a close-curl type, normally O'Connor's favorite, the right horn was near perfect, and only moderate brooming marked the left side. The head had relatively little mass and no real length. It probably would have scored in the high 150s, but if it was ever measured, I have never heard of it. A shot of Jack with the ram in the field appeared in the photo section of *The Last Book*, although it was incorrectly captioned. A similar photo appears in this book, this time with a correct caption. Although O'Connor had this head mounted by Coleman Jonas, he never seemed to have much pride in it. It hung in his Tucson trophy room and also in the trophy room in Lewiston after the O'Connors moved to Idaho in 1948. It can be seen in isolated early pictures of Jack's Lewiston trophy room, but sometime later it disappeared, and Jack may actually have given it away. Though not one of his better rams and obviously not an O'Connor favorite, the head would be very valuable today if it ever resurfaced and could be verified.

That ram was the second of only three Rocky Mountain bighorns that O'Connor collected in his entire life. One year later in Wyoming, he would kill a ram somewhat inferior to this one, and yet he went on to write long and prolifically about the Wyoming ram. Whatever the real reasons that he seemed to take so little pride in his lonely British Columbia bighorn—if there ever were any—they are gone with the only man who was on the scene.

Early in 1944, the situation regarding shortage of hunting material was much the same at *Outdoor Life* as it had been in

1943. So once again Editor Ray Brown dispatched O'Connor on a big hunt to gather material for the magazine. (Poor Jack—what a hardship!) We can almost envision him moping around as he made his arrangements with Wyoming outfitter Ernie Miller for a long mixed-bag hunt in Wyoming's Thoroughfare country!

There were several reasons for O'Connor's choice of Wyoming. Both he and Brown felt that stories about a hunt in the United States would be well received by *Outdoor Life*'s readers. Brown also believed that readers would see a U.S. hunt as being more feasible in terms of their planning a similar trip and that it would help sell magazine advertising. From O'Connor's standpoint, although he had hunted elk several times in Arizona and taken a bull or two, he had yet to collect a big 6x6. Of course, a ram was again the main focus of the trip, but he hoped to get a big bull elk along with a Shiras moose.

Jack's 1944 hunt took place on the Buffalo Plateau, a long bench connected to Pendergast Mountain just south of Yellowstone Park.

The first day of the Wyoming sheep season, 3 September 1944, saw one of the few screwups in Jack's thirty-nine-year sheep-hunting career. He and guide Charlie Peterson were completing a stalk on a bunch of three rams, including a near-black, blocky old-timer with heavy three-quarter-curl, broomed horns that Jack wanted. He had the chosen ram marked down, but in the very last stages of the stalk, the animal changed positions with another ram that Jack had not even seen. The nickering of Jack's and Charlie's horses tied high above on the mountain alerted the rams. At this point, Our Hero simply got a good case of the jitters. With the rams about to run, Jack tumbled into a sitting position and, without checking them again, knocked the center out of the wrong ram at a range of about two hundred yards. For trivia nuts, O'Connor took this ram with his flat-bolt custom .270 Mauser, barreled by Bill Sukalle and stocked by Alvin Linden, one of his two or three main sheep rifles of the period.

When Jack and Charlie toiled across a canyon and up to the dead ram, Jack was disappointed and mad at himself. Instead of the big, dark old-timer, there lay a slender-horned seven-year-old that would have scored about 150.

But apparently Jack's disappointment and anger subsided rather quickly, and he readily owned up to his mistake. He even titled his *Outdoor Life* story "A Slight Case of Ram Fever," the same title it carried later in *Jack O'Connor's Big Game Hunts* (1963). On page 342 of this book is a photograph of Jack with the young ram. A laugher of a caption reads: "When I saw those handsome curling horns, my ram fever subsided. He was a ram for the records." The "ram for the records" part is an absolute howler. Of course, Jack wrote those captions personally. But what he was thinking when he wrote that one is anybody's guess. He must have been into the Scotch a little early that day!

I do not believe that O'Connor ever had this head mounted, for two better heads were already hanging in his trophy room. His young Wyoming ram was his last bighorn.

Gamewise, the rest of his Wyoming hunt was a success. He got a big 6x6 bull elk, another smaller bull, a nice Shiras moose, and a black bear. He finished it off by taking a couple of average antelope on the Red Desert near Rawlins, Wyoming. However, he didn't enjoy Wyoming's dry, arid country as much as he had Alberta and British Columbia a year earlier. Also, the altitude, much of it around 11,000 feet, bothered him more than he would ever admit. Ernie Miller was a good hunter and guide, but compared to organizational whizzes Roy Hargreaves and Frank Golata, with whom Jack would later hunt, Miller's outfit ran rather haphazardly.

On his return home, Jack figured to take a restful passenger train to the West Coast, stay a night or two, and then take another train home to Tucson. Even his carefully planned return trip got screwed up. When he finally did get home, though, he quickly found himself yearning for another mixed-bag hunt to the Canadian North. He soon settled on the Yukon Territory. For many years, he had wanted to hunt the beautiful, snow-white Dall sheep of the subarctic. There were also grizzlies, moose, and caribou. Again he found Ray Brown ready and waiting with *Outdoor Life*'s checkbook in hand.

Locating a good Yukon outfitter was a difficult proposition. The Depression and World War II had taken most outfitters out of the Yukon. O'Connor finally decided to go with brothers Gene and Louis Jacquot, who outfitted out of Burwash Landing. As it worked out, the Jacquot brothers really did not do much more than provide an outfit. Much of the guiding and actual work was done by Indians, of whom one, Field Johnson, was destined to become Jack's very good friend.

On the Yukon hunt, O'Connor really piled 'em up. His regular license allowed two Dall rams, two caribou, two black bears, and a moose. Grizzlies were unprotected. In addition, Jack had obtained from the Arizona State Museum a permit to take another Dall ram. (For O'Connorphiles, the Arizona State Museum is *not* affiliated with Arizona State University in Tempe. It is just what it says it is: a state museum, housed on the University of Arizona campus in Tucson, where Jack had recently resigned as the head of the journalism department.) If Jack failed to collect anything on his regular license, it is news to me. He also killed at least three grizzlies, which never failed to get him pumped. But although the other stuff was fun and made great story material, for Jack sheep were what the whole business was really about.

His hunting companion on the trip was N. Myles Brown, an industrialist from Cleveland, Ohio. Jack always referred to him as a pneumatic-tool "tycoon" (one of Jack's favorite words). O'Connor stated that Brown "weighed 275 pounds and was one of the world's most unlikely sheep hunters." Whether Jack and Myles had ever met or corresponded prior to the trip is unknown. But Brown made a fine hunting pal, shared later hunts with Jack, and became a dear friend.

Jack, guided by the already much-respected Field Johnson, killed his first Dall ram in a steep-walled canyon on Mount Nagahat above the Klutlan Glacier in the Solomon Mountains. This was in early September of 1945. O'Connor always claimed that he smelled the ram (a very real possibility) as he and Field were crossing the canyon to begin a big climb on the other side. At any rate, the two men flushed the previously unseen ram; Jack fell into a prone position and took the animal on the run at about 175 yards. His first shot knocked the ram down, but it needed a finisher. O'Connor always remembered the sharp cracks of his two .270 Remington Bronze Point bullets and wondered in print at times if this might have been the very first ram ever taken with Bronze Point bullets.

The ram was a very nice trophy at 38½ x 13¾ inches. It succumbed to Jack's Linden-stocked flat-bolt .270 Mauser, the same rifle he had used on his Wyoming ram the year before. Appropriately, Jack entitled his subsequent *Outdoor Life* story "One Whiff of Yukon Ram," and it carried the same title in his 1963 book, *Jack O'Connor's Big Game Hunts*. Later in this same hunt O'Connor collected two other Dall rams that he liked more, so I believe that his first ram is the one he eventually decided to give to the Arizona State Museum from whence his permit had come. It was later mounted by the museum and displayed there for many years, although a check with museum authorities recently (2001) revealed no trace of its existence today.

With the pressure off and two ram tickets still in his pocket, Jack could afford to be a little choosy. But it almost didn't happen.

Jack and Field spent much of the remaining hunt in little spike camps looking for big rams. Finally, almost two weeks later, with time running out, they found themselves one bitterly cold, overcast afternoon on a mountain high above the Yukon's St. Clair River. They were worn out, and the weather was rapidly deteriorating. Then, high up in a dark basin across the river, they located a group of six good rams. Wasting no time, the two men practically fell off the mountain, waded the St. Clair, and began a steep climb up the other side in weather getting colder and darker by the minute. It had also started to snow. It seemed certain that the snow and approaching darkness would make getting a shot impossible.

But finally they were under a little rimrock across a canyon from the rams. The range was over three hundred yards. Jack got into a solid prone position, placed his rolled-up down jacket in a notch in the rocks, and laid out extra cartridges. I should mention that the reticle cell in the Noske scope on the Linden flat-bolt .270 had become loose a few days before, rendering the rifle useless. It may have been the best piece of sheep-hunting luck that Jack ever had. For now he had in his hands what would eventually become the most famous O'Connor rifle of them all—the old Minar .30-06 Springfield.

At more than three hundred yards, the Minar's old 2.25X Zeiss Zeilklein scope with its post reticle didn't show him much. The rams were all bedded in two little groups of three. It was snowing harder by the second, and the light was fading. Looking through his binocular, Jack decided on two rams. One looked much like a bighorn, with heavy, broomed horns. The other was typical Dall all the way, with long, slender horns that Jack guessed would hurry forty inches. With Field calling his shots, O'Connor started shooting.

Jack always called his account of the event "Rams in the Snow" wherever it appeared, in *Outdoor Life* and later books. It's likely Jack's best sheep writing. Even O'Connor himself called the story "one of my favorite hunting tales." Again, I'm damned if I'll tell a poor substitute version of Jack at his absolute best. Suffice it to say that O'Connor sent five of the Minar's 180-grain Core-Lokts howling across the dark, snow-filled chasm. All were hits. It was incredible shooting under such trying conditions and with such a low-power scope. And when it was all over, Jack had his two chosen rams.

The typical Dall was a dandy. O'Connor related that it had "curls of over thirty-nine inches" with bases of 13½ inches. The bighorn-type ram was, however, a relative dwarf. Its horns were only 35 and 34½ inches, with bases that were barely 13 inches. Both of the rams became long-time favorite trophies of Jack's, largely because of the tough conditions under which he had killed them. Once again Jack used the taxidermy services of Coleman Jonas. Around 1970 Jack apparently gave the typical 39-incher away, as there is no trace of it in O'Connor trophy-room photos after that time.

The dwarf Dall ram remained one of Jack's all-time favorites. Jonas mounted it in a half-sneak position, and (true to his word, as you'll see below) it hung in Jack's trophy room until his death. In various photos of the trophy room, the little guy can be seen peeking out from among much larger and more impressive rams. In *Sheep and Sheep Hunting*, Jack said of the ram:

> I have the mounted head of an old Dall ram. It misses the record book by a mile. The horns are broomed off and are only about 35 inches long. But I'll always keep that head. Looking at it brings me back the days when I was younger, had good lungs and iron legs.

An obscure photo remains today of Jack with another ram, obviously also taken on the 1945 trip. The ram is a sickle-headed dink, and it seems unlikely that it was taken by Jack. The photo appears in this book with a lengthy caption. If Jack indeed plugged this little guy, he and Field must have been really hungry.

His hunting pal Myles Brown was the first man Jack ever met who had actually shot a Stone sheep. Brown and a friend, Tom Bright, had taken Stones on British Columbia's Prophet Bench a few years before Jack's and Myles's Yukon Dall hunt in 1945. During the 1945 hunt, Jack pumped Myles for information about Stone hunting. Brown felt that he could not in good conscience recommend the man who had been his and Bright's outfitter. However, he remembered another outfitter they had met on the trail. Brown had been much impressed with the outfitter and found himself wishing that he and Bright had made their hunt with him instead. The man's name was Frank Golata.

Jack came home from the Yukon already thinking about a Stone-sheep hunt to British Columbia the following fall. An introductory letter to Golata brought a quick response and a reference. The reference was a previous client of Golata's who had taken a pair of big Stones a few years before. He was Dr. Wilson L. DuComb from Carlyle, Illinois. Jack wrote to Dr. DuComb. The two men set up a dinner date at the St. Louis Athletic Club for the early spring of 1946 to coincide with a family trip that Jack and Eleanor had planned back to Missouri to see Eleanor's family.

Suffice it to say that their dinner was a success and the two men hit it off very well. In fact, the whole process started such an itch in Dr. DuComb's trigger finger that he decided to accompany Jack on the hunt.

Without a doubt, the 1946 trip was the most successful sheep hunt of Jack's career. It lasted forty-five days. Golata took O'Connor and DuComb all the way from Buckinghorse Creek on the Alcan Highway to the head of the Muskwa River and back again. The outfit traveled nearly four hundred miles and was on the trail for all or parts of twenty-eight days, leaving the Alcan Highway around 21 August and returning to it on or about 3 October. O'Connor always remembered that the trip began in late summer and ended with winter fast approaching.

The hunt produced three of the best rams that O'Connor ever killed. He got the first far from classic sheep mountains, out in what was almost prairie country. One afternoon on or about 25 August, the outfit wound its way along a shallow stream called Neavis Creek, with steep canyon walls on either side. As they rounded a bend, Frank Golata, at the head of the packtrain, saw a group of seven Stone rams bedded high on the cliffs across the creek. He pointed them out to O'Connor and DuComb. Since DuComb had previously taken Stones, he had agreed to give Jack first crack at any rams they saw. Jack dropped off his horse with his .270, planted his butt on the sandy creek bank, and, from 225 yards, sent the best of the rams plummeting in a free fall into the waters of the creek.

The story of the taking of the Neavis Creek ram formed the beginning of Jack's famous story "The Grand Slam Caper," which appeared in *Outdoor Life* and later in his book *Sheep and Sheep Hunting*. Jack remembered the Neavis Creek ram this way: "He was an excellent ram and on that forty-five day trip I saw few better."

The horns of the Neavis Creek ram were around thirty-eight inches, heavy and massive. It is inconceivable that Jack would not have had the ram mounted inasmuch as it was his first Stone. But whatever became of the head is unknown.

After that success, the party hunted a couple of days on the Prophet Bench, finding only average mature rams. They then pulled out, eventually traveling and hunting all the way to the head of the Muskwa River and back.

Three weeks later, the party returned to its previous sheep camp on the Prophet Bench. There, in late September, O'Connor killed his great 175⁶/₈ Stone ram. By this time the hunt was winding down, and they faced several long, cold days in the saddle to get back out to the Alcan Highway.

Two days before (or possibly the day before) he collected his great Stone ram, what is to me the strangest event in all of Jack's sheep-hunting experiences occurred. To some this may seem inconsequential, but for those who have mulled over O'Connor's sheep-hunting career, the event was, at the very least, unexplainable.

Three weeks before, when Jack and Frank had first made the killer climb to the Prophet Bench, they had found rams everywhere, but all were just average mature animals, and none had tickled Jack's fancy. Keep in mind that some three and a half weeks before, O'Connor had taken the Neavis Creek ram (his first Stone) and it was a great trophy, old and massive. He had hoped to get something better, but to this point he hadn't seen what he wanted. Also, O'Connor had not one but two ram licenses remaining in his hip pocket. I believe it is unlikely that he had a museum permit to take a third ram on this hunt. It seems more probable that he was simply able to buy an additional ram license from the British Columbia Game Department.

In any event, on a frosty but clear morning around 20 September, with the hunt a few days from being over, O'Connor and Golata once more labored up to the top of the Prophet Bench, and this time things were different. Old-timer rams were everywhere.

Their first hunting day was uneventful. However, in the late afternoon of the second, a not-too-difficult stalk and a clean 250-yard heart shot brought what is probably the least-known, least-talked-about ram of Jack's entire northern-sheep hunting career. And one of the best.

O'Connor always referred to it as his "bighorn-type Stone," and it is easy to see why. The ram looked for all the world like an Alberta bighorn. The horns were heavily broomed and well over 38 inches long, with bases better than 15 inches around. The head was one more that Jack had mounted by Coleman Jonas. I have seen this head several times. It scores 167²/₈ B&C (it must be the biggest 167²/₈ in history; it looks more like 180!) and appeared in the record books until it was bumped by increasing minimum scores. It had greater mass than Jack's 175⁶/₈ ram. Given the same length as Jack's "big" ram, it would have scored higher. The head is owned today by Bradford O'Connor.

Now, here comes the mystery: O'Connor chose to write one, and only one, in-depth account of the taking of his great "bighorn" Stone. It appeared in the January 1947 issue of *Outdoor Life*. He called the story "Stone Rams Don't Come Easy." It was typical Jack, with a dynamic description of the stalk, the shot, and the excitement. But parts of the story are weird and downright misleading.

Jack had this to say in his account of the last stages of his stalk on the ram: "The fact that I was that close to taking my *first stone ram* [italics mine] gave me a case of buck fever." Then, after the ram was down, Jack went farther with the "first ram" nonsense: "Since he was the *first Stone ram* [italics again mine] I had ever examined, I was very interested in him." What O'Connor meant by these "first Stone ram" comments is anybody's guess. His reference to the bighorn-type Stone as his "first Stone ram" is a pure-and-simple fib. Had he forgotten taking the Neavis Creek ram some three and a half weeks before? Was he so absorbed with his second ram that he handily forgot the first? Was O'Connor up to his old (and completely legitimate) trick of separating his stories and wringing every bit of mileage out of this hunt?

Another example of O'Connor double-talk (or at least denial) regarding this ram occurred in the excellent 1963 book *Jack O'Connor's Big Game Hunts*. It occurs in a chapter entitled "A Day in Ram Heaven," which actually deals with the taking of Jack's best Stone (175⁶/₈), which he got on the same Prophet Bench no more than a day or two after he killed the bighorn-type ram. On the day he killed his biggest ram, Dr. DuComb was hunting on the same mountain a canyon or two away. In mid-afternoon DuComb connected on a couple of nice rams. However, O'Connor and Golata *never joined up with DuComb and his guide that day*. But for some unknown reason, on page 50 of the book O'Connor felt compelled to show a photo of Frank Golata with Jack's bighorn-type ram (taken a day or so earlier). O'Connor's caption reads: "Frank cradles the handsomely curled horns of one of *Doc DuComb's* [italics mine] rams." This (as Jack himself would say) is pure applesauce. But again, it would appear that O'Connor did everything he could to make his bighorn-type ram disappear through the cracks, even to the extent of palming it off as one of Dr. DuComb's rams!

Whereas O'Connor had been very open about the fact that he had taken three rams on his 1945 Yukon Dall sheep hunt, in 1946 he seemed bound and determined to keep secret the fact that he had taken three Stone rams. What his rationale was in this (if he had one) has never been known. The rams were all first-rate trophies. There can be no doubt that all were absolutely legal. O'Connor was too smart and had too much to lose for such shenanigans.

O'Connor did admit, in a somewhat left-handed way in the pages of *The Last Book*, that he had taken three Stones by 1946. In recalling a conversation with Herb Klein, he mentioned the taking of three Grand Slams by 1946, which necessarily would have included three Stone rams. But after his *Outdoor Life* account of his second Stone ram, Jack clammed up forever about the matter.

There is the possibility that when O'Connor killed his largest Stone ram a day or two later, he was so excited and enthralled that the second ram got sort of "folded under" in his memories. But that doesn't seem much like Jack.

Here and there in his books is a photograph of Jack with this mysterious ram, usually with a caption that is vague or misleading. One such photo graced the inside back dust jacket of *Sheep and Sheep Hunting*. I realize that I have been very nitpicking in the matter of Jack's second Stone ram and, more specifically, his subsequent close-mouthed attitude about it. It was a classic stalk, a clean kill, and, for my money, Jack's third-best existing sheep trophy. Jack never owed us an explanation, but his reluctance to talk about one of his best-ever rams remains intriguing.

A day or two later, O'Connor and Golata were back on the Prophet Bench again, with one license to fill. O'Connor filled it in spades, taking the 42½-inch x 15½-inch ram that became his best Stone trophy. Because of the great number of trophy rams that he and Golata saw that day, Jack called his account of the hunt "A Day in Ram Heaven" wherever it appeared (in *Outdoor Life*'s April 1947 issue and subsequent books).

The years 1943 through 1946 saw O'Connor at the height of his sheep-hunting career. His hunts in Alberta and British Columbia (1943), Wyoming (1944), Yukon Territory (1945), and British Columbia (1946) also launched him into national fame and recognition as a big-game hunter and authoritative gunwriter. Those hunts produced nine rams (and possibly as many as eleven). Of course, there were many other noteworthy events during these trips, but I'll leave those for other parts of this book.

O'Connor would go on to hunt North American sheep twelve more times from 1947 until the end of his sheep-hunting career in 1973. But never again would he be as keen, as enthusiastic, or as productive as he was in those long-ago years of 1943–1946.

In 1947 he was again off to Stone-sheep haunts—this time British Columbia's Selkirk Mountains on a hunt arranged by Roy Weatherby. It has been suggested that Weatherby stoked O'Connor's hunt financially to curry favor with Jack. No way. Actually, Weatherby put together a group of hunters in order to strike a better deal for himself. As was its custom during those days, *Outdoor Life* paid for O'Connor's hunt. Editor Ray Brown (as well as Jack himself) looked long and hard at any gun or scope makers they perceived as trying to buy O'Connor off. For that matter, throughout his career O'Connor steadfastly refused to "get into bed" with any such companies, feeling that to do so would compromise his integrity and make it difficult to remain true to himself and his readers, something he deemed of utmost importance.

Among those on the 1947 expedition were Sheldon Coleman of the Coleman Company in Wichita, Kansas;

Jack's father, Andy O'Connor, with a bag of Gambel quail shot in Arizona before 1920. Andy noted on this photo that his shotgun was made to order by Lefever at Syracuse, New York. (Photo courtesy of Eduarda Yates.)

In his very early desert-sheep days, Jack often carried his riflescope in a small pouch on his belt while climbing in the roughest country. Later he would slip the scope into its mounts on his rifle. Here he takes a peek through his scope. This may have been one of the occasions when his "funny little French binocular," as he called it, was on the blink. Photograph taken in the Sierra Los Mochos, Sonora, Mexico, 1936.

This is one of the strangest photographs in the entire O'Connor collection. At first glance, Jack appears to be carrying the head of a freshly killed ram down off a mountain. But closer examination shows the ram head to be mounted. This was actually Jack's second desert ram, killed in Sonora in late 1937. This photo was taken, probably by Eleanor, in the desert outside Tucson sometime after the ram had been mounted. By this time, Jack was writing almost exclusively for Outdoor Life, *and his desert-sheep exploits were a significant part of his hunting background. For several reasons—among them the fact that he often hunted alone and had no self-timed cameras—Jack had few desert-sheep kill photographs. This contrived shot was one he had made to build "photographic inventory" for future magazine pieces, although it never appeared in print. This in no way casts doubt on the authenticity of his desert-sheep hunting. Jack shot his own stuff; of that there can be no doubt.*

O'Connor and Frank Seibold tie a 5x6-point Arizona whitetail to the saddle. This buck was shot on the Seibold Ranch near Patagonia, Arizona, in 1939 by Jack's friend Dr. Charles Sarlin, who probably took the photograph.

Jack's desert-sheep-hunting mentor Charlie Ren takes a look at Jack's new Model 71 Deluxe .348 Winchester, probably in 1937. Jack bought the Model 71 when it first appeared on the market in 1936 and used it to take at least one desert ram. His use of this rifle for sheep seems a bit strange considering that he owned several scope-sighted, bolt-action sporters at the time. But then, Jack loved guns for their own sake. Perhaps he became enamored with the idea of taking a ram with the big lever gun. He did pull the trick off, but nothing is known of the ram he killed with it. The ram head at Ren's feet is a pickup.

Jack's first and best-ever desert ram, killed on triangular Tepopah Mountain near the Sonoran coast in September of 1935. Jack got the ram with one rear-end shot from his aperture-sighted, Minar-Sukalle 7mm Mauser as it ran over a ridge at less than fifty yards. With horns 36½ and 37½ inches long and bases 16½ inches around, the head would have placed very high in modern B&C records. O'Connor had the head mounted, but it was later stolen. Jack was accompanied on this hunt by a Mexican friend, José Del Rosario. Just why O'Connor never had his photo taken with this ram is unknown.

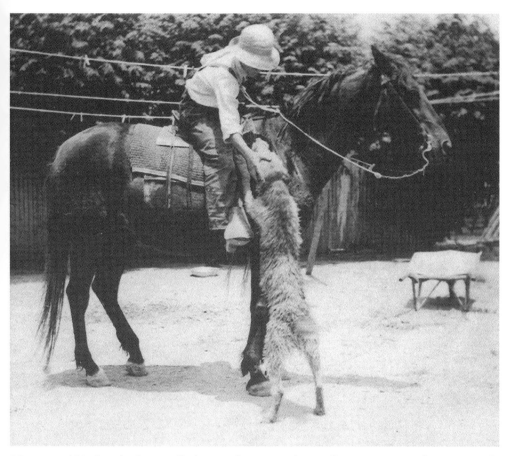

Nine-year-old Jack on his horse, Billy, leaning down to pat his Uncle Jim O'Connor's dog, Major. The photograph was taken at his Uncle Jim's Box O Ranch near Florence, Arizona. Jack was a horseman from boyhood, often going on long, solitary jaunts into the desert at a very young age, armed with a Model 92 Winchester in caliber .25-20. During these jaunts he killed his first game, a javelina, and later a young mule deer buck.

This photo of Eleanor O'Connor and a Coues deer she shot in the Cucurpi Mountains of Sonora in December 1935 first appeared in Jack's December 1936 Sports Afield *article "On the Trail of Mystery Deer." Eleanor downed the buck with a fusillade of shots from her .257 Roberts at an estimated 500 yards, shooting across the basin in the background.* (Photo courtesy of Henry Kaufman.)

Carroll Lemon, left, was one of Jack's favorite hunting companions and also helped answer Outdoor Life *fan mail for Jack during the busy war years. Jack took this photo of Carroll and Eleanor with an antelope jack rabbit in 1940, several miles south of Oracle, Arizona.*

Eleanor O'Connor with two javelina shot in 1936 in the Cubabai Mountains of northern Sonora for the Arizona State Museum in Tucson. The larger boar was her first javelina. In her right hand she holds quail taken by Jack with his .30-06 for their supper.

The Ithaca Grade 2 double 20-gauge, shown here with Eleanor on a 1937 Arizona quail hunt, was a gift from her husband nearly ten years earlier. With the stock shortened and a recoil pad added, the gun fit Jack's diminutive wife well.

Doris Seibold, left, and Eleanor O'Connor with an outstanding atypical Coues deer shot by Doris in 1945. This buck had eluded hunters for years, and was the first deer the ranchwoman had ever shot. In an Outdoor Life *story, Jack stated the buck had a total of eighteen points.*

Although not known as a handgunner, Jack owned several and used them for plinking and small game. Here Eleanor fires Jack's Colt Officers Model .22 during a family picnic in the Arizona desert.

Eleanor doing a little housekeeping on some of Jack's early trophies in the late 1930s. One of Jack's first desert-sheep heads can be seen at the left, and it ain't much to write home about.

This outstanding pronghorn was shot by Eleanor on opening morning of Arizona's first antelope season, 20 September 1941. She took it near Hay Lake on Anderson Mesa with her Remington 30-S in caliber .257 while hunting with Jack, Carroll Lemon, and the Ronstadts. Jack had campaigned for a limited open season for the previous seven years.

O'Connor with a raghorn 5x5 bull elk. This photograph was taken in September 1944 in Wyoming on a sheep and elk hunt Jack made with Ernie Miller as his outfitter. Jack killed a big trophy 6x6 bull on this same hunt. Why he elected to shoot this bull is anybody's guess. Perhaps their camp needed some protein. Maybe Jack shot the bull just as a barrel-warmer.

Jack killed this Kaibab buck literally in its tracks with one shot from his Sukalle-Minar 7x57 Mauser during a horseback hunt in the fall of 1937. The buck, posed with Eleanor, has occasionally been captioned as her kill. In truth, she bagged a forkhorn on this hunt.

Jack with a jack in the Arizona desert in the early 1940s. The rifle is his old Minar-stocked .30-06 Springfield, one of O'Connor's front-line big-game rifles in the 1935–1946 period. During those years he did much of his practice on running jack rabbits with big-game calibers. He always stated that the skills he learned from such practice stayed with him throughout his life.

Eleanor and Jerry. Eleanor is exactly what she appears: a young, vibrant mother loving her child. Jerry's face shows no indication of the demons that would haunt him in later years. Here he is only a young boy needing and getting affection from his mother.

Eight-year-old Jerry retrieves a whitewing dove for his mother while Brad looks on. At the time of this photo in late August 1939, Eleanor was nearly eight months pregnant with her last child, but still went on dove shoots, which were usually family outings.

This Ford station wagon carried the O'Connor family and their camp gear on countless hunting trips throughout Sonora, Mexico, and Arizona prior to and during the World War II years. It also provided local transportation for family picnics and plinking sessions in the desert, as shown here with Eleanor and young Jerry.

The O'Connor girls, Caroline and Catherine, admire the colorful feathers of a rooster quail during a family hunt southeast of Tucson in 1946. Cathy holds a desert gourd in her hand.

This outstanding buck was shot by Jack in 1943 in the Canelo Hills of southern Arizona. He used the same Linden-stocked Model 70 in .270 that he took to Alberta earlier the same year.

Jack's younger son, Bradford, was thirteen when he shot his first buck on Major John Healey's ranch in the Huachuca Mountains with his mother's lightweight Mauser .257.

Eleanor and Jerry O'Connor inspect a prairie dog shot in a high mountain meadow near Slade Ranch during one of their last vacations there at the end of World War II. The numerous prairie dogs were eradicated through government poisoning programs by the early 1950s. (Photo courtesy of Washington State University Library, Special Collections)

Idaho held its first open season on sage grouse in 1949. Vernon Speer flew Jack and his son Brad (second from right) to Caldwell and took this photo of the successful hunters.

O'Connor's best elk, a bull scoring in the 330–340 B&C range. Jack's old friend Les Bowman outfitted him on this Wyoming hunt. At 300 yards, O'Connor put his first 150-grain .270 bullet into the big bull's lungs. Before he could reload and get off another shot, the bull was down and out. Absaroka Range, Wyoming, September 1954.

Vernon Speer, founder of Speer Bullet Company, and Jack with a pair of Idaho pheasants. Vernon was greatly responsible for Jack's move to Idaho and also introduced him to pheasant hunting.

This desert mule deer buck was shot in the foothills of the Rincon Mountains east of Tucson by Jack's older son, Jerry.

Jack's older daughter, Catherine, takes aim with his Model 70 Winchester in 7x57 a couple years after it was built in 1957. This was the main rifle Jack used on his last African safari, to Southwest Africa and Rhodesia in 1972.

Caroline O'Connor poses in 1953 with an Idaho pheasant and the Remington Model 11-48 Deluxe in 28-gauge with which her father taught her to shoot skeet.

Eleanor holds a limit of California valley quail shot in the fall of 1948 right after the O'Connors moved from Arizona to Idaho. These birds were taken across the Snake River in Washington and retrieved by their cocker spaniel, Pat.

Coleman chief designer Dean Olds; Weatherby crony Ken Niles; Weatherby; O'Connor; Arthur C. Popham, Jack's old pal from his Sonora days; and three or four other hunters. Just how enthusiastic Jack may have been about the whole deal will never be known, for he was still flushed with the success of his three-ram British Columbia hunt with Golata the previous year. The large size of the party gave the hunt a sort of clambake flavor, which would have been anathema to Jack's lone-wolf heart. But he went along anyway and took a goat but not a ram. He wrote an account of the trip in the November 1947 issue of *Outdoor Life*. The trip was significant in that it was Jack's first opportunity to take any game with the .300 Weatherby Magnum. He came away from the experience suitably impressed.

By the late 1930s, Jack had become an avid reader of the writings of Charles Sheldon, the great sheep hunter and naturalist who was also the first Grand Slammer. Jack's favorite among Sheldon's works was *The Wilderness of the Upper Yukon*, an autobiographical account of Sheldon's hunting and study of the Fannin sheep of the Yukon's Pelly Mountains and other ranges during the years 1912–1913. Sheldon personally created a series of accurate drawings of the various color phases of Fannins in various areas as he had observed them in his studies. How the Stone sheep of British Columbia "graded" into the classic Dalls of the Yukon and Alaska also held a special fascination for O'Connor—so much so that many years later, in 1969, Jack included Sheldon's sketches in his own classic, *Sheep and Sheep Hunting*. By the late 1940s, O'Connor had resolved to get a good Fannin ram. This was such a high goal for Jack that he personally orchestrated and went on three Fannin hunts stretching over a twenty-four-year period from 1949 to 1973. His Fannin fetish wasn't something he verbalized very much, but his failure to get a real trophy Fannin ram was a disappointment to him till the end of his life.

He organized the first of his Fannin hunts during the late winter of 1949. It was to be into the Pelly Mountains of the Yukon, an area Jack had long wanted to hunt. If he ever mentioned the name of the outfitter, I have never heard it. However, he insisted that the outfitter take along Jack's old friend and guide from 1945, Field Johnson. O'Connor had high regard for Field as a person and felt that he could do much to make the trip a success. It may also have been that Field needed the work and Jack saw the hunt as an opportunity to give him some much-needed employment. Jack's old hunting pal from 1945, Myles Brown, was again to be his partner.

The entire trip was a faux pas. The outfitter was poorly organized, there was not enough food, and they saw no sheep and little other game. Jack blew away a traveling grizzly with his .300 Weatherby, the second game animal he had taken with the caliber, and he continued to be impressed with the killing power of the cartridge. This hunt was, I believe, Myles Brown's last. Not too long after the trip, a stroke ended his hunting days. It also ended Jack's first quest for a Fannin ram. But he wasn't through.

In September of 1950 Jack made his third Dall hunt. Again he went to the Yukon, and this time he was outfitted by the pioneer and excellent Yukon firm of Davis and Berard. This was the first of three hunts that JOC would make with Davis and Berard. He hunted with them again in 1956 and on Eleanor's first sheep hunt in 1963. Accompanying Jack in 1950 were Herb Klein, whom Jack had met through Roy Weatherby, and Herb's pal from the Texas oil patch, Red Early. Jack got along well with Herb, who was quiet and soft-spoken. Such was not the case with Red, who was loud and boisterous and grated on Jack's nerves. (Jack should have taken the trouble to get to know Red better. Despite his larger-than-life personality and booming voice, Red Early was one of the kindest and most charitable men I have ever met.) It is possible that Klein had hunted Dalls before. Red had not. Both men hoped to get Dall rams as steps toward their Grand Slam, which was just beginning to be known as a great North American hunting feat.

Herb was really excited about the prospects of having Jack along on the trip as a sort of "playing coach." But a throat infection sidelined Herb in Dallas and later in Seattle and kept him from going into camp with the rest of the party. He caught up with them in two or three days, being flown in and landed on a nearby lake. While "playing coach" O'Connor waited around for his main protégé, he calmly rode out on the first day of the hunt with his guide, Moose Johnson, and collected what is arguably his finest North American sheep trophy— after what he always said was the easiest stalk of his entire sheep-hunting experiences.

It happened this way: After spotting a small group of rams early in the morning, Jack and Moose rode around the left flank of the big crescent-shaped mountain on which the rams were bedded and climbed the rather gentle slopes on the back side. After arriving at a spot just over the ridge from where the rams were bedded, they tied their horses and made a short climb—really not much more than a stroll. They got in so close that O'Connor's raising of his rifle to shoot alerted the rams and they took off. Jack killed the ram on the dead run at long quail-flush range. So easy was the whole deal that Red Early went along on the stalk and got another good ram from the same bunch.

The taking of the 1950 Dall marked the last time Jack would kill a ram with any caliber other than a .270. In 1947, when it had become apparent that his beloved Minar Springfield was over the hill, Jack had another .30-06 made up. This particular rifle was the second of many that Al Biesen would build for him. O'Connor killed the big 1950 Dall with his three-year-old Biesen .30-06.

With its great, unusual, bow-shaped horns, Jack's big Dall head is unique. I have seen it many times, and it seems to grow larger every time I do. The head is a part of the O'Connor collection on display at the University of Idaho in Moscow.

A minor point of interest is the fact that Jack's big Dall ram officially scored 177$\frac{1}{8}$ B&C and appeared with that score in every record book until the 1988 edition. In that book, the ram's score was inexplicably dropped to its present score of 176$\frac{7}{8}$. Why this happened is a mystery.

Oddly and for whatever reasons, O'Connor wrote little about this ram, his finest of all. It was almost as though he felt a little unworthy of his great trophy, given the ease with which he had collected it.

By 1950 Jack had killed a boxcar load of moose, caribou, and grizzlies. Therefore, on the 1950 hunt he killed no game other than his big ram. It was the beginning of a trend toward smaller bags that would continue to the end of his life.

In the early spring of 1951, Jack came down with another case of "Fannin sheep fever." He decided to make a hunt that fall in an area east of Atlin Lake in northwestern British Columbia. His choice of areas was a strange one indeed, as this was far from typical Fannin country. O'Connor explained his decision in *Sheep and Sheep Hunting*: "Since I am a romantic fellow who likes to hunt in all the classic areas, I made a trip there (Atlin) in the fall of 1951." But the Atlin Lake area was anything but "classic" sheep country. No outfitter had operated there since before the Depression. So, by mail and telephone, O'Connor assembled his own outfit consisting of his Yukon friend Watson Smarch and British Columbia guides George Edzerza and Harry Johnson, neither of whom knew much about the area.

The hunting party consisted of a first-time sheep hunter, seventy-year-old Dr. E. G. Braddock of Lewiston, Idaho; Jack's bullet-making friend Vernon Speer; and Jack's eighteen-year-old son Bradford, also on his first sheep hunt.

Jack had visions of big, goggled-eyed, saddle-backed Fannin rams with heavy, sweeping horns. He couldn't have been more mistaken. Each hunter collected a ram, but all were very small in both horns and body size. In fact, Jack called them "the smallest North American sheep I have ever seen." Brad's ram was nine years old, but its horns were only 34 inches in length. Jack referred to it as a "big old ram in miniature." Jack's own ram was an old-timer of eleven years, but the headgear was barely 30 inches long!

The hunt was an especially big success for Brad. Besides his ram, he got a nice goat and a tremendous mountain caribou, which scored 408⅝ and won him a gold medal at the 1952 Boone and Crockett competition.

Jack's account of the entire hunt appeared in the March 1952 issue of *Outdoor Life*. Jack titled it "The Dwarfs of Turn Creek," after the size of the sheep and the Eva Lake-Turn Creek area where they were taken.

The 1951 Atlin Lake hunt was an interesting chapter in Jack's sheep-hunting life, although not a particularly successful one in terms of ram quality. Jack had the Turn Creek rams mounted, and presented Brad's to him as a present. But over the years both rams have disappeared from the scene. The whole affair failed to cure Jack's yen to get a big Fannin. But it was one sheep-hunting goal he was never to realize.

For all his life, Jack O'Connor had an interesting habit that showed his softer side. He liked to reprise interesting experiences of his past and share them with people he cared about. He especially enjoyed doing this with packtrain trips and sheep hunts. Jack's 1950 Yukon hunt with Herb Klein and Red Early had been wonderful, with great game, solid hunter success, and a great outfitter. Like the outfits of Roy Hargreaves in 1943 and Frank Golata in 1946, Yukon pioneer Alex Davis's outfit had run sewing-machine smooth.

In the spring of 1956, Jack found himself hurting all over for an encore Yukon hunt with the Davis outfit. He prevailed upon his good friend Fred Huntington, RCBS tool and die maker from Oroville, California, to come along. Also on the trip was Jack's new editor at *Outdoor Life*, Bill Rae. Jack cared greatly for Bill Rae, and Rae was one of the few men who had O'Connor's absolute respect. Another O'Connor friend, Red Cole, rounded out the outfit.

The hunt began in early September and lasted thirty days. Again the Davis outfit ran, for the most part, like clockwork. Game was plentiful. All the hunters got rams, and most of the party collected either moose or grizzlies. The taking of Jack's own ram provided yet another example of his tremendous rifle skills. As the ram bumped along at an uneven run just under a ridge line some 250 yards away, O'Connor shot four times and connected every time! His first bullet broke the skin on the ram's back, sending a shower of white hair into the air. The second just cut the hair on the ram's chest. The third bullet broke the animal's jaw and spun him around. The fourth was right in the engine room and put the ram down. Carrying curls of 40¼ and 39¾ inches, the ram was the third and last 40-plus-incher of O'Connor's career. If he ever had the ram officially scored, he never mentioned it in print. In those days, the Boone and Crockett minimum for Dall sheep was 160. Jack's ram certainly scored in the low-to-mid 160s and would have made the book at the time. Why O'Connor never pursued this is unknown.

For the most devoted O'Connorphiles, it is worth mentioning that Jack collected this ram with his "grizzly loads." Because the Dawson Range country was crawling with the big bears, Jack kept his Biesen-remodeled Model 70 in .270 filled with cartridges loaded with 150-grain Nosler Partition bullets ahead of 58½ grains of No. 4831 powder. It marked the only time Jack ever killed a ram with any .270 bullet weight other than a 130-grainer.

On the 1956 hunt, O'Connor pulled one of the dumbest stunts of his hunting career. As it worked out, nothing bad came of it, but it made no sense whatever. When a mixed bunch of rams and ewes filed by at sixty yards just above timberline, Jack thought long and hard about taking the best of the rams, which was about 40x35 inches. He finally decided to pass it up. But then he decided to see if he could just clip the hair on the ram's back without hurting the animal. The ram was standing behind a ewe with just his back line showing. Fortunately, Jack's bullet did just what he set out to do, clipping the skin and sending a shower of white hair into the air. The ram ran off unhurt. But there was nothing to be gained by the stunt. Jack might have accidentally killed the ram, which he had already decided he did not want. He might have wounded and lost it. Worse still, he might have killed or wounded the ewe. In any event, it was very un-O'Connorlike behavior.

The 1956 foray was a marvelous experience in almost every way and one of O'Connor's most enjoyable sheep hunts. In *The Best of Jack O'Connor*, he described his feelings about a morning early in the hunt, saying: "It was a wonderful day. The air was like spiced wine and life was wonderful."

After that Yukon hunt, Jack was out of the North American sheep-hunting business until the fall of 1961. A severe automobile accident 15 January 1957 near Spokane cost O'Connor that entire year in healing and rehabilitation. In 1958 and again in 1959, he was occupied with African safaris.

The fall of 1961 found Jack again up to his old trick of attempting to recreate the past. He had always remembered with great fondness his 1943 Canadian hunt with Alberta outfitter Roy Hargreaves. Everything about the hunt had been near perfect: efficient outfitter, great hunting success, good camps, beautiful country. Although Roy was no longer in the business, Jack made arrangements with another outfitter to go back into the same old country. This time he took Eleanor along on what was really her first sheep hunt, and also their daughter Caroline, who had just graduated from college. Also accompanying them was Fred Huntington Jr., son of Jack's buddy, Fred Huntington Sr. Instead of finding his beloved hunting country as he had left it in 1943, Jack and his family arrived in what was essentially a mountain slum. Development and mining had ruined it, further convincing Jack that man in his greed and shortsightedness would eventually spoil everything in the world.

Jack took Eleanor with him again on his third and final hunt with the Alex Davis outfit in 1963. This time they hunted in the Yukon's famous Ruby Range, a long-time Dall-sheep El Dorado. Jack did not take a ram, although he had his chances. Eleanor got her first sheep, a magnificent 44½-inch ram, after a long stalk on a windy, freezing day. The ram officially scored 177⁴/₈ and won her a first-place medal at the 1964 Boone and Crockett competition.

Jack, Eleanor, and Bradford all hunted Stone sheep in British Columbia's Cassiars in August of 1967. Outfitter Bruce Creyke-Dennis guided the party. This was another case of O'Connor wanting to hunt in one of the classic sheep locations about which he had read since boyhood. Jack's and Eleanor's rams were the result of a "drive" on about eighty animals that had camped out in a big basin and could not be stalked in any conventional manner. A howling snowstorm that hit just as the O'Connors collected their rams put the whole affair into such a let's-hurry-up-and-get-the-hell-out-of-here mode that no kill photographs were made. Jack's ram was 36½ inches, while Eleanor's was 37¼. Jack had the rams mounted, and his can still be seen at the University of Idaho.

In 1968 Jack and Eleanor were invited on a "freebie" Stone-sheep hunt by a British Columbia outfit that was opening up a new area. Eleanor killed a nice bull caribou and caught a lot of grayling, thereby keeping the party in good "vittles," but no rams were taken.

Jack's last two successful sheep hunts were again for Stones, with well-known British Columbia outfitter Frank Cooke.

These were in 1971 and 1973. Important to these hunts was the fact that horses could be used in much of Cooke's territory. Often, only the final stalks were made on foot. This was crucial for Jack, whose big climbs were behind him. On his 1967 hunt with Bruce Creyke-Dennis, O'Connor had learned just how helpful a stout horse could be to a pooped old sheep hunter.

The 1971 ram was a dandy, broomed and heavy, scoring in the low 160s. The head was mounted and is on display at the University of Idaho.

The 1973 ram was just a ram. It had shallow curls of around 35½ inches and perfect, unbroomed points. But for a seventy-one-year-old sheep hunter, it wasn't too bad! O'Connor never had this ram mounted, and today the horns are owned by Cathy O'Connor.

I should mention that O'Connor made one final attempt at a Fannin sheep with a hunt in 1972 into the Pelly Mountains of the Yukon. The Fannins had eluded him for so long, and this hunt was no different. Jack didn't feel well, had some trouble getting around, and it just wasn't to be.

His 1973 British Columbia Stone-sheep hunt concluded O'Connor's northern-sheep career, begun thirty years earlier. During that period he made sixteen hunts for bighorns, Stones, and Dalls and collected at least fifteen rams. Eight were taken on just three hunts (1943, 1945, 1946). On seven other trips he killed one ram per hunt, and on five hunts (1947, 1949, 1961, 1963, 1972) he drew no sheep blood. His fifteen "known" rams included three bighorns, seven Stones, and five Dalls. Actually, he may have killed two or three more. Whether Jack actually killed the little 1945 Dall ram mentioned earlier in this chapter (see shot in photo section) is not known. He also makes obscure mention in some of his writings of taking one or two other rams (also Dalls) that cannot be linked in any way to any of his other kills. As far as Grand Slams were concerned, by the time Jack returned home to Arizona from his 1946 British Columbia Stone-sheep hunt, he had completed three. Later, after adding the other North American sheep species, he had all the ingredients for five Grand Slams—except that he collected only three bighorns in his life. In the Grand Slam mania of today, it is easy to forget that O'Connor *completed* three Grand Slams before the term was ever applied to North American sheep hunting.

Jack never referred specifically to the Boone and Crockett scores of any of his rams other than the big 1946 Stone sheep (175⁶/₈) and his 1950 Yukon Dall (176⁷/₈). His 1943 Alberta ram was his best bighorn, and he certainly knew its official score (178), but curiously he never made reference to it in print. The same holds true for his best "surviving" desert ram, taken in 1946. It officially scored 168⁶/₈. (Almost certainly, Jack's first desert sheep, taken in 1935 and later stolen, would have gone 180 or better.) His best bighorn (178), his best desert ram (168⁶/₈), his best Stone (175⁶/₈), and his best Dall (176⁷/₈) give O'Connor's best slam a cumulative score of 699³/₈ Boone and Crockett points, right at the mythical 700 figure, the absolute Mecca for ultra-focused North American sheep hunters.

In concluding this long, wandering chapter, allow me to return for a moment to the total number of North American rams that Jack may have taken. Sometime in the mid 1970s, after he had collected his last ram, I read an O'Connor quote in which he stated that he had taken twenty-seven North American rams. I lost track of where I read the quote, and it has haunted me ever since. I know I didn't dream this up, but I have never been able to relocate the quote, though I have looked for it off and on for twenty years. To a great extent, it would corroborate the findings in this book's two chapters dealing with O'Connor's sheep career.

But there's a capper to all this. In a June 1977 letter to Grand Slam Club Executive Director Bob Housholder, Jack had this to say regarding his ram count: "Counting Asian and African sheep, I have shot well over FIFTY. Maybe more."

Of Old World species, as far as I know, O'Connor killed no more than five Urials, two red sheep, and one aoudad, for a total of eight. Subtracting these from his stated fifty-plus ram total, we are still left with some forty-three rams in all. Jack loved to pull Bob Housholder's leg and did so frequently. But if indeed he wasn't telling a "fun fib," then we are left knowing one undeniable fact:

Jack sent a whole lot more desert rams to the cemetery than he ever told us about.

5

The Absent-Minded Professor

Beginning in the late 1930s and continuing for almost forty years, several generations of Americans who loved guns and shooting would each month await the arrival of *Outdoor Life* in the mailbox or on the newsstand. During World War II, *Outdoor Life* was the sporting magazine selected by the armed forces to be sent to military personnel in all theaters of the war effort. From New Guinea to North Africa, in trenches and in tanks, on battlewagons and in bombers, many men would read no other part of these magazines until they had thoroughly digested every word of Jack's departmental column or his popular "Getting the Range" technical advice. A full-length piece by the Great Master featuring an exciting hunting experience was icing on an already delicious cake.

For the great majority of these people, the only contact they would ever have with O'Connor was through his clear, logical writing. He had the ability to present technical data and other information in a conversational and easily understood manner. Photographs of him in *Outdoor Life* columns and feature stories presented an image of a clear-thinking and lucid, albeit rather stern and professorial, individual—a man readers just knew could always be counted on to be careful and decisive.

As we shall see, behind this cool, calculating image lurked a sometimes-bumbler capable of some rather astounding mental lapses. Most were merely funny and harmless and became the grist of family history (if anyone ever dared remind JOC of them!).

One hilarious incident occurred in 1938, when the O'Connor clan was still living in Tucson. For years Jack was an active member of a hunting and conservation organization known as the Arizona Game Protective Association. During this time he gave many talks and speeches about various subjects he deemed important to the preservation of Arizona's wildlife. One pet project was an ongoing agitation for the Arizona Game Department to declare a limited open season on antelope in certain areas of the state. On the night in question, the association was to hold its monthly dinner meeting in a downtown Tucson restaurant. O'Connor was scheduled to give a talk about his pet subject. He arrived home in late afternoon, practicing his speech in his mind. Later he changed clothes and drove downtown in the family station wagon. Parking along the street, he went in to enjoy dinner, the meeting, and the company of numerous hunting friends.

When dinner was over, the great orator delivered his passionate plea in behalf of opening a season on antelope (which happened to be curiously in line with O'Connor's hunting desires). His speech was well received, and after the meeting Jack walked out of the restaurant, chewing the fat with several of his cronies. One of his pals offered Jack a ride home. O'Connor accepted, climbed into his pal's car, and rode away, blissfully forgetting his own station wagon parked near the restaurant. A few minutes later, after telling his friend good night, O'Connor went wearily into his house and went to bed. The next morning, still feeling the rush of his talk of the previous evening, he was up early, as was his custom. He bathed, shaved, dressed, ate breakfast, and went outside to go to work. After evaluating the cold, empty garage, he burst back into the house, shouting, "Jesus Kerrist, Eleanor! Some Goddamned Sonofabitch has stolen the car!"

And then there was the Great House Painting Debacle. More than a singular mental lapse, this one was an ongoing misery of several days' duration. It occurred during the early 1950s, several years after the O'Connors had moved to 725 Prospect Avenue in Lewiston, Idaho. Jack had become convinced that the house needed a new coat of paint. He also decided that, rather than hiring the job done, he could handle it himself. He commandeered sons Jerry and Brad, both then in their early twenties, to help with the project. O'Connor daughters Cathy and Caroline, as well as Brad, who was actively involved in the agony, all remember a nightmare of precariously leaning scaffolding, spilled paint, cursing, and confusion. Once, Eleanor emerged from the house to find Jack in the process of turning the air blue after narrowly averting a serious fall. Somehow the image of the Father of North American Sheep Hunting standing on a rickety ladder and lashing angrily away with a paintbrush is one that thousands of his fans (myself included) would just as soon forget.

Forgotten cars and Chinese fire drills disguised as house-paintings were harmless, funny occurrences, destined to weave their way into the fabric of O'Connor family lore. But the slip-ups weren't all funny.

To set the stage: Writing in *The Last Book*, JOC heaped abuse on an admirer who came to visit in the O'Connor home one fine day. As many of his fans were prone to do, this citizen was interested in looking at some of Jack's fine rifles. Somehow in the course of admiring a beautiful custom .338, this character managed to get some cartridges into the magazine. From there, one found its way into the payhole, and from there . . . ear-splitting report! (*Author's Note*: Few sounds are louder than a .338. Touching one off indoors would be unimaginable.) There was a small, neat hole in the O'Connor ceiling and a much larger hole in the roof where the 250-grain softpoint exited on its way to the stratosphere. Although some of Jack's ire was aroused by the fact that the guy never made any effort to pay for the damages, O'Connor was primarily angry that this bungler had committed the unpardonable firearm sin of letting a gun go off accidentally—and in the house, no less.

Hey. Jack didn't have any room to talk.

More scene-setting: In his 1963 book, *Jack O'Connor's Big Game Hunts*, in the chapter "My Prize Wore Sable," Jack told of taking a magnificent 44¼-inch sable during his first African safari in 1953. Few O'Connor admirers know that Jack "killed" this sable twice—once in Tanganyika and once where it hung above the staircase at O'Connor's home in Lewiston!

O'Connor was no different from many fine rifle shots in that he did a great amount of dry-firing. One day in his upstairs gun room/study, Jack picked up a rifle (caliber unknown, but something ostensibly capable of one-shot kills on sable). Raising the bolt to set the firing pin, he centered the cross hairs on the big bull and gently squeezed the trigger. As Gomer Pyle probably would have said, "Surprise! Surprise!! Surprise!!!" O'Connor's bullet took the sable bull high in the shoulder, dropping it for the count (or off the wall), much as it had happened years before in brightest Africa.

On another occasion, which also took place one afternoon at the Lewiston house, Caroline, about twelve at the time, was relaxing with a magazine in the O'Connor living room. She got up from the sofa and went out into the kitchen to get a Coke. Suddenly from upstairs came a roar like that of a 90mm cannon. Another Jack miscue had sent a bullet through the upstairs floor, its path running right through where Caroline had been sitting only a few seconds before and ripping through a bookcase before finally embedding in the wall. Son Bradford was in the upstairs bathroom getting policed up for a date. A shy lad, he burst from the bath clad strategically in a towel and a lot of foamy hair shampoo. A screaming Eleanor rushed upstairs to check for casualties. She met a shaky Jack coming down the stairs carrying a couple of rifles. Although he looked as white as a sheet, he brazened it through, announcing laconically that he was "going out to sight in a couple" despite the fact that it was nearly dark outside.

And just once, one of these firearms goof-ups caused blood to flow. This was during the Tucson years, in the summer of 1938. Eleanor was pregnant with the O'Connors' third child. She and Jack had driven into the desert outside Tucson for an afternoon of jack rabbit hunting. O'Connor did much of his running jack rabbit shooting with deer-rifle calibers. On this day, in the process of coaling up his favorite .270, the rifle discharged accidentally, striking him in the left foot and neatly blowing off the second largest toe. Jack went down like a pole-axed steer, screaming in pain. By the time he could get his boot off, blood was everywhere. Eleanor, although early in her pregnancy, was not feeling all that well, and the panic, blood, and withering Arizona heat didn't help matters. When Jack pulled his bloody foot out of his boot, the toe remained in there. At this sight, O'Connor, not surprisingly, passed out. As some of us have found out to our chagrin, even a small man, when unconscious, weighs somewhere in the neighborhood of five thousand pounds. It must have been a herculean task for the trim Eleanor, in her somewhat delicate condition, to load the dead-weight, bloody Jack into the car for the harried drive back into Tucson.

An interesting sidelight of this event took place some two months after Jack had assassinated his toe. He was in Sonora on one of his frequent hunting excursions there and stopped at a ranch where he often hired a local guide or packer. He wasn't able to make connections with the man he usually hired; in fact, the place was deserted. So O'Connor went off alone on his hunt. A little later, the local man showed up at the ranch and saw Jack's boot tracks in the dust. Several weeks later, when O'Connor was back in Sonora again, he ran into his local amigo, who said: "Señor

Jack! I saw your tracks the other day at the ranch and I saw from them you had hurt your foot. You OK now?" This incredibly observant man had not only recognized O'Connor's tracks but had also detected from them Jack's recent foot injury!

Another lifelong O'Connor boondoggle involved the relatively mundane process of driving an automobile. Most people enjoy driving a car. They take to it like a duck to water, and driving becomes almost second nature. Most do it casually, remaining relaxed but alert. Not so with Jack! All his life, driving a car remained an awkward and fretful experience. In his case there seemed to be no marriage of man and machine (or even an uneasy truce, for that matter). The automobile seemed an area of life in which he was determined to hold back time. Although he grudgingly accepted the auto's necessity, a succession of O'Connor station wagons, Jeeps, and other vehicles remained the most basic of conveyances and were generally devoid of all amenities such as heaters and radios. Behind the wheel, Jack clattered along keeping mostly to the right and viewing every driving situation as a sort of personal Armageddon.

But it is worth mentioning that his driving record was good and that he was not at fault in his January 1957 accident near Spokane, Washington. Two of his greatest attributes—a keen interest in all that went on around him and his great powers of observation—worked against him when he was behind the wheel. Virtually nothing along the road escaped his hunter's eyes. He was wont to roll along, taking in everything on all sides and occasionally behind him, to his passengers' alarm—all the while blissfully unaware of other traffic, pedestrians, and whatnot. A drive with Jack was not something to be lightly entered into.

As Brad related in his foreword to his father's *The Last Book*, published in 1984 after Jack's death, O'Connor mixed with any type of newfangled gadget about like nitroglycerine mixes with a bumpy road. But despite the above-mentioned firearms gaffes, dumb though they were, there is no indication that O'Connor was less than careful in the overall sense. For example, the handloading of ammunition is no time to have a brain fart, and by all evidence, O'Connor was a careful handloader. He just didn't dwell on the tiniest nuances of the handloading procedure, as has become fashionable with the gun scribes of recent years.

On yet another tangent, O'Connor was proficient with cameras from an early age, and most of the cameras he used over his lifetime were pretty persnickety. Then again, we all tend to develop a reasonable degree of skill with things we like to do, and photography was one of Jack's minor passions.

Of course, Jack's mental hangfires, especially the firearms incidents, never reached the eyes of his readership. Such news certainly would have tarnished his image as the guru of the American gunwriting trade. Obviously, lapses in firearm safety are never excusable; however, knowledge of these screwups would have done much to put several layers of mere mortality on the old king of the .270.

Whether we realize it or not, each of us tends to view people within the context of the environments that they construct for us. This is certainly true with Jack O'Connor. His long face with its sad, wise countenance, his writing style, even his eyeglasses conjure up an image of prudence and carefulness. And although those aberrations certainly did happen, somehow the idea of an O'Connor miscue or goof-up remains hard for us to envision.

6

Jack and Roy

I mentioned in this book's introduction that for all of his life, Jack O'Connor was a man who revealed little of himself that was personal in nature. Therefore, any relationship, behavior pattern, or other information that helps to piece together the complex tapestry that was O'Connor the man is welcome indeed. For these reasons, Jack's thirty-two-year friendship with Roy Weatherby, his interaction with the Weatherby Company, and his service on the Weatherby Award selection committee merit some consideration. Through Roy and his company, O'Connor made many new friends, directly or otherwise. Several of these friendships were lifelong. Jack's service as a Weatherby Award judge brought him still more friends and contacts. But more importantly, the entire O'Connor-Weatherby thing is a veritable treasure trove of opportunities to see Jack in action—to see him pout, to see him criticize, to see him laugh, and occasionally to see him step on himself. Subtle though these opportunities are, they all provide picture windows directly into the brain and the diverse personality that was Jack O'Connor. It's an interesting tale, so let's take a look.

By the end of World War II, from his position as *Outdoor Life*'s shooting editor, Jack had already correctly foreseen that the post-war big-game hunter and shooter was going to be a very different breed. This new hunter would be smarter, more sophisticated, and more demanding. O'Connor realized also that the use of telescopic sights on hunting rifles would become almost universal in the years to come. He understood that along with scope sights would come increased usage of and demand for flatter-shooting, high-performance cartridges. His incredibly heavy fan mail during the war, much of it from servicemen anxious to get home and go hunting, formed the basis of these foresights. Throughout his long career, O'Connor always relied greatly on his readers to keep him informed of trends and developments and remained very responsive to their interests. His attentiveness to his readers was one of the secrets of his success.

So it came to pass that from his Tucson home/office in the early part of 1946, O'Connor began to hear vague rumblings in the land. They came mostly in Jack's monthly mail and concerned the activities of a brash young California insurance salesman by the name of Roy Weatherby. Seems the young Weatherby had begun developing a red-hot line of big-game cartridges that really had people talking. Although the backbone of the Weatherby line is now and has always been the .300 Weatherby Magnum, it was not actually the first Weatherby offering. That distinction went to the .270 Weatherby Magnum. Although no one knows exactly when it occurred, we can almost imagine Jack's ire when he saw his first wicked-looking .270 Weatherby Magnum cartridge with its sexy, double-radius shoulder. He probably felt that the new upstart was invading the hallowed grounds of his beloved .270 Winchester. The infidels had to be stopped!

At first he was merely skeptical. After all, he had seen these kinds of ninety-day wonders before. New wildcat cartridges had a way of being more smoke than fire. However, when the mailbag continued to reflect more and more interest and questions regarding the Weatherby line, he resolved to investigate for himself. The great bulk of such interest seemed to center on the .300 Weatherby Magnum caliber. Since Jack was never one to answer his readers without checking things out for himself, he set out to get a .300 Weatherby built.

Jack's route to his first Weatherby was a bit indirect. In the first place, he was damned if he would just knuckle under to the young upstart riflemaker by calling Weatherby up and ordering one of the new bolts-of-lightning. No, sirree. He'd do it his way.

At the time, O'Connor owned a .280 Halger rifle built on a square-bridge magnum Mauser action. He first sought out the services of his old buddy, Tucson barrelmaker Bill Sukalle. He had Sukalle remove the Halger barrel and then fit a medium-heavy 25-inch-long barrel with a 12-inch twist chambered for the .300 H&H Magnum. Sukalle then sent the barreled action to Roy Weatherby's South Gate, California, shop, where it was rechambered to .300 Weatherby Magnum caliber. Weatherby's ace stockmaker, Leonard Mews, recheckered the stock, did some other minor stock alterations, and sent the rifle back to Sukalle. After taking delivery from Sukalle, O'Connor fitted a 4-power Weaver scope and began to work up some 180-grain loads. He shot the rifle quite a bit at the range, was impressed with its accuracy, then sat back to await an opportunity to use the rifle in the field. (In later years, much was made of the fact that O'Connor never actually used Weatherby "rifles" per se. He certainly used Weatherby calibers, most notably the .300 and the .257. The plain facts are that most of Jack's use of Weatherby calibers came during the late 1940s and 1950s, before the distinctive Mark V action came into being.)

During this period, Weatherbys were built on FN Mauser actions, Model 70 actions, 1917 Enfield actions, and other types. Therefore, the fact that O'Connor never owned any Weatherby-built rifles should not be construed as a lack of endorsement of Weatherby products on his part. By this point in his career, O'Connor was well connected with the custom gunmaking trade. For the great gunsmiths and stockmakers of the day, it was an honor to work for Jack. In terms of rifles chambered for Weatherby calibers, he simply got what he wanted made the way he wanted. For the record and to my knowledge, O'Connor owned and used only two Weatherby calibers to any degree, his first .300 and a second .300 that he had built, and a later .257 Weatherby Magnum that he had made up and used rather extensively on his first safari to Africa in the summer of 1953.

Ironically, Jack's first hunting opportunity with his initial .300 came in the fall of 1947 during a hunt to British Columbia's Selkirk Mountains—arranged by Roy Weatherby himself. Roy had not done much big-game hunting on his own and was anxious to increase his hunting experiences. He put together a large party of eight or nine hunters, including O'Connor, for the British Columbia trip. Roy assembled this rather large group so that he could get a better deal for himself. The hunt was to be primarily for Stone sheep and goats. As it worked out, there were few sheep in evidence but goats aplenty.

In Jack's first combat action with his homegrown .300, he figuratively blew the doors off a big billy at a range of over three hundred yards. In the February 1948 issue of *Outdoor Life*, he commented:

> My Rocky Mountain goat shot at about 300 yards and hit in the lungs with a broadside shot was killed instantly. The Remington 180-gr. Bronze Point bullet was used, and the whole far side of the goat appeared at first glance to have been blown off. Actually the exit hole was 7 or 8 inches across.

Another comment regarding the performance of the .300 Weatherby appeared in the same article:

> To say that (.300 Weatherby) 180-gr. bullets pushed along at a muzzle velocity of from 3,200 to 3,300 foot seconds have terrific killing power would be practically an understatement.

Jack's next experience with the .300 Weatherby came in the fall of 1949. He booked a sheep and mixed-bag hunt in the Yukon and arranged for his old friend and Yukon guide, Field Johnson, to come along as his own personal guide. The hunt was generally a failure, with little game taken. But one afternoon, while Jack and Field were taking a break, they spotted a big grizzly traveling over the tundra right in their direction. Years later, in a chapter of *The Hunting Rifle* entitled "The .30 Caliber Magnums," O'Connor described the incident:

> He was walking rapidly and about 100 yards away when I bushwhacked him. The 180-grain Remington Bronze Point driven by 78 grains of No. 4350 hit him high through the lungs. He dropped in his tracks. On the off side was a hole you could stick a fist in and bright against the green grass was a fan-shaped spray of blood and bits of lung and bone.

Like it or not, JOC had to admit that Roy Weatherby's big thirty was Old Death and Destruction itself!

As far as I know, a long shot he made with the .300 Weatherby on an ancient, dwarflike Stone ram in British Columbia's Atlin Lake district in the fall of 1951 more or less completed O'Connor's North American hunting experience with Weatherby calibers. Thereafter, he went back to his old favorite, the .270, with occasional use of the .30-06.

But on his first safari to Africa in the summer of 1953, Jack took two Weatherbys, a lightweight .300 and a .257 Weatherby Magnum that he'd had made up. He used the .257 quite a bit, with great results, mostly on plains game and smaller antelope. He may have used this rifle more than he otherwise would have to placate his good friend Herb Klein, who was along on the trip. The .257 Weatherby Magnum was Klein's lifelong personal favorite Weatherby caliber. Getting Jack to comment favorably on Weatherby products in his columns was just as important to

Herb Klein as it was to Roy, for the simple reason that by this time, Herb had a big, big chunk of cash invested in the Weatherby Company. On this same safari, O'Connor used his .300 Weatherby to take one of the greatest trophies of his hunting life, a tremendous 44½-inch sable. He killed it with a single .300 thunderbolt, prompting him to comment: "I aimed for a high lung shot at about 150 yards. I squeezed off and the next thing I knew I could see all four feet in the air."

So, however grudgingly O'Connor may have handed out compliments regarding Weatherby products, at least in the early years he certainly knew that Roy Weatherby, the buoyant, happy fellow from South Gate, California, really had something in his line of laser-beam calibers.

In fact, O'Connor's praise for Weatherby products wasn't always so grudging. It reached perhaps its zenith with this comment from *The Rifle Book* (1964): "The .300 Weatherby Magnum is the easiest caliber to hit with at long range that I have ever used." In another comment from an *Outdoor Life* column, he stated: "The .300 Weatherby Magnum has made perhaps the most enviable reputation for one-shot kills on soft-skinned game of any caliber."

Of course, it is well known that Roy's flamboyant stocks, with their fore-end tips, Monte Carlo combs, and exotic woods, were way too "Hollywood" for the ultra-conservative Jack. Probably too much has been made of this, for it was simply a matter of different tastes. Then, too, the extroverted, happy Roy was in the business of selling rifles and did a pretty darned good job of it, too!

One minor opportunity to hoot at Señor Jack took place in 1958 and involved his comments about Weatherby's new Mark V action, which had just appeared on the market. He wrote about the revolutionary bolt-action in his *Outdoor Life* column, giving it high praise for its strength, new locking-lug system, and great camming power. However, he couldn't resist one little jab to Roy's kidneys, saying rather testily on several occasions that the Mark V was a little too "bulky" for his tastes. This was a howler inasmuch as when O'Connor had had his own first .416 Rigby built a few years before, he had it made up on a 1917 Enfield action, which for all its own great strength was rather "bulky" itself, with all the clean lines and streamlined look of a garden tractor!

O'Connor continued to comment, mostly favorably, on new Weatherby offerings and developments throughout the years, although these comments declined about 1960. In the early years of the Weatherby Company, Roy openly sought favorable reviews from Jack for his line of cartridges and rifles. Actually, Jack's only real quibble with Weatherby was its markedly different tastes in stock design. True to form, O'Connor "called 'em just like he saw 'em." Jack took great pride in his candor, absolute integrity, and personal honesty in his assessments of shooting equipment. With Weatherby products, however, O'Connor's opinions may never have sold one Weatherby—or prevented anyone from buying one, either, for that matter. Weatherby buyers and users were and are a pretty headstrong, think-for-themselves bunch!

The 1947 hunt was Jack's first opportunity to spend any significant time with Roy Weatherby. He found Roy to be upbeat, light-hearted, and fun to be around. In short, it was almost impossible *not* to like Roy Weatherby. He was a real "people person," an extrovert at heart, and a natural salesman. O'Connor once called him a "male Pollyanna in a business suit." Jack himself had little or nothing of the salesman mentality in his makeup. With his cynical, dour, rain-on-your-parade personality, it was difficult at first for him to like the exuberant, kid-like Roy Weatherby.

But Roy grew on everybody he ever knew, and Jack was no exception. Secretly, O'Connor admired Roy for his promotional skills, his abilities with people, and his attitude toward life in general. Oh, he poked plenty of fun at Roy on numerous occasions, usually about the far-out, fancy stocks that adorned Weatherby's rifles. Many years later, Jack wrote good-naturedly and humorously in *The Last Book* about Roy's splashy appearance on the gun scene: "Roy Weatherby came sky-hootin' over the horizon in the middle forties!" Of course, there were other aspects to the Jack-and-Roy friendship. But each man was undeniably the better for having known the other. The few thorns along the way were simply the results of two dynamic, hardheaded personalities in association and occasional conflict. It was mostly in good fun, and Jack respected Roy for his nerve and daring to try things on his own. When Jack looked at Roy, he may have seen his own long-since-abandoned novelist career and wondered again what might have been if he had kept on with his early life's passion. One thing is certain: During all of his life, Jack O'Connor admired the self-made man. And Roy Weatherby was just such a man.

There are really three parts to the O'Connor/Weatherby saga. We have taken a look at their friendship and reviewed some of JOC's ideas and thoughts about the Weatherby line. But the third aspect of their relationship was something else again. In fact, it was such a bone of philosophical contention that it became a source of frustration and often even disgust for O'Connor for the rest of his days.

JACK AND THE WEATHERBY AWARD

That third element of the O'Connor/Weatherby saga has to do with O'Connor's winning the Weatherby Award in 1957 and his subsequent role as a member of the award selection committee. Although Jack basically enjoyed his twenty-two years of service to Roy as a Weatherby Award judge and the experience brought him many new friends and contacts among the elite of the hunting world, it proved to be a philosophical burr under his saddle. More of that later.

The four-foot-high, forty-six-pound Weatherby Big Game Trophy was Roy Weatherby's 1955 brainchild and almost certainly his greatest promotional success. Its significance and continuity are reflected in the facts that the award, presented every year to a deserving hunter/conservationist, is alive and well in the year 2001, is as prestigious as ever, and is still considered to be the "Oscar of the Hunting World."

Did Roy Weatherby have any notion of the long life and impact his idea would have on the world's hunting community when he first toyed with the notion of the award in the summer of 1955? Maybe. It has been suggested that Roy initially conceived the trophy idea to honor his good friend Herb Klein—business partner, financial backer, and worldwide big-game hunter. Klein had been a staunch supporter of Roy and user of Weatherby rifles for over ten years. He was also perhaps the most famous hunter of the day. But Roy was never one to think short-sightedly, and he quickly saw the promotional benefits and interest levels that could be attained by presenting the trophy on an annual basis. Make no mistake about it— Roy knew the award would sell Weatherby rifles!

The first selection committee was formed before the first trophy was presented to Klein. This committee consisted of General Nathan L. Twining, Chairman of the Joint Chiefs of Staff; General Robert L. Scott, author of *God Is My Co-Pilot*; Joe Foss, Governor of South Dakota; Coleman Jonas, famous Denver taxidermist; Warren Page, arms editor of *Field & Stream*; Pete Brown, arms editor of *Sports Afield*; Ken Niles of radio fame; Jack O'Connor; and Roy himself. Roy polled the committee, and they all agreed that Herb Klein had perhaps accomplished more in the world's hunting fields than any other individual. But the decision to honor Klein with the trophy was ultimately Roy's.

The first-ever Weatherby Big Game Trophy was presented to Klein in July 1956 at the housewarming for a beautiful north-Dallas home that Klein had just completed. The trophy room in this house was almost two thousand square feet in size. The selection committee attended the event, as did many of Klein's hunting friends, both local and from around the world. A cousin of mine who was a friend of Herb's was there and remembers seeing O'Connor strolling around in a gray suit, nursing a scotch and water, looking droll, and spending most of his time talking with his old buddies, Colonel Townsend Whelen and famous Mexican hunter Julio Estrada.

Just how functional the original selection committee was in the early years of the Weatherby Award remains to be seen. Since 1957 winner O'Connor and 1958 winner Warren Page were both on this committee, they would have been in the strange position of considering themselves for the trophy. It seems more likely that the real decision-making as to who got the trophy in its second and third years was probably left to Roy Weatherby, Ken Niles, and Herb Klein, who became a member of the committee immediately after winning the award himself.

Much has been said and written over the years indicating that the second Weatherby award was given to O'Connor to curry favor with him because of Jack's prestige as America's foremost gunwriter. While this was almost certainly in the back of Roy Weatherby's mind, O'Connor was absolutely deserving of the award. His North American big-game hunting experience was unparalleled. In addition, he had hunted Africa (1953), India (1955), and Iran (1955). There was probably no more-experienced big-game hunter in the world in those long-gone days than O'Connor—with the possible exception of Klein, and he had already won the award.

Jack did not really become a part of the selection committee until after he himself had won the award in 1957. Some of O'Connor's comments in print over the years left readers with the undeniable impression that Jack resented his responsibilities as a Weatherby Award selection judge. He actually did not resent these responsibilities nearly as much as he wanted everyone to think. However, certain elements of the award itself as well as some of its aspirants stuck in Jack's craw like a cocklebur. Of that, more a bit later.

Before we can understand Jack's less-than-affirmative attitude toward the Weatherby Award itself, some background material is necessary: O'Connor was what I like to call a "regional" hunter as well as a "progressive" hunter. As a boy in southeastern Arizona he had hunted the animals native to his area. His first big-game animal had been a javelina boar that he capped with a Model 92 Winchester carbine in .25-20 caliber. Some two years later, he killed his first mule deer, a scrawny four-point buck. Along the way there were doves, quail, and the occasional duck as well as jack rabbits and coyotes. He did not actually kill his first Arizona Coues whitetail until the fall of 1923, when he was twenty-one years old. He took a few more whitetails and desert mule deer during his twenties and a few antelope in Mexico. He did not take his first desert ram until he was thirty-three, and his first elk came the same year. O'Connor never hunted outside Arizona, Mexico, and the Texas Big Bend before 1943. That year, *Outdoor Life* paid for him to take a thirty-day pack trip in the Alberta Rockies for sheep, grizzly, moose, caribou, and other game. That was O'Connor's first real "assignment" hunt in pursuit of magazine material. Many more sheep hunts, African safaris, and Indian shikars followed.

But in the years after World War II, a new type of hunter began to emerge. There was much greater affluence, airline travel was cheap, and hunting horizons began to widen. Many of the new breed of hunters were intensely competitive men who had made a pile and were looking for a new hobby. They may have heard some hunting stories at a cocktail party and decided it was something they wanted to try. In some cases, the new breed had done no hunting in boyhood, had no hunting heritage, and had no general interest in wildlife. This is not to say that many of these individuals did not become skilled, knowledgeable, and ethical big-game hunters. But the start-at-the-top, go-go-go style of the new breed griped the daylights out of O'Connor. He felt that most of them had not served a hunting apprenticeship, had not done their hunting homework, and were in the game for the wrong reasons. His primary lament had to do with how this new-age hunter affected his beloved sheep hunting.

He focused on the sheep situation in his famous *Outdoor Life* article "The Grand Slam Caper" and later in his book *Sheep and Sheep Hunting*. While he railed at the furor over "Grand Slamming," the article thinly disguised Jack's disgust at some of the men in pursuit of a Grand Slam or other big-game hunting hurdles.

With notable exceptions, but increasingly after 1960, this hard-driving, ambitious, moneyed, gung-ho set of hunters spawned most future Weatherby aspirants and eventual winners.

The criteria for winning the Weatherby Award were largely established by Roy Weatherby himself. But as mentioned before, certain of these criteria were like fingernails scraping on a blackboard to the conservative Jack. Here are the early Weatherby Award guidelines:

> The Weatherby Big Game Trophy is an annual award, not for a particular record, but for an individual who has made the greatest lifetime achievements in the world of big-game hunting . . . a person who has collected the greatest number of average as well as record animals

throughout the entire world . . . the difficult and rare animals . . . for the various continents hunted and the number of hunts . . . for unusual accomplishments, such as bagging all species of sheep with representative or record heads, or collecting such rare animals as the bongo, glacier bear, etc. . . . a person who has contributed greatly to conservation and whose character and sportsmanship are beyond reproach.

It was the "greatest number of *average* [italics mine] animals" portion of the criteria that really gave O'Connor pause. At the hunting level of Weatherby aspirants, this and other elements of the award criteria encouraged a "pile 'em higher and deeper, whack 'em and stack 'em" mentality that made the ultra-restrained Jack want to puke.

Beginning in 1958, O'Connor served as a Weatherby Award judge for eighteen years, or until the end of his life. In the early years, a typical Weatherby Award winner was an individual who had hunted extensively in North America, probably collected a Grand Slam of North American sheep, and had several African safaris under his belt, probably including the taking of the Big Five. Most of these hunters had also been to India and taken a tiger. That was generally about it. These feats pretty well defined all the horizons available in the hunting world back then. Certainly the award winners prior to 1960 were notable hunters, but in those balmy days the award had something of a "who do we give it to this year?" aura about it.

But beginning in 1960, when the great hunter Elgin T. Gates won the trophy, the new breed of Weatherby Award winner was on the scene to stay. Gates was the first of the great hunter/collectors to win the award. Because his hunting accomplishments were so widespread and comprehensive, it may well also be said that he was the first winner who really fit Roy's criteria. Thereafter, winners would increasingly fit the "mission statement" of Roy's award. But for some hunters interested in the award, this created a unique sort of problem.

After 1960, many of the world's elite hunters found themselves "shaping" their careers around the Weatherby Award criteria. To win the award or even become a nominee, a hunter's greatest priority had to be collecting a great number of species. Though trophy quality was important, the comprehensiveness of one's "collection" was even more so. This placed hunters in the position of having to "collect" many animals in which they may have had no real interest. It was all a part of "putting up the big numbers." Some of these feats, such as taking all of Africa's spiral-horned antelope, were without doubt great hunting achievements. The award criteria undoubtedly had a great impact on the proliferation of "pioneering" expeditions into previously unhunted areas, primarily in Asia. The awarding of the annual Weatherby trophy placed great weight on such far-flung expeditions. This in turn sparked much of the expansion of the hunting-agent business and the discovery of new hunting areas worldwide.

In terms of the breadth of their collections, many of the Weatherby Award winners of the early days would never even become nominees today. So competitive has pursuit of the award become that today 250 different species is more or less a requirement, and a candidate without complete or nearly complete collections from North America, Africa, Asia, Europe, and the South Pacific has no real chance to win the trophy.

O'Connor always felt that the big-game hunter had a responsibility—to himself as well as to his sport—to conduct himself with restraint and conservatism. During the 1960s, O'Connor grew to feel that the competitiveness, the zeal, the shenanigans, and the occasional corner cutting that went with the pursuit of the Weatherby Award had gotten out of hand. At the height of his disgust, he wrote the hilarious "How K. R. Bolz Won The Krautbauer Trophy," which appeared in the 1968 *Gun Digest*. The story, filled with Jack's barbed humor and biting cynicism, is a takeoff on the Weatherby Award and its pursuers. According to O'Connor, the hero of his story, K. R. Bolz, was "not a portrait of anyone, but combined the characteristics and background of several candidates."

During his service on the award selection committee, Jack often felt he was being patronized, saying in *The Last Book*,

> As one of the judges, I was deluged with fancy presentations with 8x10 color prints of candidates posed with various defunct mammals—tiger, elephants, sheep, bear, and what not. I was also offered free meals, free hunting trips and enough booze to intoxicate a brontosaurus!

But in truth, he loved the prestige and attention that went along with being a judge. He and Eleanor regularly attended the Weatherby Award dinners. In the course of writing this piece, I had occasion to look at many dozens of press photographs taken at various Weatherby galas over the years. These invariably show Jack beaming as the center of attention or alternately looking stonily superior. Through his service to Roy as a judge, Jack made many, many new contacts and friends, and it also helped him keep his finger on the pulse of the big-game hunting world.

In the end, though, his frustrations over the award and its requirements remained unresolved, and it was these frustrations that undoubtedly gave rise to what is arguably the most famous O'Connor quote of them all. Writing in *Sheep and Sheep Hunting* in 1974, Dinosaur Jack commented:

The idea of collecting one each of every variety of game found in any country or on any continent brings me down with an acute attack of the vapors. I have, for example, about as much desire to bump off a muskox or a tapir or for that matter a woodland caribou as I do a giant Costa Rican banana-eating fruit bat, if there is such a thing!

7

Africa's Big Five

Long before Jack O'Connor first set foot on African soil in the summer of 1953, he already had two favorites among African animals: the lion and the greater kudu. Extensive reading about African hunting and conversations with those who had been on safari had led him to these choices. (Interestingly, nineteen years and nine safaris later, he had not changed his mind.) So when he embarked on his first safari—a sixty-day, two-country marathon in June of 1953 with Herb Klein and Red Early—lion and greater kudu were the two animals he most wanted to collect. As for the other Big Five animals, he was mildly interested in leopard and Cape buffalo. He thought he had a certain responsibility to *Outdoor Life* to get a buff, since a buffalo story would make good reading and *Outdoor Life* was footing his bill. Beyond that, Jack wasn't a Big Five guy. He may have relented a bit during the long flights and hotel stays en route from the United States as he listened to the enthusiastic cocktail conversations of Herb and Red, who were both hot to get all of the Big Five during the course of their first safari. But only a bit. Jack, a man who never let anyone do his thinking for him, arrived in Africa with his own plan. To hell with the Big Five.

Nevertheless, before Jack was done with the safari trail, he had collected all of the Big Five. How he did it is an interesting study in mind changes, flukes, feelings of responsibility, and benevolent accidents. And because it gives us a few more long looks into O'Connor's mental processes, passions, opinions, and eccentricities, it's worth a closer examination.

LION

"Most of all I had dreamed of someday knocking over a great maned lion, this grandest of the cats, this epitome of all that is Africa." (JOC, "Lions Don't Come Easy," *Outdoor Life*, November 1953)

Jack breathed African air for the first time 20 June 1953 in Nairobi, Kenya. With him were Texans Herb Klein and Red Early. Their outfitter was Ker and Downey, the most famous and prestigious safari firm in all of British East Africa. Although the safari was outfitted from Nairobi, the first hunting camp would actually be over the border to the south in Tanganyika (now Tanzania). After three and a half days of red tape, preparation, and travel, Jack, Herb, and Red found themselves in their first safari camp amid a mixed-game paradise on northwestern Tanganyika's Simiyu River.

Klein and Early used the Simiyu camp to obtain a general bag. Not Jack. A big lion was his absolute priority, and he was prepared to spend a great part of his safari getting it, perhaps to the exclusion of other game. So, except for an occasional Thompson gazelle or a bait animal, he and his PH Don Ker looked neither right nor left for eight long days as they pursued a big lion. Jack later wrote that he shot the seventy-eighth lion that he saw. (In other writings, he stated that it was the eighty-seventh lion. No matter. He looked at a *lot* of lions.) Whether he shot the seventy-eighth or the eighty-seventh, it was certainly *not* the first lion that he shot *at*, and as JOC himself would have said, therein lies a tale—as well as one of Jack's very few embarrassing big-game moments.

In the course of their search, Jack and Don hung baits. They tried stalks based on the early-morning roaring of lions making their way back to heavy cover to bed down after a night's hunting. But mostly they simply cruised around in the hunting car, hoping to spot a big male lying up in the shade.

To digress briefly: Before the 1953 safari, Jack had planned to use his .300 Weatherby Magnum as his lion rifle. Although this rifle is discussed at some length elsewhere in this book, a few more details here are not out of order for the purposes of this story. Jack's .300 was a Weatherby in caliber only. The rifle itself was "home grown" in that O'Connor had had it built and stocked to his specifications in about 1946. At the time of the 1953 safari, O'Connor had this to say regarding his .300: "That .300 Weatherby Magnum is one of my favorites. It is a short-barreled, scope-sighted featherweight, so accurate that it will keep five shots on a silver dollar at 200 yards." Obviously, Jack had great confidence in the rifle and his ability to use it. Prior to his first lion stalk, he had a mental picture of himself settling Old Simba's hash with just one of the .300's 220-grain softpoints right in the engine room. Although it was no fault of the caliber, it just didn't work out that way.

So the .300 Weatherby was in the rack of the hunting car on the second or third morning of lion hunting as Jack and Don bumped over the terrain in search of an old he-lion. In the first rays of an early sun, the two men spotted two male lions lying on a flat rock near a water hole in a donga. Both were big. One was black-maned, and the other was a blond. They were a couple of hundred yards away. After looking the pair over with glasses, Don Ker quickly drove the hunting car three hundred yards farther away before beginning the stalk. Jack grabbed his .300, bailed out of the lorry (truck), and took off in a hurried trot behind Ker. In later years, O'Connor would state that he had been almost beside himself with excitement. He felt that in a few moments he was going to get a shot at the trophy he had dreamed of for over forty years. But the sheer excitement, the panic of the stalk, and the running did Jack in.

In short order, he and Ker were in shooting position a hundred yards from the two lions. But the animals had seen them and were alerted. O'Connor would have liked an anthill to shoot over, but none was available. So, dropping into a sitting position, he took a look at the big black-maned lion through his scope. What he saw wasn't at all encouraging. The cross hairs were wavering all over the lion. Worse, he was afraid the animals would run at any second. The net result of all these factors was a howling miss—one that was completely understandable, given the circumstances, but a miss that would dog O'Connor for the rest of his days.

At the shot, the big black-maned lion unhurriedly walked off the rock and out of this story. But the blond lion was still there, so Jack quickly rolled another cartridge into the .300's chamber and swung over onto lion Number 2. Missing the first one apparently helped get rid of Jack's jitters, because this time the cross hairs settled down rock-steady behind the lion's shoulder. However, the result was no different from his first shot. Like his buddy before him, the blond lion gazed around after the shot and strolled unconcernedly off about his business.

O'Connor felt he may have jerked his shot at the first lion, but he was confident that he had been right on the money with the second lion. So, a little later in the day, when he missed a couple of shots at a kongoni, he took his first close look at the .300. The rifle had taken a terrific pounding in the rack of the safari car for several days. Not only the rifle's guard screws but also the scope-mount screws were loose. He didn't have the time, place, or opportunity to resight the .300, so Jack decided to shelve it and continue the lion pursuit with his .375.

I have gone into some detail in the above account for this reason: Had it not been for the loose screws on his .300 Weatherby, it is most likely that Jack would have killed one of the two lions cleanly. If so, it is also very probable that the .300 would have become his regular lion medicine on subsequent safaris. This might well have led to routine usage of the caliber for other game. Then, in later years, Jack's grudging and obtuse admiration of the .300 Weatherby and other Weatherby calibers might have been more open and vocal. It's just a thought.

To resume our story: Jack's next opportunity to stalk a lion came on the morning of the fourth day. He and Don again spotted two big males from the hunting car. But by the time they drove a suitable and legal distance away, parked the lorry, and made their stalk, the lions had run. The men took up the trail and followed it for more than five miles before they came upon the animals again. This time they jumped the pair at close range, but heavy cover prevented Jack from getting a shot. At a flat-out run, Jack and Don chased the lions almost a quarter-mile, getting their last look as the two big males moved off at a range of three hundred yards. A winded and shaking Jack declined to take any risky shots.

After this stalk failed, Jack and Don would spend four more grinding, disappointing days before their luck turned.

At the end of eight days of lion hunting, the entire safari ground to a halt. Both Herb Klein and Red Early had taken lions and leopards as well as the other game they had wanted from the Simiyu camp and were ready to move on to other areas for other animals. However, good sports that they were, they waited patiently for Jack to come to grips with the lion of his dreams. O'Connor and Ker were about whipped. They had ridden hundreds and walked dozens of miles in the previous eight days. And they were still lionless.

On the ninth day, O'Connor and Ker set off very early to inspect the first of three lion baits they had hung. Feeding on the first bait was a young male lion with a fair mane. O'Connor probably would have taken the lion, but the ever-hopeful Don talked him out of the idea.

The second bait was a bust. But then and there, the gods of the hunt decided that the fifty-one-year-old kid from old Nogales had suffered enough. And when they decided to present Jack with a lion, they gave him a lion to end all lions.

The third bait had been fed upon. In the dirt were the enormous paw prints of a monster male lion. Don quietly told Jack that he felt the lion had been gone from the bait for only a few moments and was still nearby. Don slowly drove the hunting car the regulation quarter-mile away and parked it out of sight. Then he, Jack, and their gunbearer set out to stalk the bait. After walking only a couple hundred yards, they arrived at a point where they could see the bait. Sure enough, a huge lion was sitting in high grass nearby. This time everything was absolutely perfect. This time the obliging anthill was right where it should be. It allowed O'Connor to steal forward unseen by the lion. He slipped up behind the anthill and peeked over. The lion had not moved. It was all so simple. Jack eased his big .375 over the top of the hill and rested the fore-end in his left hand. The strain, failed stalks, and hard work of the previous eight days seemed to have drained all the nervousness out of him. O'Connor's calmness was born of fatigue. Placing the rock-steady cross wires on the base of the big lion's neck, he pressed the trigger.

But the lion still gave Señor O'Connor one more adrenaline rush. At Jack's shot, the big male shot a full ten feet into the air! Then a series of blood-curdling death roars so unnerved Jack that before he realized what he was doing, he himself rushed forward to get in some clinching shots and put a stop to all the bedlam.

To say that O'Connor was thrilled would be a huge understatement. The thrill and excitement of taking his first lion never abated. In fact, twenty-four years later, in 1977, he would state that other than his first desert ram, no other trophy in his entire hunting career excited him as much as his first lion.

At the time Jack killed his 1953 lion, Don Ker had been hunting professionally in Africa for twenty-seven years. Upon examining O'Connor's big lion, Ker told Jack it was the largest lion that he had ever seen in his hunting career. Ker estimated its weight at five hundred pounds. The lion was 9' 7" long, measured "on the straight" (from the tip of the nose to the last joint of the tail). Ker was by nature restrained and conservative, so of course his statement about the lion's size flattered O'Connor. Ker and later Syd Downey further told Jack that they doubted whether an honestly measured ten-foot lion had ever been taken. Because O'Connor liked the two men and valued their opinions, he bought heavily into this statement—so much so that in later years any nimrod who told Jack he had killed a ten-foot lion in Africa was sure to incur an O'Connor outburst or, at the very least, Jack's best go-to-hell stare.

Jack collected his second lion during a minor misadventure in one of Africa's most unlikely lion spots. It all took place on Jack's second safari in January of 1958. He and thirty-four-year-old Elgin Gates journeyed to French Equatorial Africa (now Chad) in the southern Sahara to hunt scimitar-horned oryx, addax, dama gazelle, greater kudu, and aoudad sheep. O'Connor had not bought a leopard license on his first safari in 1953. But beautiful leopards taken by Herb Klein and Red Early on that trip had him kicking himself later for not doing so. Chad had a few big leopards and the occasional lion. This time Jack bought a leopard license and, of course, a lion license.

It happened this way. In the predawn light of a bitterly cold desert morning, Jack and his outfitter, Mickey Micheletti, stalked a bait they had previously hung in a thorn tree. Peeping over a dune from a hundred yards away, Micheletti almost fainted. There feeding on the bait was what he thought to be the largest leopard he had ever seen. The light was still bad, showing everything in a shadowy monotone. Micheletti motioned Jack up beside him. Here was the leopard for which O'Connor had waited five years! He eased off the safety of the big Griffin & Howe .375 and slapped a 270-grain softpoint through the huge cat, killing it tombstone dead with one shot. The two men ran to the monster to find not a leopard at all but a middle-sized, rather moth-eaten, and totally maneless lion! The whole affair left gun editor O'Connor rather chagrined and was not necessarily his finest moment.

However, an incident a few days earlier confirms that O'Connor would never have shot this animal at all had he known it was indeed a lion. In the earlier incident, Jack and Micheletti had cut the tracks of a big lion at dawn one morning and followed them for two hours. Finally they had gotten a look at the lion some two hundred yards ahead. It was maneless, and O'Connor declined to shoot it. This event seems to make it obvious that Jack's taking of his leopard-lion was a clear mistake, but certainly understandable, given the conditions. The killing of his second lion perhaps received less ink from O'Connor than almost any other event in his hunting life. About all that could be said about his Chad lion is that it *was* a lion. The whole business left him still smarting for a good leopard and with a bad taste in his mouth that only the taking of another trophy lion would wipe away. As we shall see, he only had a year and a half to wait for another big lion payoff that resulted from probably the best shot of Jack's entire hunting career.

After the passage of those eighteen months, Jack went to Tanganyika in October of 1959 for his third safari (Eleanor's first). This trip was a gift to the O'Connors from the safari firm of Ker and Downey in gratitude for the greatly increased bookings that had resulted from Jack's *Outdoor Life* stories (more than a dozen) based on his first (1953) Ker and Downey safari. The trip was in many ways O'Connor's most rewarding and enjoyable African experience. For one thing, in two previous trips he had taken most of the animals he had any real interest in collecting. Still, his main goals for this trip were again lion, leopard, and greater kudu. (What a surprise!) Then, too, Jack was happy to have Eleanor along and to be sharing with her the experience of Africa.

The O'Connors spent the first portion of the hunt in northern Tanganyika, where Jack got a good leopard after some hard hunting. Lions were protected in this area, and the O'Connors saw many, including the finest Jack ever laid eyes on, a huge male with a mane flowing halfway back to its hips near Serengeti Park. Northern Tanganyika was the finest lion country in the world, a land of high, cool plains with little or no thorns to tear the hair out of lions' manes. But because the area was closed for lion, Jack planned to do his lion hunting in southern Tanganyika on the second part of the safari. After seeing the monster Serengeti lion, Jack asked his PH, Syd Downey, if there would be much chance of finding such an animal down south. Syd told O'Connor that the lions in southern Tanganyika were not as well-maned and that the country was hot and thorny. Still, when Jack and Eleanor left by small plane for southern Tanganyika and the second portion of the safari, all Jack could think of was the five-hundred-pound, heavy-maned giant that he was leaving behind.

Jack killed his third lion in southern Tanganyika almost before the hunting began. So in need of a lion "fix" was O'Connor that at dawn on the second morning, he was asleep and dreaming of lions roaring when PH John Kingsley-Heath and a gunbearer burst into Jack and Eleanor's tent. Jack hadn't been dreaming after all! Not a quarter-mile from camp, a pride of lions were roaring like fiends as they made their way back to cover after a night of hunting. As Eleanor watched the proceedings wide-eyed from under the covers, the gunbearer grabbed Jack's .375 and a handful of cartridges, and John threw Jack's clothes in his direction. In a moment, a gummy-eyed

O'Connor stumbled from the tent, tripping over his bootlaces and with his shirttail flapping, and headed off for a dawn face-off. So close were the lions that the three men left the camp on foot, heading toward the roars. They had gone only a quarter-mile when they saw a lioness poke her head out from some high grass 150 yards away. In a few seconds, a heavy male burst from the same cover, quartering slightly away in a hard, flat run. Jack raised his .375. It had been eleven years since he had shot any running jack rabbits, but his old skills didn't let him down. Jack would later say that the cross hairs rolling along ahead of the running lion's chest presented a perfect sight picture and the old .375 seemed to go off all by itself. O'Connor heard the clap of the heavy bullet, and, with a heavy grunt, the big lion was immediately into the high grass and out of sight.

What could have been a very tense follow-up of a wounded and dangerous lion never came to pass. John and Jack found the animal dead only a few yards into the high grass. Jack's 270-grain bullet had blown its heart to shreds.

The very large, heavy male was an excellent lion for the Tanganyikan "bush" country, although it was not as long or heavy-bodied as his 1953 lion or the final lion that he later took in Zambia in 1969. Most notable about the whole business was the beautiful 140-yard running shot that O'Connor made, almost certainly the best big-money, high-pressure shot of his entire hunting career. Jack called the story "Lion on the Kilombero" when it appeared in the January 1961 issue of *Outdoor Life* and later in *Jack O'Connor's Big Game Hunts* and *The Best of Jack O'Connor*. The 1959 safari also marked the O'Connors' first meeting with John Kingsley-Heath and the beginning of what was to become a lifelong friendship.

O'Connor went on to take two more great lions before the end of his safari days. He got the first of these (his fourth lion) in August of 1962 near the Caprivi Strip in Angola's Mucusso Concession. For this hunt, Jack and Eleanor were outfitted by

Angola Hunting Safaris, a company owned by Robert M. Lee, O'Connor's New York pal and an avid hunter. Jack nailed this lion on a frosty morning with two shots from his trusty old Griffin & Howe .375. This lion was 8' 9" between pegs, a little smaller than animals he had taken in 1953 and 1959. However, the Mucusso lion had a beautiful ginger-brown mane and was, up to that time, Jack's best-maned lion. (See "The Big Lion of Mucusso," *The Best of Jack O'Connor*, Amwell Press, 1977.)

Jack saved the best of his lions for last. His next-to-last safari, to Zambia in October of 1969, produced the longest-bodied (9' 8" over the curves, 9' 4" on the straight) and best-maned lion that Jack ever killed. He took it with his .416 on the twenty-ninth day of a thirty-day safari in a straightforward stalk led by PH Keith Rowse. O'Connor always stated thereafter that his Zambia lion was the best he *had ever seen* in Africa other than the Serengeti Park lion in 1959.

In conclusion, O'Connor killed five lions in four different countries over a sixteen-year span from 1953 to 1969. Of the five, four were great trophy males, the lone exception being the maneless desert lion he took in Chad in 1958. In fact, O'Connor to the end of his life said that he collected four of the five best lions he ever saw in Africa, the other being the above-mentioned Serengeti Park monster. All four were long, heavy-bodied, and well-maned, although he always felt that his first, taken in 1953, was his heaviest lion. O'Connor grew to be a great connoisseur of manes, always his greatest criterion in judging lion trophies. He had each of the four best lions shoulder-mounted, and they are currently on display at the University of Idaho in Moscow.

Only the lion among the Big Five really struck fear into Jack's heart. He felt that elephant, rhino, and buffalo were all potentially deadly for sure, but with the use of good judgment, trouble with them could almost always be avoided. The lion was a different matter altogether, and what made it different was its speed. A big lion lounging in the shade a hundred yards away could be on you in about four or five seconds. After another second or two, it could have your head in its enormous jaws and crush it like an eggshell. O'Connor further thought that the lion was the most naturally irritable of the Big Five and the most likely to attack unprovoked. This, combined with its great speed, made the lion, in O'Connor's lifelong opinion, Africa's most dangerous game. His opinion of the lion as a game animal was so high that he was moved to say with his characteristic dry wit on more than one occasion: "If lions had horns like rams, they'd be just about perfect!"

CAPE BUFFALO

"But the die was cast. I didn't have much to say about it and I was going to get in a ruction with a buffalo whether I liked it or not." (JOC, "Buffaloes Shoot Back!" *Jack O'Connor's Big Game Hunts)*

In his writings after his first African safari in 1953, Jack reflected that prior to the trip he had been rather reluctant about the idea of hunting Cape buffalo. But afterward he had to admit to himself that buffalo bespoke the very flavor of Africa almost as much as lion and elephant. Too, he was very mindful that his upcoming safari had been made possible through the kindness of *Outdoor Life* and his editor there, Ray Brown. He was also well aware that he had been sent on the trip to produce material for the magazine. As lukewarm as he was originally to the Cape buffalo idea, he also had to admit that any story of tangling with a big buff would probably make pretty exciting reading.

Still, there is at least one indication that Jack may not have been as cool to the buffalo-hunting idea as he would later state in print. Months before the safari kicked off, he went to considerable pains to get a "heavy" rifle custom-built. His choice of caliber was the .450 Watts, a wildcat chambering that was the forerunner of the .458 Winchester Magnum. O'Connor definitely had no initial plans to hunt either rhino or elephant, so we are left to wonder: What would the .450 be used for? The answer could only have been that he had plans to collect buffalo, at least in the back of his mind.

In describing O'Connor's lion-hunting experiences above, I mentioned that he and PH Don Ker concentrated almost totally on getting a big lion in the early days of the 1953 safari. However, one exception to their tunnel-visioned lion hunting was the quick twenty-minute side stalk that resulted in Jack's first and finest Cape buffalo.

One fine morning, Jack and Don were rolling along in the hunting car in their lion search when they saw the bull of all buffalo bulls in the midst of an early siesta under a thorn tree. A pandemonium-filled half-hour later, Jack sat down near the defunct monster, shaking so hard that he couldn't light a cigarette.

To fill in the details: After spotting the bull and the obligatory drive-off in the lorry, Jack and Don planned a hasty approach. Jack took his big .450 Watts from the gunbearer, and Don grabbed his .475 double. Being a bit naive about buffalo ammo, Jack had the .450 stuffed full of 480-grain softpoints and was about to learn a very scary lesson. In short order, O'Connor, Ker, and their gunbearer had closed to within fifty yards of the still-sleeping bull. With the bull quartering away, Jack whispered to Don that he would try to drive one of the heavy .450 bullets through the bull's upper lungs and also break the spine. Dropping to one knee, O'Connor made what seemed to be the perfect shot. The buffalo went down as though dynamited. Ker told O'Connor to shoot again. This time, Jack's bullet blew the big bull's heart to shreds. It seemed that no animal could have been any deader.

But Jack had never shot any animal with the unbelievable toughness and cardiovascular reserve of a Cape buffalo. He was reloading the .450 when the "dead" giant roared to his feet and came for the men like an express train. Twin blasts from Don's .475 and Jack's .450 stopped the bull as though he had hit a wall. As the hulk staggered away, O'Connor put still another bullet into his heart, finally putting him down to stay.

Only after the bull was down and out did Don Ker learn that Jack had been using softpoint bullets. This brought a stern admonition from him that solids were the bullet of choice in dealing with buffalo. Nevertheless, Don wanted to see how O'Connor's bullets had performed, so they did what Jack referred to as an "autopsy" on the bull. (An "autopsy" on a two-thousand-pound Cape buffalo strikes me as being roughly akin to field-dressing a Brontosaurus!) Sure enough, Jack's first 480-grainer had gone right where he had held, ripping through the lungs and striking the backbone. But instead of breaking it, the bullet had flattened on the cable-steel spine like a wad of bubblegum on hot pavement. It was something O'Connor never forgot.

The big bull had a heavy boss with massive, deep-curling horns and a spread of 44 inches, which eventually shrank a bit to 43½ inches. No matter. Jack never bettered his first bull despite more Cape buffalo hunting than he ever actually admitted. In his usual clear and direct manner, he told the story of taking his great bull in the pages of *Outdoor Life* and again in a chapter titled "Buffaloes Shoot Back!" in *Jack O'Connor's Big Game Hunts*.

O'Connor later killed a 41-inch bull in 1962 on a safari near the Save River in Mozambique and another on a Botswana safari in 1966. The Botswana bull, carrying two seemingly lethal O'Connor bullets, charged him and PH John Kingsley-Heath and absorbed a veritable thunderstorm of heavy lead before finally giving up the ghost. Jack took his last bull with his pet .416 Rigby on his next-to-last safari near Sichifula, Zambia, in 1969.

By the end of Jack's Cape-buffalo career, he had killed five bulls—one (his first) with the .450 Watts, two with his old Griffin & Howe .375, and two with the .416, a rifle and cartridge with which he had a quiet love affair during his later years. Three of the bulls took one or more killing shots from Jack's rifle and then came after him, which left him with an unending respect for the buff's great vitality. In terms of trophy quality, all five of O'Connor's Cape buffalo had spreads of forty or more inches, which has always been the yardstick for trophy bulls. However, the final disposition of the great sets of horns is unknown. Jack undoubtedly gave some of the heads away. Because of their great size and weight, Cape buffalo were not "mounting trophies" as far as he was concerned. He put the horns of some of his bulls on wooden shields and let it go at that. Only his best bull made it into the O'Connor collection housed at the University of Idaho, where it is on display today.

RHINO

Of all the animals that compose the African Big Five, the rhino held the least fascination for O'Connor. Long before he ever landed in Africa, he correctly saw the black rhino for what it was: a holdover from a few million years before, truculent, stupid, near-blind, certainly dangerous, but probably avoidable. O'Connor had no particular interest in playing host to thirty-five-hundred pounds of prehistoric armored car that would come trundling up to get a closer look at and perhaps run over him. The rhino also fell into Jack's "too big" category—trophies really too cumbersome to mount and that, if mounted, might pull down a wall at 725 Prospect Avenue in Lewiston, Idaho.

Jack's 1953 hunting companions Herb Klein and Red Early both had the hots to get rhino. But they were going to do their rhino hunting in the second half of the safari up in Kenya's Northern Frontier District, where rhino were more plentiful and horn quality was better. Jack had his own plans for that part of the safari, and they didn't include rhino. If he was going to take a look at a rhino, it would have to be in the very early days of the big show.

127

As things worked out, the three bwanas spent the first days of their safari in a beautiful camp near Tanganyika's Simiyu River. Herb and Red hunted on a general basis, while Jack used nine days of this time trying to get a good lion. At the end of the period, he had his lion and a magnificent 43½-inch Cape buffalo that just fell into his lap during the course of his lion looking. After winding up operations in the Simiyu River camp, the entire company moved south into Tanganyika for an entire month. Because Jack's hunting goals were much more modest than either Herb's or Red's, he was left at loose ends for a short period in the early stages of the second segment of the safari.

Although Jack's aspirations hadn't really included a rhino, at this point he may have let Herb's and Red's rhino enthusiasm get to him. Whatever. Anyway, accompanied by his boy wonder PH Myles Turner, Colonel Jack, as Herb called him on occasion, found himself in the small Kenya village of Mbalu buying a rhino license. A local who knew Myles came up to chat with the two men. After introducing O'Connor, Myles mentioned that they were buying a rhino license for Jack.

Right then and there, Jack's big rhino was essentially presented to him gift-wrapped.

"You don't say," intoned the local man in so many words. Seemed he was just in town for the very purpose of reporting to the district officer about the activities of a great rogue bull rhino at nearby Lake Eyasi. He further told them that the big bull had run down and tossed a native village woman who had been out gathering wood. The local man thought that the rhino had perhaps been wounded and gotten unusually mean and ornery. Somebody had to go out and dispatch the creature, and Señor O'Connor got the job on the spot.

So impromptu was his little sidebar safari-ette that Herb and Red didn't even accompany Jack. Syd Downey, one of the two major-domos of the famous Ker and Downey safari firm, and Myles quickly rounded up a couple of tents, some groceries, and three or four safari boys, loaded all this along with Jack into a couple of big lorries, and bumped off in the direction of Lake Eyasi.

The group arrived in the area a little after noon. While the safari boys were setting up camp, Jack, Syd, and Myles paid a visit to the local village and saw the native woman who had been tossed by the big rogue rhino. The locals told them that the rhino came out to feed in late afternoon along the lake.

Lake Eyasi turned out to be less a "lake" than a large, flat, low basin that caught the waters of the heavy seasonal rains. The water would then be a foot or two deep. As it receded, rich, heavy grass sprang to life in the "lake," and game flooded into the area.

Later that afternoon, after a belated lunch and a nap, Jack, Myles, and Syd set out to find the rhino. In a short time, they caught a glimpse of him feeding in low brush at the edge of the low plain that was Lake Eyasi. Piling out of the big safari truck, the three men took up the chase. But the rhino was on the move, and catching up to him required more than a half-mile of travel at a steady trot. As they closed in, the run, the excitement, and Jack's thirty-year cigarette habit had him sucking wind big time. But when they were within 150 yards of the big bull, O'Connor found an opening to shoot through, dropped to one knee, allowed a bit for the rhino's forward travel, and stuck the first shot from his big .450 Watts right through the chest cavity, a little behind the heart. The bull turned and ran.

By this time in his hunting career, Jack had been a scope man for twenty years. But his .450 was an aperture-sight affair and Jack had hardly shot it at all other than to sight it in prior to the safari. His lack of recent experience with aperture sights may have contributed to what happened next.

When the big rhino ran, Jack's second 480-grain bullet was a complete airball, boring a .45-caliber hole in the cool, late-afternoon air in Tanganyika. The third shot was more like Jack. It went through the rhino's lungs and did the damage. Before the bull went down, Syd and Myles each hammered away with their big .470 doubles.

Everyone rushed over to get a look at the rhino. Its 19½-inch horn was a good trophy, but O'Connor couldn't get very interested in the whole deal. As far as he was concerned, he had a rhino and that was about it. The bull had turned mean after a native had plinked it with an arrow.

Despite his lack of enthusiasm for the entire affair, Jack's rhino misadventure *did* give rise to one of his most delightful self-deprecatory remarks. His second shot that missed the rhino as it ran quartering away at a range of 150 yards had been completely forgivable—easier to do than one might imagine. But for the rest of his life Jack would occasionally chuckle and admit that he was a charter, if red-faced, member of the Missed-A-Rhino Club.

And so ends this little tale of how the Arizona Kid strummed his one and only rhino. O'Connor's own wistful account of the proceedings appeared in his delightful 1963 book *Jack O'Connor's Big Game Hunts* in a chapter entitled "Iron-Plated Tinhorn." A kill photograph of Jack with the bull appears on page 328 with a caption by Jack that says in part: "I gaze sadly upon the rhino, wondering why I shot the huge pea-brained beast." This statement pretty well summed up his thoughts about the whole affair. In later years and on subsequent safaris, he had absolutely no interest in collecting another rhino.

Interestingly enough, Herb's and Red's best-laid plans to get big rhino didn't materialize. Herb Klein's bull had a 20-inch horn, which was only a half-inch longer than Jack's. Red Early's rhino was a bit smaller. O'Connor had his rhino horns mounted on a wooden shield. They are now on display at the University of Idaho.

LEOPARD

On O'Connor's first safari in 1953, he had a mild interest in collecting a leopard, but a Loliondo game warden told him he probably wouldn't even see one. The leopard license would have set O'Connor back $75, so thrifty Jack held onto his wallet. Of course, he saw no fewer than ten leopards during the course of that safari. He also saw the trophy cats taken by his hunting cronies Klein and Early. In death, leopards had a look that Jack liked, all clean and satinlike. There was none of the worn-out tan-carpet look of a dead lion. Jack began to kick himself for not buying a leopard license and continued to do so for five years until January of 1958, the start of his second safari, in French Equatorial Africa (Chad) with Elgin Gates. There, leopards were on the general license, and Jack wanted one badly. Again he failed to get one, but this time he saw the enormous desert leopard taken by Elgin, and this only whetted his leopard appetite all the more.

I mentioned earlier that Jack's third African safari, to Tanganyika in October of 1959, was a freebie hunt courtesy of the East African safari firm of Ker and Downey. It was also Eleanor's first safari. The trip reunited Jack with his old friend Syd Downey, one of the best leopard men in all of Africa. This time, a leopard was a high-priority goal with O'Connor. He spent the first part of the trip in northern Tanganyika and there finally collected a big tom. However, the operation was not without its tricky moments.

Syd planned to produce a leopard for Jack by the traditional East African method of baiting. A series of baits were hung in suitable trees where the prevailing wind was right and where the trees themselves could be stalked or ground blinds could be built nearby to hide the hunters while they awaited a cat's appearance. Such trees had to be large enough to hang the baits out of reach of lions and hyenas and to provide feeding leopards a sense of

131

concealment. Their first bait, a large zebra stallion (Eleanor's first African kill), was cut in half and hung, and the wait began.

The next morning the hunters found a large male leopard on a high limb a few feet above where the bait was hanging. But the leopard was itself "treed" by a fine male lion on the ground at the foot of the tree, growling angrily and looking hungrily up at the bait. With typical British understatement, Syd observed dryly that the treed leopard didn't exactly constitute a sporting opportunity and that Jack would have to forgo his first leopard chance.

The situation went downhill from there.

Leopards were plentiful, but the area was awash in lions. As fast as Jack and Eleanor could kill bait animals and the safari crew could hang them, they were eaten or torn down and stolen by the aggressive lions. The lions intimidated the smaller leopards and generally fouled up the hunt. The process of shooing off the lions soon deteriorated into low comedy. Once, to lend variety to the leopard fiasco, a wandering band of Masai drove a large herd of cattle up a donga, right past the hunters' two best bait trees, totally ruining the area for two or three days.

Jack, remembering his rifle problems during the 1953 lion hunt, faithfully fired a sighting shot every day with his .30-06. Every day it was right on the button. Then one day, lulled into complacency, he failed to check his rifle. Sure enough, that very afternoon he undershot a big tom at sixty yards from a ground blind, just grazing the skin on the leopard's chest. Sometime since his last sighting shot, his scope had taken a hard bump on top of the eyepiece, causing the rifle to shoot low. So once again Jack brought his old Griffin & Howe .375 into the battle.

Syd said it would be futile to expect to get another chance at the big leopard that Jack had missed. Though this proved to be true, at noon the next day the two men found that the same bait had been fed on by yet another leopard. This put Jack and Syd back in the same blind where Jack had failed to connect only twenty-four hours before. And sure enough, at the last possible shooting light, another big tom slipped in to the bait and began to feed. O'Connor took him out with one 300-grain Silvertip through the lungs.

Jack had now taken four of the world's great carnivores with his faithful old .375 (Alaskan brown bear, lion, tiger, and leopard). O'Connor never offered any precise details about the weight or length of his leopard, saying only that it was "a large, heavy male, chunky and powerful." When the story appeared in *Outdoor Life* and later in *Jack O'Connor's Big Game Hunts*, Jack called it "Leopard at Long Last." The title gives the impression that O'Connor had two or three futile safaris tied up in the securing of a leopard. In reality, 1959 was the only time he really focused his energies on collecting a leopard, and despite the laughs, confusion, and one missed opportunity, he got an excellent tom after only five days of hunting.

Jack had his big tom made into a full rug, but in the passage of time, it has disappeared from the scene.

ELEPHANT

Of all the major big-game species with which he came in contact over his hunting life, Jack O'Connor almost certainly wrote less about the African elephant than any other author did. And even then, much of his "elephant" writing came about indirectly in the course of his unabashed praise of the life and accomplishments of W. D. M. "Karamojo" Bell, one of O'Connor's great heroes. Bell was almost certainly the most famous of Africa's great ivory hunters and a man of great energy, courage, and toughness. Jack never tired of extolling Bell's virtues. Of course, it is well documented that Bell did most of his ivory hunting with the .275 Rigby, known elsewhere as the 7x57 Mauser, Jack's personal mid-caliber favorite. Obviously, Bell's accomplishments with the "little seven" fascinated Jack, corroborated his opinions about the cartridge, and did Jack's own vicarious relationship with Bell no harm!

Throughout his safari experiences, Jack seemed to have no real desire to take an elephant. Most of the animals in which O'Connor was interested (lion, kudu, sable) were usually on the "general" African hunting license. Elephants were routinely not available on such a license. O'Connor was always rather tight-fisted with his own and *Outdoor Life*'s license money and therefore simply didn't purchase any special elephant licenses. In his safari writings, however, he never failed to comment on sightings of the great animals. He loved seeing elephants and felt correctly that they were a wonderful, romantic part of the African scene. Elephants were so magnificent in O'Connor's eyes that he did not really think of them as game animals per se. But the hulking creatures secretly saddened O'Connor, perhaps because he felt that they were eventually doomed to extinction, thanks to their ivory value, sheer size and conspicuousness, and poaching problems.

In the summer of 1969, Jack, Eleanor, and son Bradford arrived in Zambia for a safari they had booked with Zambia Safaris, Ltd. Operated by two Brits, Ron Kidson and Keith Rowse, Zambia Safaris was a crack outfit. It was Brad's first safari, Eleanor's fifth, and Jack's eighth.

Lo and behold, the O'Connors found that elephants were included on the general Zambian license. Furthermore, the great beasts were so plentiful in the floodplain of the Zambezi River that their feeding habits were destroying a lot of their own habitat. The license deal and the sheer numbers of elephants in the area apparently put hunting them in a little different light for Jack. In any event, he, Eleanor, and Bradford decided to "take a whirl at elephant hunting."

As it worked out, Eleanor was the first of the O'Connors to actually take a bull. She and Ron Kidson closed to within fifty yards of a bull carrying around fifty pounds of ivory per side. As cool as icewater, the still-trim Eleanor dropped the elephant with the neatest of brain shots and a single 220-grain solid from her little .30-06. So much for that!

In the end, we'll never know just why Jack chose finally to kill an elephant. He'd had numerous chances in the past. Although he had not bought any elephant licenses on past safaris, he could certainly have done so had he really wanted a bull. Perhaps he felt that his African hunting experiences would be incomplete without the taking of at least one elephant. Perhaps he looked forward to the challenge of attempting the somewhat tricky brain shot, about which he had read so much in the Bell writings. And just maybe, Eleanor, his bride of forty-two years, had thrown down the gauntlet a bit with her calmness in taking her own first bull.

A day or so afterward, Jack and Ron Kidson stood quietly watching an average mature bull from a range of about seventy-five yards. Perhaps the bull saw the two men, because he turned and began walking purposefully in their direction. So in the very end, Jack's elephant-killing decision was made for him. He stood quietly, observing the bull's advance. At forty feet, he raised the .416 and centered the cross hairs between the bull's eyes and a bit low. At twenty-five feet, he squeezed off a 300-grain solid. The ground shook as the bull collapsed, and although Jack had entered into the whole business with something of an "Oh, why not?" attitude, he was finally, after sixteen years and eight safaris, an elephant hunter.

Jack's bull was almost a twin of Eleanor's in the size, weight, and shape of the tusks. When Bradford took his own bull a few days later, its tusks were almost identical to those of Jack's and Eleanor's bulls. In fact, all six of the tusks weighed between forty and fifty pounds. (In photos, Jack's tusks appear smaller.) One of these sets of tusks strangely disappeared at some point during the thirty-plus years since they were taken. The two other sets still remain in the O'Connor family, but even Brad does not know with certainty to which bulls they belonged.

With the braining of his elephant, O'Connor came to the end of the Big Five, one of Africa's most prestigious hunting achievements. (He would probably have referred to it as "The Big Five Caper.") But the whole business had happened in a rather left-handed way. The only Big Five animal that he had been hot to get in the beginning was the lion. He was *always* a passionate lion hunter, grew to like Cape-buffalo hunting, but collected his single rhino, leopard, and elephant in a very matter-of-fact way, with the rhino being nothing more than the result of a set of good circumstances. Curiously, within two weeks of his arrival in Africa for his first safari in 1953, he had three of the Big Five. But it took him sixteen more years and seven more safaris to complete the circuit.

It is interesting to note that the term "Big Five" occurs almost nowhere in all of Jack's writings, and he wrote nothing at all about his own pursuit or accomplishment of the feat. In fact, given that he was an iconoclast and inclined to be something of a "reverse snob," we are left to wonder whether, had he seen the Big Five as a great hunting hurdle, he might have found a way to *avoid* pulling it off. O'Connor was no man to be chivvied around, and no one was going to tell him what to hunt—or to do with any other facet of his life, for that matter. Jack's Big Five just sort of *happened*, without much sense of purpose or plan. Still, his collection of the Big Five and the offhand manner in which he did it remain a significant barometer of the depth and breadth of Jack's safari experience.

8

Jack as a Trophy Hunter

For more than fifty years, Jack O'Connor was an avid hunter of big game in North America, Africa, and Asia. He did not make his first African safari until 1953, when he was fifty-one years old.

But after that he went on eight more safaris, his last in 1972. He made the first of his five Asian hunts, or shikars, to India for tiger and other game in 1955. He hunted tiger again in 1965. His three other shikars were to Iran in 1955, 1959, and 1970 for Urial sheep, red sheep, ibex, and wild boar. O'Connor felt and said that his writings about African and Asian hunting experiences were well received by his readership at *Outdoor Life,* and of course they added to his authority and reputation.

However, his reputation as America's foremost gun authority was solidly in place long before he ever hunted abroad, and this reputation was built on his vast experience as a hunter of North American big game. Over his long career, Jack related these hunting experiences for many different reasons: to demonstrate bullet performance, stalking techniques, hunting methods, animal behavior, the effect of weather conditions, etc. Last, and most significantly for hundreds of thousands of his readers, he told us his stories for our sheer enjoyment.

But Jack's hunting history is spread over fifty years and scattered in hundreds of *Outdoor Life* feature pieces and columns, other magazine articles, and a dozen or so books. In other chapters of this book, we have dealt with his desert and mountain-sheep-hunting career and taken a close look at Jack's hunting of Africa's Big Five. Here we'll home in on what the word "trophy" truly meant to Jack O'Connor.

NORTH AMERICA

As a seeker of mountain sheep, O'Connor was the purest of trophy hunters. Although he had a few slip-ups (as do all long-time trophy sheep hunters, whether they will admit or not), he held to a very high standard in the quality of the rams he killed. His main criteria were always age, horn mass, and horn length, in that order. The current Boone and Crockett scoring system for sheep and other North American species was developed in 1950. This was long after Jack had developed his own trophy standards for rams. As mentioned in other places in this book, it is almost eerie how the B&C sheep-scoring system followed O'Connor's personal trophy-ram criteria.

But Jack hunted much other game, and it was in the hunting of those other North American species that he was almost certainly *not* a pure trophy hunter. He tried to take good stuff at all times, but he was much more an "everyman" hunter or a "hunter of opportunity" where game other than rams was involved. The title of this chapter is not meant to cast any aspersions on O'Connor as a selective hunter. But as far as I know, in all of his writings O'Connor gave the B&C scores of only two of his trophies: his best Stone sheep, taken in 1946, with an official score of $175^6/8$, and his best Dall sheep, taken in 1950, which scored $176^7/8$. If he ever stated in print the scores of other personal trophies, it is news to me. To be sure, he collected some very good North American trophies besides rams, but he always seemed curiously disinterested in their measurements, scores, or ability to qualify for the records.

Furthermore, he never developed the habit—as is the norm for today's hard-core trophy hunters—of referring to animals by their scores alone. And although he served the Boone and Crockett Club as both a measurer and a competition judge and heartily approved of its conservation principles, he was always wise enough not to get caught up in the "one-upmanship" into which trophy hunting can unfortunately degenerate.

How many elk did he take? Where? How good was his best bull? How many caribou, and over what time frame? How big? How many grizzlies? Moose? Antelope? His best antelope? How many deer? (Even Jack didn't know the answer to that last one.)

It has taken some digging, but here, perhaps for the first time, is something of a comprehensive overview of O'Connor's North American career apart from sheep hunting. This chapter will take a look at the various species, numbers, and quality of animals taken, the timing, some minor mysteries, and a few unanswered questions. A little later we'll examine his African and Asian hunting from the same perspectives.

Grizzly

In his *Outdoor Life* column in the late 1960s, O'Connor stated that he had taken thirteen grizzlies in his career. He killed no more grizzlies after that writing. In the article, he went on to say that he had taken ten of the big bears with the .30-06, two with the .270, and a single bear with the .300 Weatherby Magnum. Of those bears taken with the .30-06, most were killed with his Sukalle-built, Minar-stocked Springfield, which he fondly referred to as his "bear rifle." O'Connor's best grizzly was his very first one, collected in Alberta in 1943 while hunting with Roy Hargreaves. According to Jack, the bear was 9' 6" long from the tip of its nose to the end of its tail as it lay on the ground. Jack conjectured that it "might have weighed 900 pounds." If so, the bear would have been an all-time heavyweight of interior grizzlies. No matter, it was a very big bear.

O'Connor has no grizzlies listed in any editions of the Boone and Crockett record books. Given the size of his Alberta bear, it very likely would have made the book, assuming O'Connor had kept the skull and had it measured as soon as the B&C system was devised in 1950. At that time, the grizzly minimum score for inclusion in the book was 23. Jack had a bear rug or two made, but what became of most of his grizzly hides or skulls is unknown.

If O'Connor killed any grizzlies after 1949, I do not know of them. If he did not, this compresses the killing of his stated thirteen grizzlies into four hunts (Alberta in 1943, the Yukon in 1945, British Columbia in 1946, and the Yukon in 1949). Of course, grizzlies were unprotected in all those provinces during those years. Still, that's a bunch of grizzlies!

The grizzly was one animal that never failed to excite Jack. In fact, he jokingly stated on a few occasions that a big grizzly was the one animal that he "might have interrupted a ram stalk for." Then he would laugh and say: "Of course, the ram would have won out!"

Caribou

In a chapter entitled "Outsmarting the Caribou" in the book *Hunting on Three Continents with Jack O'Connor*, Jack had this to say about his caribou-hunting career: "In thirty years of off-and-on caribou hunting, I have shot my share. Of maybe twenty-five that I have taken, I can remember that only two required more than one shot." This quote is not recounted here to prove Jack's shooting record on caribou but rather to state his own estimate of how many bulls he had killed. O'Connor hunted in caribou country on fourteen separate

When the Winchester Model 71 in .348 came out in 1936, Jack bought the Deluxe model shown here with the bolt peep sight. He liked the rifle's stock design very much.

Jack's first Dall ram, with horns 38½ inches long and bases 13¾ inches around. Jack killed it as it climbed out of a basin that he and guide Field Johnson had been crossing, using his Linden-stocked, flat-bolt .270 Mauser. O'Connor wrote that he thought this ram was one of the first heads of big game ever taken with a Remington Bronze Point bullet, and he remembered hearing a peculiar, sharp crack as the bullet struck the ram. Klutlan Glacier, Yukon Territory, September 1945.

O'Connor looks over the best caribou he ever collected. He got the 359⅛ B&C bull with his tried-and-true Minar .30-06 Springfield at the Generc River, Yukon Territory, September 1945.

O'Connor with his largest Stone ram, taken on British Columbia's Prophet Bench during the last week of September 1946. It scored 1756/8 B&C and was No. 10 in the 1952 and 1958 record books. The rifle was Jack's third custom .270. It began life as a Krieghoff 98 Mauser action, which was given to O'Connor by a returning military friend. In the spring of 1946, O'Connor had it rebarreled to .270 by Tucson gunsmith Bill Sukalle. It was then stocked by Bob Owen. Jack's two previous custom .270s had been a little on the heavy side, and this was his first real lightweight.

Guide Field Johnson looks down on the second of two Dall rams killed by O'Connor from a bunch of six spotted above the Yukon's St. Clair River. Because the ram had thin horns, Jack did not care much for the head and later gave it away. Generc Glacier area, Yukon Territory, September 1945.

Jack with his first Stone ram in August 1946. O'Connor killed it off the cliffs in the background at a range of 225 yards, sending it tumbling down into the shallow, noisy waters of Neavis Creek, British Columbia. Jack's outfitter, Frank Golata, had seen a small group of rams as the packtrain rounded a bend in the creek. He called to Jack, who piled off his horse, sat down on the sandy creek bank, and collected the best of the bunch. Despite the steepness of the cliffs in the background, the ram was actually taken in "prairie"-type country a long way from any traditional sheep habitat. Although he did not know it at the time, the ram made O'Connor the fifth-ever Grand Slammer.

Jack's first "mystery ram," an average mature bighorn taken in September 1943 in British Columbia a few miles west of the Alberta border. This photo has appeared in other publications with an erroneous caption. O'Connor actually killed this ram during the second half of an Alberta-British Columbia hunt. He had previously taken a 178 B&C bighorn during the Alberta phase of the trip. Jack took this photo with a self-timed camera. He collected the ram at a salt lick while he was actually in the process of stalking a goat late in the afternoon of a traveling day with outfitter Roy Hargreaves's packtrain. For some reason, he wrote little in later years about taking this ram, telling the story in any detail only once (see "The Rocky Mountain Bighorn," page 42, Sheep and Sheep Hunting*). The ram was the second of only three bighorns that O'Connor ever killed. All were taken in 1943 and 1944.*

Roy Hargreaves (left) and O'Connor with Jack's first and best Rocky Mountain bighorn, taken on the first day of the 1943 Alberta sheep season. The ram officially scored 178 B&C and appeared in the 1952, 1958, and 1964 Boone and Crockett record books before the bighorn minimum was raised from 175 to 180 in 1968. O'Connor got the ram with a Model 70 in .270 Winchester custom-stocked by Alvin Linden. Chocolate Creek, Alberta, September 1943.

Another "mystery" ram. Taken on Mount Olympus, British Columbia, in September 1946, this was Jack's second Stone ram, and it completed his second Grand Slam. The ram, which looks for all the world like a bighorn, was an excellent trophy, scoring 1672/8 and ranking nineteenth in the 1952 record book. One day after he killed it, he was back on the same mountain with his outfitter, Frank Golata, and got the best Stone of his life, a 1756/8 B&C ram. But strangely, O'Connor chose to write almost nothing about the ram pictured above.

Jack admires the 9¾-inch horns on his first mountain goat, taken on his 1943 trip to Alberta. Jack lost a goat a few days earlier when a broken shell casing stuck in his Model 70 in .270 and prevented the needed follow-up shot.

Bill Weaver, first to design and mass-produce quality telescope sights at a reasonable price, is seen here on the right during a break in a pheasant hunt with Jack near Lewiston about 1951. Note the 1X scope Bill used successfully for wingshooting.

The rifle on the left, a custom 7x57 Mauser built by Tom Burgess and Russ Leonard in 1951, was used by Eleanor O'Connor on countless big game worldwide. It wears a Leupold 3X scope.

Jack receives congratulations on his best-ever North American sheep trophy from guide Moose Johnson. Jack killed the 176⁷/₈ B&C ram after what he always contended was the easiest sheep stalk he ever made. The other ram head, lying in the left background, was at first a mystery. It was not killed by O'Connor. In later accounts, Jack indicated that he and guide Moose Johnson made the stalk alone. But a check of Jack's original January 1951 Outdoor Life *story revealed that his hunting pal Red Early went along on the stalk and collected the other ram. Sifton Range, Yukon Territory, August 1950.*

O'Connor downed five Cape buffalo during his safari career but never improved on this 43½-inch, which he killed on his first safari to Tanganyika in early July of 1953. The rifle is a custom-built .450 Watts, a forerunner of the .458 Winchester Magnum. O'Connor had the rifle built before the safari for heavy game.

O'Connor with his first lion, a 9' 7", 500-pound monster taken in Tanganyika on his first African safari in 1953 after eight days of very hard hunting. Jack had dreamed of killing a lion since childhood and always stated that no trophy in his entire life, other than his first desert ram, gave him a greater thrill than his first lion.

Jack dropped this excellent 27¾-inch lesser kudu in Kenya's Northern Frontier District in 1953. The taking of both greater and lesser kudu on the same safari has always been a difficult hurdle, but Jack was able to pull it off, to the considerable amazement of his hunting pals Herb Klein and Red Early.

A magnificent 44½-inch sable taken by O'Connor on his first safari in 1953. Here he is shown receiving congratulations from his PH, Syd Downey. The rifle, used extensively on this safari, is the second .300 Weatherby Magnum Jack owned. On various safaris, O'Connor collected numerous African animals eligible for inclusion in Rowland Ward records, but curiously, this sable is one of only two that were ever entered.

Jack poses with a brown bear taken during a drenching rain on Admiralty Island, Alaska, in May of 1956. He used his Griffin & Howe Model 70 in .375 Magnum, shown here with the scope temporarily removed.

*"Beat" elephants stand unconcernedly by as Jack looks over his first tiger, a huge male measuring 9' 9"
between pegs. Jack took it in a classic elephant beat as the tiger bounded by in high grass. Jack looks
reserved in the photograph. He wasn't. Although it was one of his greatest hunting thrills, the tiger's death
made O'Connor strangely sad. In a story about the event, he had this to say: "I'd have his hide tanned
and his head mounted. I'd spend the rest of my life with him, yet I hardly knew him." Kashipur, India,
March 1955.*

O'Connor with his second Persian red sheep, a 26½-incher taken with a 300-yard shot at an elevation of 12,000 feet during Jack's first Iranian shikar in May 1955.

Jack gets a handshake from Prince Abdorreza Pahlavi for this big Persian wild boar taken on a drive during Jack's first Iranian shikar in May of 1955. Two boars were Jack's first Iranian trophies, and boar hunting proved to be a lot more exciting than Jack had anticipated.

Jack and Ken Niles look over some British Columbia mule deer taken by their party on a hunt cooked up by Roy Weatherby in the fall of 1947. Jack brought along his own home-grown .300 Weatherby Magnum and killed his first game, a goat, with it.

O'Connor and Khandlar Grah Shadloo with a nice Persian ibex (pasang) collected by Jack during his second Iranian shikar in November of 1959. Jack's rifle did not arrive in Iran, but he was able to make do with Prince Abdorreza Pahlavi's custom .270 (sob!).

JOC, at a Weatherby luncheon in the late 1950s, about to tie into the grandfather of all steaks. His prestige and reputation sat him down to many a fine table. His favorite restaurants and watering holes were scattered worldwide in such exotic places as New Delhi, Tehran, Nairobi, Rome, Madrid, Paris, London, New York, San Francisco, and Los Angeles.

)'Connor with a nice young 5x5 elk taken in the early 1960s. In the years after the O'Connor clan moved to Idaho, Jack made many short elk hunts, often with his winter's meat as the main objective.

Getting this 31½-inch Patterson eland was a messy business. O'Connor had to trail the wounde[d]
bull, which required five or six 300-grain Silvertips from Jack's .375 before it gave up the ghos[t].
Tanganyika, November 1959.

Eleanor did not begin hunting sheep until 1963, but once she got started, she did so with a bang, killing this 44½-inch Dall ram on a day of howling and bitter cold wind in the Yukon's Dawson Range. In this photograph, a happy but near-frozen Eleanor looks down at her ram as guide Frank Isaac looks on. The ram scored 177⁴/8 and won Eleanor first place in the next Boone and Crockett competition. Ashihik Lake, Yukon Territory, September 1963.

Jack admires his new custom Mauser .280 Remington, stocked by master craftsman Earl Milliron, right. This rifle, made in 1966, was the first of three custom .280s Jack had made. The last, by Al Biesen, was finished after Jack's demise.

This mule deer buck received both a .270 bullet from Jack and a 7mm from Eleanor as he jumped from a brushy rim in Idaho's Snake River breaks. The buck, shot in 1964, weighed 182 pounds field-dressed.

Jack retrieves a Canada goose shot during a gun-company seminar in Maryland in 1965.

Jack O'Connor and Peter Alport take a lunch break during a pheasant hunt in the 1960s. Alport was head of Norm Thompson, a Portland, Oregon, outdoor supply and apparel company that used some of Jack's designs for leather gear. Alport was the recipient of some O'Connor firearms.

Jack swings on a going-away bird during a red-legged partridge drive in Spain in late 1967. The O'Connors used their Winchester Model 21s on this shoot.

occasions (1943, 1945, 1946, 1947, 1949, 1950, 1951, 1956, 1961, 1963, 1967, 1971, 1972, and 1973). He killed no caribou in 1950, 1967, 1971, 1972, or 1973. If his own twenty-five-kill estimate is correct, then for the remaining nine years he would have had to hammer caribou at a rate of about three bulls per trip. That's putting a lot of protein on the ground. He killed one bull with a 7mm Ackley Magnum (wonder where *that* came from?). The rest were taken with .270s or .30-06s. He did all of his caribou hunting in Alberta, British Columbia, and Yukon Territory. The great majority of his bulls were mountain caribou, or what Jack referred to as "Osborn" caribou. But he also killed a few barren ground caribou in the Yukon. His best-ever bull was taken in a high, lonely basin near the Yukon's Generc River on a cold, dreary day in September of 1945, and this bull showed up in the 1952 Boone and Crockett record book with an official score of 359⅛. He enjoyed seeing caribou and never tired of watching their hilarious behavior. O'Connor thought and said that the caribou was probably North America's most beautiful big-game trophy, and likely the dumbest. However, he also thought them a great part of the romance and mystique of hunting in the Canadian North.

Goat

O'Connor never gave any final tally in print of his take of mountain goats, saying only that he "had shot a few." In fact, he may have killed as few as three goats. He got his first two in Alberta in 1943 while hunting with Roy Hargreaves. What Jack generally refers to as his first goat was a heavy-based 9¾-incher that he killed in early September of the 1943 hunt. Jack described the action on pages 131–133 of *Hunting in the Rockies* in a chapter appropriately entitled "The White Goat." Jack and Roy made a stalk up a steep mountain from below a big billy. When they got into shooting position at the top of a small bluff, the terrain was so steep that when Jack lay down prone to shoot, he found himself sliding down the mountain. The two men solved their dilemma in a near-slapstick manner. Roy stood on a small fir tree that grew out of the near-perpendicular cliff. Jack in turn stood on Roy's shoulders for his shot at the goat! One can almost picture tall, skinny, flat-assed O'Connor standing on the shoulders of tall, skinny Roy as Jack wavered off three salvos (all solid hits at three hundred yards) from his .270—pretty good shooting, given his shaky foundation! The scene must have been hilarious, but it sure worked.

Curiously, however, on page 38 of *Hunting on Three Continents with Jack O'Connor*, he refers to a different animal as his "first goat," saying: "Actually, the first goat I shot was feeding on the other side of a little canyon and about 200 yards away. I rode a horse up, got off just under the ridge, and shot the goat." Of course, this is nitpicking on my part. It matters not at all which was his first billy. Jack was simply not a goat man. His goat-hunting adventures were evidently not sufficiently memorable for him to keep track of them.

He took the only other goat that I am aware of in 1947 on a hunt put together by Roy Weatherby to British Columbia's Selkirk Mountains. Jack killed a big billy graveyard-dead at long range with his homegrown .300 Weatherby Magnum (see the chapter "Jack and Roy" in this book). It was one of Jack's first opportunities (if not the first) to see the great killing power of the .300, and he was impressed.

Jack's on-Roy's-shoulders 1943 goat, with its 9¾-inch length and heavy bases, might well have merited inclusion in the Boone and Crockett record book when the 1952 edition came out. At that time, the B&C minimum goat score was 47. Almost certainly, O'Connor never had this billy scored.

Jack pretty well summed up his thoughts about the goat in *Big Game Hunting in the Rockies*: "The (goat) trophy is a unique but not spectacular one. Every big game hunter owes himself a good goat, just for the experience, but few become real goat-hunting fans." The phrase "just for the experience" seems to define O'Connor's goat-hunting motives. Of course, goats were part of the fauna of the West and, to a greater degree, Canada. An occasional goat-hunting yarn made good grist for his *Outdoor Life* mill, and he obviously knew that there were avid goat hunters among his readership. However, when all was said and done, he concluded his goat comments above by saying: "The goat just hasn't got what it takes to be in the top flight of sporting animals."

Moose

In writings long after his moose-hunting days were over, Jack claimed to have taken twelve moose, but he shot few after 1950. So most of them were collected in the years between 1943, when he made his first Canadian hunt, and 1950. Again, this is not cited to cast any doubts on Jack's claim but to show that O'Connor must have been a moose-hunting machine during the four or five trips on which moose were available.

On his 1943 Alberta hunt with outfitter Roy Hargreaves, Jack still-hunted up his first bull all by himself. This occurred at the head of Copton Creek in far western Alberta. The bull was a 52-incher, but with narrow palms. Jack was proud of how he had gotten the bull, and it is described in the only personal moose yarn that he ever told in any detail. The next year, he killed his only Shiras moose, an average bull, on his Wyoming hunt with outfitter Ernie Miller. He followed that in 1945 with another Canadian bull in the Yukon's Solomon Range; the bull, despite its rather average spread of 55 inches, was massive and a fine trophy. Then in 1946 he collected a many-pointed 59-incher at the head of Lapp Creek, British Columbia, while hunting with Frank Golata. Evidently, most of his other moose were rather mundane happenings in Jack's mind inasmuch as he never commented on them in print to any degree. Because of their sheer size, moose were not among Jack's favorite big-game animals. Ever thrifty at heart, he had this to say in *Hunting in the Rockies*: "A moose is a grand animal, but he is so enormous that I always feel a bit guilty when I kill one," adding that "much of the meat is usually wasted by the hunter. There simply isn't enough room to take it all or enough mouths to eat it." He further felt that moose were generally "too big" to mount as trophies, although he did have one mounted when he still lived in Tucson. This mount has long since disappeared. His other comments regarding moose as trophies were along the same lines as those about goats—for example, this quote from *Hunting in the Rockies*: "Every big game hunter owes it to himself to get a good trophy moose, but for some reason, I have never hunted them as avidly as, for example, I have sheep and grizzly—or even elk."

As far as I know, Jack never used B&C scores in describing any moose heads—his or anyone else's.

Given his lukewarm feelings for moose, it is rather ironic that one of Jack's last significant trips was a moose hunt to British Columbia in the fall of 1975, accompanied by his son Brad. Although Brad collected a very good bull and Jack was happy for his son's success, his own moose-hunting thrills were behind him, and he busted not a cap.

Elk

In an off-and-on (as Jack would have said it) elk-hunting career that spanned nearly forty years, O'Connor killed twenty-one elk. He stated as much in the middle 1970s, after his elk-hunting days were done. Predictably, seventeen of these were taken with the .270 Winchester. Three others were killed with the .30-06, and a single bull fell to the 7mm Remington Magnum. He got his first bull in

December of 1935 during Arizona's inaugural elk season on a hunt on the Mogollon Plateau. Jack carried and used a Griffin & Howe .30-06 Springfield on this hunt. Thinking the elk to be a hard-to-kill animal, he originally planned to use 220-grain bullets. But for whatever reason, he shot his first bull, a nice 6x6, with 180-grainers. This bull got away and Jack didn't find it until three days later. It was one of very few big-game animals that O'Connor ever lost to spoilage. In the interim he had killed another bull, a so-so 4x4. His experience with the first one reinforced his belief that elk were armor-plated, a thought that led to his acquisition of a .35 Whelen.

O'Connor's first hunt on which a big bull elk was one of his absolute priorities (along with sheep, of course!) was to Wyoming in the fall of 1944. He was outfitted by Ernie Miller and guided by both Miller and Charlie Peterson. On this trip O'Connor got a very nice bull in the 310 B&C range with what he always contended was his longest shot on any head of big game. Jack believed the shot to have been in the range of six hundred yards. This was perhaps his first .270 kill on elk. He also got a raghorn meat bull, a small 5x5, on the same hunt. O'Connor did little or no elk hunting in the middle 1940s, when he was mainly occupied with sheep and mixed-bag hunts in the Canadian North.

After the O'Connors moved to Idaho in the summer of 1948, Jack became acquainted with Les Bowman, a well-known and successful Wyoming outfitter. Bowman was a match for Jack in every way, and O'Connor had a great deal of admiration and respect for him. Les was a colorful character who in earlier life had been a stunt pilot, barnstormer, circus actor, and whatnot. He was also a rifle wildcatter, knowledgeable ballistician, and all-around gun nut. In the summer of 1959, when I was fourteen years old, I met Les Bowman and had the opportunity to be around him quite a bit. He was a salty guy with a ribald sense of humor and a sharp cookie indeed. When I knew him, he was nearly deaf. Conversations between him and hard-of-hearing Jack must have been near-shouting matches. But Bowman was one of the very few who didn't shrink from Jack in any way.

O'Connor made several elk hunts with Bowman in the early and mid-fifties. In September of 1954, high in Wyoming's Absaroka Range out of Bowman's L B Ranch on the south fork of the Shoshone River, Jack killed his best-ever elk. He described the action in a chapter of *Jack O'Connor's Big Game Hunts* entitled "Bull Elk Above Timberline." But in a strange goof-up, the five photographs and captions that Jack supplied to accompany this chapter are *not* from the 1954 hunt but rather from his 1944 hunt with Ernie Miller. Even the kill pictures on pages 39 and 43 are photos of Jack's 1944 bull. Why the usually razor-sharp O'Connor did not catch this error in the editing and proofreading of the book is impossible to know.

A good kill photo of Jack with his big 1954 bull appears on page 175 of *The Art of Hunting Big Game in North America*. Although the bull was apparently never officially scored and would not have made B&C, long-time O'Connor scholar and B&C measurer Eldon "Buck" Buckner thinks the head would have gone around 330 B&C.

After the O'Connor family moved to Idaho in 1948, Jack became an enthusiastic elk hunter in his new home state. However, here he was more of an "everyman" hunter, with good elk meat never far from his mind. He killed a nice Idaho bull here and there, his best being a 7x6 scoring around 310, taken in 1967 with outfitter Dave Christensen. This was O'Connor's lone elk taken with the 7mm Remington Magnum. But during his Idaho hunting he also killed some small bulls, a spike or two, and an occasional cow.

A really big trophy elk was one of Jack's favorite trophies, and he collected some fine ones. He would be astonished at some of the mega-bulls that are being taken today, many in his native state of Arizona. But as with most of his hunting, O'Connor relished the entire elk experience, and a great trophy was only icing on an already wonderful cake.

Black Bear

Jack collected some eighteen black bears in his hunting career. His first one came in the late fall of 1925 in the White Mountains of east-central Arizona. He dropped it with a new Griffin & Howe .30-06 Springfield sporter. Jack had graduated from the University of Arkansas earlier that year and had received the rifle as a graduation present from a "rich uncle." Later that same fall, he killed two other black bears on the Navajo Indian Reservation in the Four Corners country of northeast Arizona. For these two he used his brand-new Model 54 .270 Winchester. Jack's bear kills could very well have been the first game taken with the .270 caliber in the Southwest.

Later he collected several of what he called the "skinniest and mangiest little black bears I ever saw" while hunting whitetails in the mountains of Chihuahua, Mexico. He also took blacks in Wyoming, Alberta, British Columbia, Yukon Territory, and southeast Alaska. He got his largest black bear in the spring of 1956 along the southeast Alaskan coast, where he was outfitted and guided by famous bear guide Ralph Young. Jack's reference to the bear as his "largest" ("Black Bear Wonderland," *Jack O'Connor's Big Game Hunts*) referred to the bear's overall size. There is no indication in any of his writing that he ever set out to collect a "trophy" black bear per se. He hunted bears where and when he found them, and most of his blacks came as sidebar trophies during sheep and mixed-bag hunts for other game. He even went so far as to say that most of his blacks had been taken as happy accidents or just "pure luck." As far as I know, Jack never had any of his black-bear skulls measured with the idea of inclusion in the B&C book.

O'Connor saw the black bear exactly for what it was: totally omnivorous, almost never dangerous, highly adaptable. He always said that black bears were "great game animals." But he would usually add with a chuckle that he "resented them a bit because they didn't have horns like rams." He also stated that the possibility of an encounter with a black bear made deer country more exciting and romantic whether it was in Pennsylvania, upstate New York, Montana, or Maine.

Antelope

Jack began seeking antelope in the late 1920s. Some of his first antelope hunts were in the Mexican state of Chihuahua, a manageable trip from Jack's home in Alpine, Texas, where he was teaching at what was then Sul Ross State Teachers College. The Chihuahua hunts involved a long, rough drive down through the Texas Big Bend over almost nonexistent roads to Presidio, where he would cross the border into Mexico. He also did some antelope hunting in Sonora and Texas.

In fact, prior to 1941, Jack's antelope hunting was confined to Texas and the Mexican states of Chihuahua and Sonora. His home state of Arizona had not had an open season on antelope for many years. In October of 1936, however, Jack did collect an Arizona buck and doe on a permit issued by the Arizona State Museum in Tucson. The buck was a handsome $15\frac{1}{8}$-incher and was listed in the 1939 Boone and Crockett record book. Of course, no B&C score was given as this book tabulated trophies on the basis of horn length only.

Antelope were the subject of some of Jack's first hunting articles. In fact, his very first *Outdoor Life* piece, which appeared in the magazine's May 1934 issue, was titled "Arizona's Antelope Problem." In those years, Arizona had one stagnated antelope herd of two or three thousand animals. It must be remembered that in 1908 the entire antelope population in the United States had been down to only fifteen thousand animals. Jack's article was generally a conservation piece. But in an unusual recommendation for the times, he contended that a limited season and some intense game management were needed if Arizona's antelope population was to grow and thrive. Another early *Outdoor Life* piece was called "Stalking America's Speed King," in the July 1937 issue. In it he rated the antelope second only to the bighorn as a desirable trophy. Later, in "Antelope to Order" in the April 1939 issue, he wrote of taking the Arizona State Museum buck and doe. He wrote glowingly of antelope in his excellent 1939 book *Game in the Desert*. He thought of them as the consummate plains animal and felt that a truly big buck, fairly stalked and taken, was a trophy to be greatly prized. During the decade of the 1930s, he fairly salivated when he thought of the enormous bucks he saw occasionally on Arizona's Anderson Mesa south of Flagstaff. Jack always contended that a few of these bucks had horns exceeding twenty inches in length. The idea of getting a crack at one of them was no doubt in the back of his mind in the late thirties as he lobbied the Arizona Game Department for an open season on antelope.

The state did finally establish an inaugural season for antelope in the fall of 1941. But that affair was something of a personal low for O'Connor. He could not turn up one of the monsters he had seen in years past. The area had seen harsh winters in 1938–40, and most of those old-timers hadn't made it. To collect his buck, he made what he said was his longest shot on an antelope (535 long paces through a boulder field with his Minar .30-06 Springfield). The buck was a heavy 14½-incher, but nothing like he had hoped for. I believe his failure to get a truly magnificent buck on this hunt was more of a personal disappointment than he ever revealed to anyone and may well have taken some of the wind out of his trophy-antelope hunting sails.

In 1943 *Outdoor Life* made possible the first expansion of Jack's hunting horizons by paying his way on a sheep and mixed-bag hunt to Alberta and British Columbia. Over the next few years, these horizons would expand to game fields all over the world as the magazine sent Jack off again and again in pursuit of adventure and story material (tough life!) Slowly but surely, this forced Jack to de-prioritize antelope hunting. Often, there just wasn't time.

After the early 1940s, Jack's antelope hunting was scattered and infrequent. In the wake of his 1944 Wyoming sheep and elk hunt, he collected two nice pronghorn bucks in the Red Desert near Rawlins, Wyoming. He killed a nice buck around Gillette, Wyoming, in 1950, and a freak-horned buck near Cody in 1954. In 1958 he also collected a nice 15-incher with his brand-new pet rifle of the day, the very last 7x57 ever chambered by Winchester.

Jack's very last venture into North American game fields was an antelope and deer hunt in Montana in the fall of 1977, a few months before his death. It was made possible and was guided by Jack's good friend Jack Atcheson of Butte, Montana. The hunters located a big buck for Jack, but he was unable to score. It seemed that time had at last caught up with big-game hunting's Grand Old Man.

As with his other quarries, O'Connor never formed the habit of referring to antelope trophies by their Boone and Crockett scores, as many of today's hunters routinely do. As far as I know, he never stated in print the score of any of his antelope, if indeed he even knew. In 1951, before Boone and Crockett's new scoring system was initiated, the antelope minimum record-book score was 70. This was raised to 75 in 1953. Almost certainly, some of Jack's early bucks would have qualified for the 1952 book. He may not have even owned these heads by this time. For whatever reasons, he never pursued any plan to have his pronghorn heads officially scored.

I have been unable to discover the whereabouts of a single one of Jack's antelope trophies.

Had his hunting world not expanded so greatly, Jack might well have become the hardest of hard-core antelope hunters. He lived in great antelope country, and other great antelope states of Nevada, Wyoming, and New Mexico were within driving distance. He thought antelope beautiful animals in general and loved the complicated stalks and long-range shooting challenges involved in hunting for trophy bucks. To him, it was a sort of poor man's sheep hunting.

It would interest O'Connor to know that today antelope continue to thrive and antelope hunting retains its wide appeal. There is also a small near-cult of dedicated trophy hunters who pursue buster bucks with as much zeal as any sheep hunter. Of this group, Jack would no doubt be an enthusiastic member.

Deer

O'Connor killed more deer of various kinds than any other species of big-game animal. By his own estimate, he took more than a hundred deer in his life. In the early 1930s, he hunted Rocky Mountain mule deer in Arizona's Kaibab National Forest and took his best bucks there in the years from 1931 to 1934. He hunted Coues deer and desert mule deer in Arizona and Sonora from boyhood until 1947. He collected his very best desert mule deer in Sonora 31 December 1941. This heavy-horned 7x6 can still be seen in the O'Connor collection at the University of Idaho. He was more focused on obtaining trophy heads in his early deer hunting than in later years. As Eleanor developed into an interested hunter and skilled rifle shot, and later, when the O'Connor sons Jerry and Brad were old enough to hunt, deer hunting became a family sport enjoyed by all the clan. As with antelope, the great expansion of Jack's hunting world in

151

the 1940s and 1950s de-emphasized his deer hunting to a significant degree. After the O'Connors moved to Idaho in 1948, Jack continued to hunt deer, but less frequently than in times past. One point worth mentioning is Jack's personal lament that he never obtained a really good "northern" white-tailed buck, as he referred to them.

There is no intent here to pay scant attention to Jack's deer-hunting career. In fact, his deer adventures are enough to fill several books. But Jack has written about these experiences well and prolifically, and they are available in many of his books. Any effort on my part to retell an O'Connor deer hunting tale would be like putting paste wax on the Hope Diamond.

AFRICA

I have commented elsewhere in this book that O'Connor had definite hunting goals before he ever went on his first African safari in 1953. His two main trophy aspirations were lion and greater kudu. He was also interested in collecting a trophy sable. He was successful in obtaining absolutely first-rate trophies of all these species on his first try, although he had to hunt hard to pull it off. He took a 9' 7" lion, and later a 54-inch greater kudu, and a 44½-inch sable. The kudu and sable are the only trophies from any of Jack's safaris that are listed in the Rowland Ward record book. The two listings were almost certainly done in O'Connor's behalf by Jack Block, managing director of Ker and Downey, the East African safari firm that outfitted O'Connor's trip.

Interestingly, O'Connor's ideas about what constituted Africa's premier trophies changed little over the course of nineteen years and eight more safaris. Lion and greater kudu remained his main hunting goals whenever and wherever they were available, and he hunted sable successfully on numerous other occasions.

Furthermore, Jack apparently never really cared whether one of his record-book-eligible African trophies made it into the Rowland Ward record book or not. A prime example is the excellent 60-inch greater kudu he killed on a 1959 Tanganyikan safari. This was perhaps Jack's finest African trophy of all and the one most personally prized by him. It was also one of the largest greater kudu ever taken in East Africa up to that time. John Kingsley-Heath of Ker and Downey guided Jack to this great bull. The opportunity to get the big kudu into the Rowland Ward record book through Ker and Downey was available. Certainly Jack could have pushed for it. But it never happened. We are left to surmise that a record-book listing just wasn't important to O'Connor.

Another observation: Although Jack enjoyed observing all species of African game, he never viewed certain species in terms of their trophy potential. For instance, he had little to say about a 28½-inch roan antelope that he got in 1953. This is arguably his second-finest African trophy and would have been at the very top of the record listings at the time. But his roan held little appeal to Jack. Ditto for a near-world-record 20½-inch puku that he obtained in Tanganyika in 1959. To Jack, the circumstances of any stalk and kill were always important considerations in the taking of any trophy. In the case of the puku, John Kingsley-Heath knew its whereabouts and took Jack to it, Jack made a clean but matter-of-fact shot, and in about twenty minutes the whole deal was over and done. This undoubtedly took some of the luster off the puku business. Then, too, the puku was not on Jack's "must-get" list.

And though he took many a Thompson gazelle for the frying pan and was hell on bait animals such as topi and kongoni, Jack's total career African bag was relatively small in numbers of species and total animals. An educated guess is that he may have taken in the neighborhood of 125 African animals.

O'Connor had the opportunity to hunt with some of Africa's finest professional hunters. Among them were Syd Downey, Don Ker, Myles Turner, John Kingsley-Heath, Mario

Marcelino, Harry Manners, Ron Kidson, Keith Rowse, Volker Grellman, Peter Seymour-Smith, and others. These individuals were indispensable in making it possible for O'Connor to achieve most of his African hunting goals.

Perhaps Jack's one regret involving Africa is that he never got the chance to take a big elephant. As noted earlier, he took the one and only bull of his life in Zambia in 1969, and it was only so-so (about fifty pounds of ivory per side). Afterward, he began to have thoughts about a hunt for a bigger bull and made various inquiries along these lines. But time, failing health, and financial considerations more or less caught up with him, and it never came to pass.

INDIA

From boyhood, Jack was always deeply interested in the India of British colonial times. He was an avid fan of the writings and poetry of the India of this period. One does not have to read much O'Connor stuff to find a Kiplingesque phrase or a line from a Kipling poem. Remember, O'Connor was an incurable romantic; to him, the Raj was the most romantic of times and places. And to Jack, the embodiment of the flavor, the danger, and the intrigue of India was the great Indian tiger.

Had Jack ever been forced to pick the world's greatest game animal, he might well have chosen the tiger. He referred to it as the "greatest of the cats" (with apologies to his other cat-hunting passion, the African lion). Long before he made the first of his two hunts to India in 1955, he had read everything he could on tiger hunting and tigers in general. He was a particular devotee of James Corbett, the great English hunter of the early 1900s who had lived in India and taken many of the great man-eating tigers and leopards of the time. Later, Corbett wrote of his adventures with man-eaters and other game in *Man-Eaters of Kumaon, Man-Eaters of India*, and other classics. Corbett's simple, yet descriptive and absolutely riveting writing style was one that Jack loved, and he had devoured all of Corbett's works long before he journeyed for the first of his tiger hunts.

Of course, a tiger was the main focus of both of O'Connor's Indian shikars. He made the first one in May of 1955 with his New England hunting pal Lee Sproul. The two men hunted in northern India near Kashipur, in the Kumaon District, Corbett's old tiger-hunting haunt. Both men got tigers. But Jack had to endure several frustrations before he killed his in a classic elephant beat. His tiger was 9' 9" between pegs, and O'Connor called it "distinctly larger and heavier than my African lion" (the very large and heavy male lion he had taken in 1953).

Sproul and Jack also had a fine time hunting blackbuck on the plains near Meerut. Jack killed several, with the two best measuring 23 and 23½ inches. He also enjoyed hunting axis deer, saying they were "the most beautiful deer in the world."

In keeping with his habit of wanting to share happy past experiences with people he cared about, Jack took Eleanor to India with him on his second shikar in 1965. Eleanor had excellent tiger luck, taking a large male and a large tigress. Jack also killed a large tigress. The two also killed several nilgai, or blue bulls.

To Jack, the India hunts were much more than just two listings on his hunting résumé; they were as much social, cultural, and travel experiences as they were hunts. But to be sure, the tigers were two of his most valued trophies and provided some of his best hunting memories.

IRAN

Jack O'Connor's three fine shikars to Iran would probably have never come to pass had not His Imperial Highness, Prince Abdorreza Pahlavi, begun a mail correspondence with Jack when the prince was an undergraduate student at Harvard during the

1940s. At a very young age, Prince Abdorreza was an avid hunter, a rifle nut, and a diehard O'Connor fan. O'Connor answered the prince's questions, and a friendship quickly began to grow. In time, O'Connor introduced His Highness to Al Biesen of Spokane, Washington, one of Jack's favorite custom gunsmiths. Over the years, Biesen built and remodeled many rifles and shotguns for the prince. There was always a great deal of mutual respect between Jack and Prince Abdorreza, and they remained friends until the end of Jack's life.

Jack made his first shikar to Iran in May of 1955, accompanied by his friend Lee Sproul. The two were returning to the United States after a month-long tiger shoot in India. Jack and Lee took Persian red sheep, wild boar, and ibex (*pasang*) during their stay in Iran. O'Connor loved the country because much of it was similar to his native Southwest. Prince Abdorreza rolled out the red carpet for the two men, and for Jack the cultural experience was always a wonderful part of any hunt to a foreign land.

O'Connor returned to Iran in November of 1959. This time he planned to meet his friends Herb Klein and Elgin Gates, who were returning from an exploratory *Ovis poli* hunt in the tiny kingdom of Hunza near Pakistan. Illness felled Gates in Pakistan, and he was unable to join the others. But Jack and Herb had a wonderful hunt for Urial sheep and ibex. Jack collected four Urial rams, the best two of which went 38½ and 37½ inches. Both heads had good mass. (In later correspondence with Bob Housholder, Jack claimed to have taken five Urials, but he may have included a wounded ram that he had finished off for Herb with a fine shot at very long range.) Jack's ibex were average mature billies, and one of them, about a 32-incher, is still owned by Cathy O'Connor. Jack's best Urial heads might have qualified for the listings of the Counseil International de la Chasse, the European record-keeping organization of the day, but as far as I know, they were never measured for such.

On Jack's third Iranian shikar in November 1970, he took Eleanor, and she was successful in dropping a nice Urial ram. On this trip Jack killed no game.

During those three Iranian shikars, O'Connor was in the capable hands of Prince Abdorreza or Yar Mohamed Shadloo, Alex Firouz, and others designated by the prince to help Jack obtain good specimens of Iranian game.

CONCLUSION

At various times and with certain species, Jack O'Connor was the most dedicated of trophy hunters. However, his interest in record-quality heads was more evident in his earlier hunting days. But even then, his ideas about trophy criteria were largely self-evolved. It must be remembered that in the beginning of Jack's career, there were none of today's modern record-keeping entities to guide him. As mentioned earlier, he thought age and horn mass were the most important qualities of sheep horns. But if pressed, he would have said that age alone was the most vital factor of all in deciding whether to take a ram. In later years he mellowed somewhat. But always he was his own man, and his main concern remained the totality of any hunting experience, with any trophy head seen as a happy bonus. He never indulged in today's record-book-speak of numbers, circumferences, G2s, G3s, and whatnot. Of course, it has only really been in the past twenty years, after Jack passed away, that this jargon became the language of the trophy hunter.

Finally, O'Connor had too much class and dignity ever to become caught up in the rat race that trophy hunting has become in certain circles today. In his best Menkenian style, he expressed his disgust for this phenomenon at length in *Sheep and Sheep Hunting* and later in *The Last Book*. Usually he referred to the hanky-panky as it existed in the sheep-hunting business, but he realized that trophy obsessions went far beyond sheep. I'll never forget a statement he made to me in 1975, voicing a sideways swipe at "trophy-mad" hunting types:

"Always remember that there is one thing that will forever be in very short supply in our world, and that one thing is *restraint!*"

9

Jerry

The first of Jack and Eleanor's four children was a boy, born in Alpine, Texas, on 23 November 1930. The proud parents named their new son Gerald Barry O'Connor, Barry being Eleanor's maiden name. Almost from the beginning, the boy was simply called Jerry.

Jerry weighed over ten pounds at birth. The petite Eleanor was in labor many hours, and it was a difficult birth. Perhaps this was an omen for the strange and sad life that lay ahead for the infant.

Little is known of baby Jerry's very early life, for the simple reason that no one remains to tell the story. Alpine was isolated from Jack's and Eleanor's families, and apparently nothing much about the baby's infancy was passed along by the O'Connors to their relatives or to the other O'Connor children born later.

In spite of his large size and apparent health at birth, Jerry suffered from an inexplicable malady known today by the medical term "failure to thrive." Indeed, that term defined Jerry from the beginning.

Though little is known about his early boyhood, it would seem that Jerry was lonely and troubled even at a very young age. But there is not much information about Jerry until he reached about twelve years of age, by which time he had a younger brother, Brad, two years his junior, and two younger sisters, Cathy and Caroline.

Even as a young boy of ten or twelve, Jerry loved hunting and was a natural hunter. He made long sojourns alone on foot or on an old bicycle into the desert outside Tucson, where the O'Connors lived at that time. Almost always he carried a shotgun or a .22.

He was fascinated with rattlesnakes, always searching for and observing them. On many of these outings, younger brother Brad tagged along. Once, when Brad was struck on the ankle by a small rattler, the resourceful Jerry quickly found a piece of broken glass, made several incisions over the fang marks (to Brad's terror), and tried to suck the poison from the wound. Then he ran a long way to a neighboring ranch for help. As it happened, the small snake had struck Brad a glancing blow, and almost no poison had gotten into the wound. But that didn't take away from Jerry's quick thinking and decisive action.

Another time, when Jerry was about fifteen, he and Brad were on an afternoon hunting expedition at the edge of town. A gang of young Mexican men showed up, drunk and threatening the two youngsters. When the young toughs attempted to steal one of the boys' bicycles, Jerry warned them against the idea. Undeterred, the thugs grabbed the bike and started off with it, whereupon Jerry coolly put a .22 Long Rifle bullet into the chest of the gang's leader, dropping him like an ox and ending the bicycle boost immediately.

It is not recorded whether Jerry told his parents about the incident when the boys returned home that afternoon. Perhaps not. However, the O'Connor family was just sitting down to a quiet dinner when the authorities showed up and took Jerry off to jail. But nothing came of it. Jack was a prominent University of Arizona professor and a well-known citizen. The men who had attempted to steal the bicycle apparently meant harm to Jerry and Brad, and they were Mexicans. It was a pretty clear case of protecting one's property as well as self-defense. Justice was still rather rough-hewn in wartime Arizona. The entire matter was somewhat simplified by the fact that, incredibly, the Mexican thug didn't die. Anyway, Jerry was released after only one night in the hoosegow. There was a rather perfunctory hearing of some kind, and the whole thing was basically over. But it did prove one thing: Jerry O'Connor had the same iron in his soul as his father and wasn't someone to be messed with!

From boyhood, Jerry's loneliness and strange behavior distressed Jack and Eleanor. But beyond normal parenting and discipline, they felt increasingly powerless to know what to do. More of this later.

With every passing day, Jerry seemed to grow more detached, less interested in daily life, lonelier. The few friends he did have were far from the mainstream of normal young people—"weirdoes," as his family would refer to them in later years. Furthermore, every effort by his parents and siblings to involve him in family life seemed futile.

Jerry attended Tucson schools and had completed his junior year in high school when the O'Connors moved to Idaho in the summer of 1948. Though obviously very intelligent, he was an indifferent, unmotivated student. Jerry entered Lewiston High School as a senior in the fall of 1948 and quickly got the nickname "Tucson." Predictably, the new friends he made there were strange, off-center types, and a little frightening. Jerry finished high school in Lewiston, graduating in the spring of 1949.

There can be no doubt that Jerry O'Connor was extremely intelligent. This was true of all the O'Connor family. His father and mother both had IQs of near-genius level. The same was (and is) true for Jerry's brother Brad and his two sisters, Cathy and Caroline. Jerry may well have been the most intelligent of them all. However, it was as though he had no emotional compass. After high school, he went for a semester to a small college in Pocatello, Idaho. But he had no real interest and no continuity, and apparently flunked out.

In 1950 Jerry enlisted in the army. Soon he was in Korea, involved in some of the most brutal fighting and terrible conditions that American forces had ever seen before or have since.

Like almost everything else about Jerry, little is known about his combat action. He was a machine gunner. He served with a twelve-man advanced reconnaissance unit. Once, Jerry's unit was sent on a particularly hazardous patrol mission behind North Korean lines. Somehow the group got cut off, with no way back to their own lines. In very heavy fighting, much of it at night, the battle lines surged back and forth. Jerry's unit was cut to pieces. Although it was never proven, there exists the possibility that some of the casualties were the result of friendly fire.

Of his patrol, Jerry was one of two survivors.

He felt that his unit had been betrayed, and there were accusations along those lines, although nothing ever came of it. But the bloodshed and the trauma had pushed the already emotionally fragile Jerry past the breaking point. The events described above occurred near the end of his hitch, and he was soon back in Lewiston. But being back home with his family didn't help. If he had been strange and distant before, now he was literally unreachable.

He lived at home with his parents and sisters for a while. (Brad was serving in Korea by this time.) Jerry came and went at all hours of the day and night, and the situation was a tense and sad one for the O'Connor family. Then he moved out.

As in high school, his friends grew ever more strange—vagabonds, itinerants, drifters, ne'er-do-wells, and beatniks, as they were beginning to be called in those days. He became the town character. At 6' 4" and rail-thin, he was often seen on winter nights when the Lewiston temperature was five degrees above zero, walking the streets clad only in jeans and a light cotton shirt.

He continued to stay around town, although no one remembers much about where and how he lived. He worked sporadically at menial jobs, but never for any length of time. It was evidently during this time that he began to drink heavily, hanging out in town bars and idly watching people come and go.

I should mention that through all of this, Jack and Eleanor were beside themselves with worry over Jerry's situation. But by this time they had done everything they knew to do. Gradually their worry was replaced by grief. It seemed that Jerry was gone forever.

It is an almost unknown fact that Jack O'Connor was a very talented cartoonist. Jerry must have inherited this talent from his dad. During this time frame, he made many paintings and drawings, most of which still exist within the O'Connor family. The themes of most of these are dark, sinister, foreboding. Some deal with military situations, several depicting military bases with military police and prisoners of war. Almost invariably, there is a cruel-seeming commanding officer in the picture. Others are of disastrous car wrecks or holdups. Still another is of a police lineup. Some of the characters are drawn in a childlike manner, but all of the depictions are very detailed, with everything in perfect perspective. Viewing them is an unnerving experience.

Jerry became more and more resistant to efforts to care for and love him. Indeed, he seemed to relish his solitude and loneliness. Then he just vanished.

It wasn't that he was never seen again by his family. But contact became essentially nonexistent, and his life from the late 1950s until his death is an absolute darkness with virtually no signs of a trail. It is possible that Jack and Eleanor did not see their son for the last ten years of his life. It is as though Jerry O'Connor wasn't even alive during this period.

He apparently wandered on the winds through various western states. He drank more and more and was in and out of different Veterans Administration hospitals, suffering from various illnesses, usually alcohol-related. Once, the VA called Jack from Denver to inform him that Jerry had been admitted to a hospital there and was badly in need of some clothes. Jack undertook the task of shopping for Jerry to spare Eleanor the grief of the affair, but he soon found himself so overcome with sadness that he was unable to face it alone. Jack's daughter Caroline remembers her dad calling and asking her to accompany him to a Lewiston store to buy jeans, shirts, underwear, and a coat for her brother. During this period, Jerry became a devotee of Malcolm X, declaring his intent to become a Black Muslim.

Sometime in the mid-1960s, Jerry made the acquaintance of a woman we'll call Mary Brown (not her real name). Mary and her husband lived in Las Cruces, New Mexico. How this relationship came about is yet another question mark in Jerry's life, but somehow the Browns became Jerry's guardians. Whether this was legal or self-appointed is unknown, as is whether the Browns acted alone in Jerry's caretaking or other individuals were involved. However, the Browns set Jerry up in a small trailer behind their home in Las Cruces. They saw to it that he was fed and cared for. The honesty of these people and any others involved in the process was exemplary. How Jerry passed the time over the years when he lived in the trailer behind the Browns continues to be a mystery. Jerry by this time was incapable of managing his own money. (But someone was. When Jerry died, he had over $20,000 in the bank.)

But sometime in the early morning hours of a bone-cold 23 December 1969, after a period of heavy drinking, Jerry O'Connor's dark life ended. His body was found later in the morning in a vacant lot next to his trailer. The coroner's report indicated that he had drowned in his own vomit, induced by alcohol consumption. But perhaps he had already been dead for a number of years, and this was just the night on which he finally turned off the last of his life-switches.

The O'Connor family learned of Jerry's death when a Christmas package addressed to him from his brother Bradford was returned with the single word "deceased" written on it. It is not known whether or not the Browns also communicated the news to Jerry's family.

Bradford and Cathy O'Connor flew to Las Cruces to make Jerry's funeral arrangements. Jerry's other sister, Caroline, was in Hawaii with her own family on vacation and was unable to attend the funeral. Jerry was buried in a military cemetery in El Paso, Texas, thus returning in the end to the soil of the state where he had been born.

Jack and Eleanor did not attend the funeral. In retrospect, this seems oddly detached on their part. But Eleanor was in poor health at the time and so grief-stricken that Jerry's funeral might well have been more than she could bear. Jack would later state that by the time of Jerry's death, he had already grieved for his older son for so many years that he had no grief left. And Jerry had been gone for a very long time.

After his death, O'Connor family members would increasingly characterize Jerry as "schizophrenic." Such a diagnosis would certainly seem valid. Webster's New Collegiate Dictionary defines schizophrenia as "a psychic disorder characterized by loss of contact with the environment and by disintegration of personality expressed as disorder of feeling, thought, and conduct." More detailed definitions of schizophrenia and associated symptomology would seem to corroborate the family's retrospective diagnosis of this haunted man.

In addition, it would seem almost a foregone conclusion that Jerry O'Connor was profoundly scarred by his experiences in Korea and that he probably also suffered from chronic depression.

Medical knowledge of these illnesses, diagnostic procedures, medications, treatment skills, counseling, and self-awareness have all increased many-fold over the years since Jerry's death. In all probability, he would have benefited from at least some of these medical breakthroughs.

Jerry's sad and directionless life had caused much strife between Jack and Eleanor for many years. They blamed themselves as parents and ultimately found fault with each other over their son. However, new medical information and books on the subject even before Jerry's death were great sources of comfort to them and inevitably helped them to realize that they were probably not to blame for Jerry's tragic life. Even so, Jack and Eleanor never got over their son's loss.

Author's Note: For various reasons, this has been a very difficult and sad piece to write. Information about the life of Jerry O'Connor is minimal at best, and facts about his later years are almost nonexistent. So his story is related here in a straightforward, bare bones, almost simplistic manner. There seemed to be no other way, and for this I apologize.

10

Spiritual Jack

"I was simply not the religious type."

JOC, commenting on his boyhood in *Horse and Buggy West*

In the wonderful autobiographical account of his own childhood from which the passage above is taken, Jack O'Connor had this to say about an early benchmark event in his spiritual life:

> Curiously enough it was a sermon on atheism that made an agnostic out of me. The preacher told his congregation about the incredible beliefs of the wicked atheists. They believed, he said, that Jesus was a mortal man, the son of a mortal woman by a mortal man, that he was a teacher, not the Son of God. These strange people also believed, he went on, that Jesus had not arisen from the dead, that there was no heaven and no hell. There were gasps of disbelief from the congregation. Some of the women were so shocked that they wept. All of this suddenly seemed reasonable and logical to me and I at once put most of what I had been taught in Sunday school in the pigeonhole where I kept the story of the stork, of Santa Claus, and the Garden of Eden.

Despite the logic of the sermon in Jack's mind—he was eleven years old at the time—it troubled him for a long while.

He finally sought the advice of his beloved paternal uncle, Jim O'Connor. Uncle Jim was a lawyer, rancher, and shrewd businessman who later became county judge in Arizona's Maricopa County. He was affectionate, affable, liked and respected by all. Furthermore, he was a keen scholar of human nature. Young Jack worshipped his Uncle Jim, who was a wonderful surrogate father to the boy.

One day Jack asked his Uncle Jim (also from *Horse and Buggy West*):

> Jack: "I heard a preacher talk about atheists. What he said they believed sounded sort of true to me. "
>
> Uncle Jim: "Did it bother you?"
>
> Jack: "No."
>
> Uncle Jim: "Well, this heaven and hell business has never sounded particularly plausible to me, but that's neither here nor there. I go ahead and try to be a reasonably decent and honorable guy every day. If I should die and wake up in either place I'd be surprised. But if the belief in either place makes some people happier and more decent and more able to endure the kicks in the tail we all have to take in this world I am all for it. I would not do anything to undermine their belief."

From that day forward and for all of his life, Jack O'Connor professed to be an agnostic. However, it would appear that his ideas about spirituality mellowed a great deal in later years. Of that, more later. But he also took his Uncle Jim's advice about being a "reasonably decent and honorable guy" very much to heart. No one who ever knew Jack O'Connor could say other than that he was honest to a fault, truthful, and honorable.

But on a different note and a lighter side, it was contacts at various times in his life with preachers, churches, churchgoers, and church environments that gave rise to some of the funniest behavior, most hilarious comments, and most biting cynicism of Jack's whole repertoire. Here are a few samples:

In 1919, when Jack was home on leave from the navy, his mother, Ida, prevailed on him to accompany her to the First Baptist Church, South, as it was known in those days, in Tempe, Arizona. Ida, a school teacher, was a hard worker who was usually so fatigued on weekends that she was not normally a churchgoer, but having her only son home safe and sound, if only for a brief period, had obviously put her in the spirit. Jack, against his better judgment, relented. Many a scornful stare from the stodgy matrons of the congregation was cast in Jack's direction as he stood, resplendent in his dress whites, beside his mother in the pew. He was duly recognized and welcomed by the minister. But all the worthy matrons remembered was the Jack of young boyhood and adolescence. Jack had been a little hellion as a child, purveyor of terrible practical jokes, near-obscene Halloween pranks, and a ribald wit. What a little punk he had been! The nerve of that young upstart, daring to desecrate the house of the Lord with his unworthy presence! As for themselves, well, they were saved! That made all the difference. So the harumphing and the condescending looks continued.

But Jack endured, giving no indication that he was aware of his spiritually unwashed state. Near the end of the service, the minister asked if there were any hymn requests from the congregation. One middle-aged woman, with a scathing look in Jack's direction, spoke up: "Pastor, could we please sing number 88?" Then the congregation stood, hymnals in hand, and the pianist began the music to "Let the Lower Lights Be Burning."

Jack, reading ahead to the chorus of the hymn, saw it coming. But it was too late. When the congregation came to *the* passage, "Some poor, fainting, struggling seaman, you may rescue, you may save," the pious matrons threw back their collective heads and sang with special gusto, all eyes in O'Connor's direction. That'd teach him!

Jack had had all he could stand. He hadn't wanted to be there in the first place and didn't have to take this crap. Today's saying "I'm outta here!" would have been perfectly appropriate for Jack's thoughts at that moment, for he was into the aisle and out the back door in a flash!

The following is a sample of a very short conversation between Jack and a man of God. It is clear proof that, clergyman or not, one had better have his verbal knives razor-sharp when he locked horns with O'Connor:

In 1954 or so, when Jack's younger daughter Caroline was about fifteen, she began attending the Episcopal church in Lewiston with some of her teenage friends. She enjoyed it so much that she soon began asking her parents to attend the services with her. Jack and Eleanor, not normally churchgoers, finally acquiesced.

On the appointed Sunday morning, Jack and Eleanor went to the Episcopal services with Caroline. As many know, high Episcopal church services are a continuing process of standing, kneeling, sitting, and more standing, more kneeling, more sitting, ad infinitum. But finally it was over. The priest had seen O'Connor in the congregation. Jack was something of a national celebrity, and certainly a big cheese in Lewiston. Having him in the Sunday morning congregation was a plume in the priest's cap. He hurried to the back of the church to shake O'Connor's hand. After the exchange of salutations, and with a good crowd looking on, Jack boomed:

"Well, Rev, I'm real glad I caught your act." Here he paused before continuing: "And we certainly enjoyed the calisthenics!"

Verbally or in any other way, it was almost impossible to get ahead of Jack O'Connor!

Another O'Connor experience with a man of the cloth occurred when Jack was recovering from a January 1957 automobile accident. He was hospitalized for many weeks in Spokane, Washington. Finally he was moved to a hospital in

Lewiston, where he continued his recovery and rehabilitation. Having Jack in a local facility made it more convenient for Eleanor and the rest of the family to visit. Thinking that it might lift Jack's spirits and speed his recovery, Eleanor sneaked a bottle of Jack's favorite Passport scotch into his room. There he would be able to ward off the hospital chill with a surreptitious late-afternoon nip.

A day or so later, a local clergyman, aware of O'Connor's hospitalization and perhaps also knowing of Jack's crusty stance on organized religion and apparently slim opportunity for personal salvation, dropped in to see him. The two men had a short visit, and the minister departed. A couple of days later the minister called on Jack again. Hospitalized though he was, O'Connor felt that he had certain responsibilities as a host. Then he remembered his stashed scotch.

"Pastor, would you care for a little drink?" Jack inquired.

The clergyman allowed as how that sounded like a capital idea. So the barkeep produced his bottle of Scotch and poured cloth-man a little shot. Almost immediately a mellow glow came over the pastor. Another tot and he warmed even further. The conversation became more animated and diverse. In time, the man said his good-byes and departed.

But the clergyman knew a good thing when he saw it. In almost no time, he became a daily visitor with apparently serious concerns about Jack's well being. (One wonders if he was at all anxious for Jack to leave the hospital!) After several bottles of Passport had gone down the tubes, Eleanor asked where it was all going, to which Jack snorted:

"Hell! If old so-and-so (the minister) doesn't quit trying so hard to save me, he's going to become a Goddamned alcoholic!"

As to the more serious matters of faith and spirituality, it wasn't the belief in a god or the need to believe that gave Jack pause. Rather, it was the edifices and the people-twist on the whole business that made him gag. It was the fire-and-brimstone preachers and their ranting, conning, threatening, frightening, and intimidating. It was televised evangelists, purveyors of snake-oil salvation, who acted and sounded as if they or their denomination had the exclusive dealership for eternal life. To him, such behavior was intolerable, especially in a spiritual vein.

Also, Jack's keen intelligence almost certainly got in the way of his becoming a blind believer or lemming-like follower. It was hard for him to put aside logic in any endeavor of life. Perhaps a spiritual playing field where faith and logic had equal footing would have been more palatable to him.

However, that same intelligence probably told him something else, because in his life he saw too much of the great sweep of nature and the depth and breadth of the world and its peoples to think that the whole thing had been a great metaphysical accident without continuity, hope, and a control panel somewhere.

Jack lived much of his life during a time when church denominational allegiances and doctrines were practically shoved down peoples' throats. The freedoms that today allow an individual to have a personal faith and to make personal interpretations about religions and spirituality were not in vogue. Nobody, but nobody, ever force-fed Jack O'Connor anything!

At the risk of contradicting Jack's own statements about matters spiritual, he probably wasn't really an agnostic. In later life, his personal family correspondence was replete with such phrases as: "I am very thankful" and "For this I devotedly give thanks to God." He even said in letters on more than one occasion: "I am still just a Southern Baptist at heart, I suppose, and I am glad I am."

And after all, the whole business of Jack's faith and spirituality was really no one's business but his own.

This previously unpublished photograph shows Jack and guide Sam Williams with Jack's 40¼-inch Dall ram taken in the Dawson Range, Yukon Territory, in September of 1956. This ram was one of three exceeding 40 inches taken by O'Connor during his sheep-hunting career. Before walking up to the ram, he thought the horns might exceed 45 inches. But although the ram was an old-timer at thirteen years of age, it was small in body size, which may have caused O'Connor to overestimate the horn length. This was Jack's second hunt with the pioneer Yukon outfitting firm of Alex Davis.

Puffing away, Jack and Khandlar Grah Shadloo admire one of several Urial rams Jack collected in Iran in November of 1959. Two others were better than this one. A smoker since early adulthood, Jack gave up cigarettes in the early 1960s.

Although a similar photo of Jack with his last Stone ram appears elsewhere in this book, this somewhat different version provides a good look at the rifle that was O'Connor's pet of pets. It is a pre-64 Model 70 Featherweight in .270 Winchester caliber, restocked by Al Biesen and topped with a 4X Leupold scope in two-piece Buhler mounts. O'Connor generally referred to it as his "No. 2 rifle" because it followed another Model 70 in .270 that he had bought and had restocked some years before. He did most of his sheep hunting after 1960 with the No. 2 rifle.

Jack with his third lion, taken with his much-traveled old Griffin & Howe .375 on a frosty, late-winter morning in August 1962 near the Caprivi Strip in Angola. While the big lion was not quite a nine-footer, it was one of the two best-maned of five lions that Jack killed in his safari career.

Jack, ever the cavalier, lights Eleanor's before his. Weatherby dinner, 1964.

Eleanor looks admiringly up at a stern-appearing Jack after an unknown dinner occasion in the early 1960s. Early financial difficulties and family stresses, including the loss of son Jerry and Eleanor's later emotional and alcohol problems, took their toll on the marriage. But Jack and Eleanor weathered the storms and loved each other with a rare passion all their lives.

Jack enjoys a light moment with an old friend, famous Wyoming outfitter Les Bowman. O'Connor hunted elk on several occasions and collected his best-ever bull with Bowman. There was great mutual respect between the two men, and Bowman was a match for Jack in any conversation. The photo was taken in the RCBS offices of Fred Huntington in Oroville, California, in 1962. Fred was another long-time O'Connor crony and hunting companion.

Jack with a good springbok, Botswana, 1966.

Eleanor and Jack talk it over in front of the Taj Mahal in February 1965. India was a cultural treat for Jack, who was a great reader of authors of the British Raj in India.

This 7x6 bull was the best elk Jack ever killed in Idaho. It was taken in November of 1966 on a short hunt outfitted by Dave Christenson. The bull had massive horns that scored around 310 B&C even though the points were short. It was the only bull O'Connor ever killed with the 7mm Remington Magnum. He never had the head mounted, and it lay in a tangle with several others on Jack's perpetually "up" garage door in Lewiston until he passed away in 1978.

Sheep hunting's Grand Old Man reflects tentside. Telegraph Creek, British Columbia, fall 1967.

Eleanor and Jack admire a pair of bookend Stone rams taken in the British Columbia Cassiars in September of 1967. The O'Connors had killed the rams the previous day on a high plateau fifteen miles from their camp. A howling snowstorm that hit just after the kills made for a long, freezing ride to camp for the hunters and their guides. The next morning, Jack and Eleanor turned out for a more relaxing look at their rams. Jack's was 36½ inches around the curls and Eleanor's was 37¼ inches. Jack was a sucker for great sheep-hunting destinations and remembered the Cassiar Range and Telegraph Creek from reading about them in the pages of Outdoor Life *as a small boy.*

Jack and University of Idaho President Richard Gibb at Pheasant Valley Preserve near LaCrosse, Washington. Jack's big-game trophy collection was donated to U. of I. because of Jack's relationship with President Gibb and Wildlife Management Professor Ernest Ables.

Jack rolls up his bedroll at Telegraph Creek, British Columbia, fall 1967. In his writings, O'Connor always contended that the best sleep he ever had was on long packtrain trips in the mountains. He also had much to say about proper bedding and bedrolls and felt that good rest was essential for an enjoyable mountain hunting experience.

Jack, left, and longtime friend and Gun Digest *Editor John Amber, admire red grouse taken during a rough shoot in Scotland in 1968. O'Connor had experienced driven grouse shooting previously, in 1959. In this photo, as before, he used his favorite Model 21 Winchester.*

Of Jack's five lions, this one was his last and best. Here he gets the glad tidings from his pro, Keith Rowse, Zambia, 1969. O'Connor killed the 9' 8" lion with a custom, lightweight .416 Rigby, his heavy rifle of choice in later years.

O'Connor with a 40½-inch Zambia sable, taken in 1969 with a .338. Sable was Jack's third most favorite African animal, after lion and greater kudu, and he hunted them at every opportunity.

Eleanor and shikaris with a nice Urial ram taken in the last minutes of a November 1970 Iranian hunt. She piled off her horse and killed the moving ram with a single shot from her little 7x57 at a range of over 200 yards. The hunt took place in the Mohammed Reza Shah game park east of the Caspian Sea. Jack, on his third Iranian shikar, killed no game.

Jack is presented with the Hunting Hall of Fame Award by his great pal John H. Batten. O'Connor and Batten were longtime friends and correspondents. The two men, both avid sheep hunters, made several plans to hunt together, but for various reasons the hunts never came to pass. However, they did make a tiger hunt together in India in 1965, along with Eleanor and John's wife, Katy.

A pensive O'Connor, seen here in later years, admires a wood carving of a greater kudu. It is not well known that Jack was an avid military historian. Visible on the bookshelf are Korea: The Limited War, A Military History of the Western World, The Two-Ocean War, William the Conqueror, *and* A Stillness at Appomattox. *For all his life, Jack was a voracious reader, devouring newspapers, periodicals, magazines, and hundreds of books.*

A morose O'Connor looks over his first, last, and only elephant, a modest-size bull taken on the Zambezi River in Zambia in 1969. Jack took the bull at free-throw distance with a frontal brain shot from his .416 Rigby. The bull completed the African Big Five for O'Connor, but there is no indication in any of his writings that the Big Five had been a goal for him or that he felt any exultation in its accomplishment.

Señor O'Connor relaxes with two attractive ladies in Mexico: Eleanor O'Connor on the left and June Brooks on the right. This photo was taken early in 1970 when the O'Connors visited the home of Oscar Brooks at Cuernavaca after taking in the bull-fights at Mexico City. Oscar Brooks was an avid international sheep-hunting pal of Jack's.

Eleanor, Fred Huntington (founder of RCBS), and Jack with a bag of pheasants shot at a California preserve during a very wet day in December 1970, following the Weatherby Awards.

Jack looks perhaps more than a little jealous of an overjoyed Eleanor and her 60-plus-inch southern greater kudu, killed in South-West Africa in 1972. After lion, greater kudu was always Jack's top safari priority. He had killed a 60-incher in Tanganyika in 1959 and numerous other excellent bulls, but the bull shown here was the best of them all.

Jack is congratulated by Otto Steinmaster for a beautiful Hartmann mountain zebra stallion. This was in South-West Africa in 1972 on what was to be Jack's last safari. O'Connor killed the stallion with a single 7x57 bullet at 300 yards. Throughout his safari career, Jack remained pretty mad at zebras, always taking all that were allowed on his general license—amounting to more than a dozen zebras of various types. Back home, Jack gave away several hides as gifts to friends.

Jack in a quiet moment with one of the last hunting horses he ever rode. Horseback hunting had been a part of his life for over fifty years. He wrote numerous articles on the subject. One of his favorite topics was the various options for hanging the rifle scabbard on the saddle. The photograph was taken at Colt Lake, British Columbia, in August 1973 during Jack's last sheep hunt.

Jack and son Bradford look over antlers from a nice moose taken by Brad in British Columbia in the fall of 1975. Moose were not among Jack's favorite animals, and he fired not a shot on this hunt, his last to the Canadian North.

Jack's last ram, a decent Stone taken in August of 1973 out of British Columbia outfitter Frank Cook's Colt Lake camp. Famous guide Rawhide sits behind the ram. Oddly, Jack got the ram a few hundred yards from where he had taken another, somewhat larger ram two years before. The ram pictured here had horns measuring 36 and 35¼ inches with average bases and scored in the low 150s. This photograph of Jack with his ram at the kill site has rarely been seen. A much more widely circulated photo showed Jack back in camp with this head. For this reason, various O'Connor detractors have hinted in recent years that O'Connor did not actually kill this ram, his last. Not true. Jack was an absolute purist in such things and could not have lived with himself if he knew he had pulled the wool over his fans' eyes. His real lament about this ram was that it was beneath his standards. By this time, he knew he had stayed too long at the party and that his sheep-hunting days were done.

A solemn O'Connor with Eleanor at dinner on board the cruise ship Mariposa, *en route back to San Francisco from Hawaii. It is not well known that Jack loved the sea almost as much as he did the mountains, and he and Eleanor went on several cruises in the last years of their lives. In this photograph, Jack was much more ill than anyone realized. In fact, I believe it is the last photo taken of Jack, and may have been shot on the evening of 20 January 1978, the night before his death.*

Brad O'Connor, retired outdoor editor of the Seattle Times, *gazes at the high mountain meadows he last saw as a boy more than fifty years earlier. This photo of Brad, perched on the Slade Ranch woodpile, was taken in August 1997. The rifle is Jack's old 2R Lovell single-shot, first used here on prairie dogs in 1942.*

Buck Buckner nailed this jack on the run near Tucson with O'Connor's R-2 in 1997, fifty years after Jack last used it.

Jack's favorite .30-06 was a custom FN Mauser built by Al Biesen in 1947. With it he took his best North American ram in 1950. It is shown here with a fringe-eared oryx it downed for its present owner, Henry Kaufman, in Kenya, January 1977.

11

Jack's Guns—Favored Firearms over the Years

by Eldon "Buck" Buckner

Jack O'Connor's interest in firearms began before 1910 while he was still wearing short pants in Tempe, Arizona. His maternal grandfather, James Wiley Woolf, a pioneer rancher, farmer, and hunter, appreciated and owned several fine guns. They ranged from a heavy Winchester 1876 scarred by a grizzly's teeth to a 1907 Purdy double 12-gauge cased with an extra set of barrels.

Although Jack's first gun was an Iver Johnson 20-gauge single-shot shotgun, received from his grandfather at age eight, his first love during his life was the big-game rifle. Jack described his sentiments best in the introduction to his first gun book, *The Rifle Book* (Knopf, 1949).

> I like a handgun. I hold a shotgun in high regard; but rifles— well, I love the darned things. To me they stand for wilderness, mystery, romance . . . the brown bighorn ram high on a rocky comb, the flash of a whitetail's fan as he bursts out of his cover and dashes for safety, the big hulking moose stalking on long, stilt-like legs through the spruce timber . . . high mountain passes, timber-line basins, green, lush, smooth as an English lawn, where a grizzly bear digs for marmots and the soaring eagle whistles.

To Jack, guns were more than tools of the hunt. Rifle or shotgun, he loved them for their own sake. That is not to say that he found all of them equally attractive. With the plethora of sporting rifles and calibers available today, it is easy to forget that such was not the case in the twenties and early thirties. Although several lever- and slide-action models were made then, a good bolt-action with a well-designed stock didn't exist until the Remington 30-S came out in 1935 and Winchester introduced its classic Model 70 in 1936. Telescope sights were still objects of curiosity. If one desired a topnotch rifle, he had to have it custom-built on either a Mauser or 1903 Springfield action.

Shotguns, on the other hand, were having their day at that time. Classy, elegant doubles were being made by several companies and reached their zenith of quality in the 1930s, fancy shotguns being a status symbol back then. American models included Parker Bros., A. H. Fox, Ithaca, LeFever, Winchester, Remington, and L. C. Smith.

Handguns were available in a variety of high-quality models, led by Colt and Smith & Wesson, but the revolver was by far the most popular design, as opposed to the current mania for high-capacity automatics.

In this chapter, I have tried to relate some detailed history of several of Jack's firearms in the order of his preference by type—rifles, shotguns, handguns—and to tell of how his forty years of writing on the subject influenced design. This information was gathered over the past forty-plus years from various sources. I have read every book, every article published in *Outdoor Life* and *Petersen's Hunting*, and many authored by Jack in other magazines. I have read and collected the writings of others about Jack, much of which is incorrect. Interesting facts have come from mutual friends and acquaintances, both living and deceased, who hunted, guided, socialized, built rifles for, or, in the case of Angus Cameron, served as Jack's book editor. Jack's voluminous correspondence preserved at Washington State University, as well as personal photo albums and scrapbooks shared by the three O'Connor children, have both entertained me and verified certain dates of interest. Last but not least, my notes made after the many conversations I shared with Jack and Eleanor years ago have been invaluable, as has our personal correspondence.

PART I: RIFLES

One of Jack's first articles written under his new contract with *Outdoor Life* was "Building Your Dream Rifle," published in 1937. Variations of this piece appeared over the next forty years and, over time, had great influence on the stock design of commercial sporting rifles later produced and still in evidence today. Jack, who appreciated quality and class in everything, always preferred the classic and functional lines of stocks, best exemplified in the 1920s and 1930s by Alvin Linden, Adolph Minar, and Bob Owen, all European-born craftsmen who stocked Jack's early rifles. As Jack wrote in 1955:

> There are almost as many different varieties of taste in firearms as there are in women. My own taste in both is on the conservative side. I like graceful shape along classic lines in either a rifle or shotgun stock.

Jack preferred stocks of European walnut with good figure, ornamented with expertly cut checkering of twenty-four to twenty-six lines per inch. Those who read the following from a 1961 gun column will have no doubt as to his opinion of carved stocks:

> Simplicity, functionalism and elegance are keynotes of the classic stock. Those who want portraits on their rifle stocks of Old Towser, the family watchdog, pictures of African lions devouring buffaloes, or of voluptuous nymphs

being chased through the meadows by satyrs, had better go to someone other than a classic stocker.

Similarly, Jack felt that good metalwork was best adorned by tasteful and conservative scroll engraving, or, if properly executed by an expert on anatomy, a combination of game animals and scrollwork. He did not care for gold-inlaid birds and animals, believing they detracted from the overall appearance of the firearm.

A good example of Jack's ability to write of such esoteric subjects as the aesthetics of stock design in a way the average man could relate to is this passage from 1964:

> Sometimes very slight changes in curves and angles make the difference between a beautiful and graceful stock and a homely and ordinary one. I am thinking now of two sisters I once knew. Both were blond, witty and charming. But one, though she was a fine cook and had a heart of gold, was a rather ordinary lass who got by on her good disposition and winning ways. The other was a stunning beauty, a creature so lovely that one look sent young men's blood pressure skyward and set them to uttering wild hoarse cries and tearing telephone directories apart with their bare hands. Yet these two girls looked much alike, and it was easy to see they were sisters. What made the difference was an angle here, a line there, small dimensional differences in features.

Those who doubt that anyone was paying attention to Jack's preachings have only to look at the classic lines of the Model 77 Ruger when it first appeared.

Over his lifetime of nearly seventy-six years, Jack owned a tremendous number and variety of rifles. Some were factory models, but most that he used much were custom-made. He experimented with different calibers but felt that most wildcats, with a few exceptions that became standard later, were not worth the extra trouble and inconvenience. He believed that moderate cartridges were more effective for the average hunter than the big super-duper magnum simply because it was easier for such a person to shoot them accurately and thus put bullets in vital areas. Following are notes on some of Jack's and Eleanor's significant rifles:

Griffin & Howe Springfield Sporter .30-06: Acquired as a gift from an uncle (probably as a college graduation present in 1925), this was Jack's primary hunting rifle until the mid-1930s. Equipped with a Lyman 48 receiver sight, it had a hooded front sight typical of G&H rifles through the years. Jack used this rifle extensively in Texas. Shortly after moving to Flagstaff in 1931, the O'Connors sold all their guns but three to pay doctor bills. The Springfield was Jack's sole big-game rifle, which he used to hunt the Kaibab during the next three years. With it he took his widest mule deer buck—37½ inches. This rifle is believed to have been the one destroyed when its broken firing pin caused an accidental discharge in 1939, injuring Jack's hand.

Winchester Model 54 in .270 Winchester: This was Jack's first .270, purchased the summer of 1925 when the caliber was first introduced. It was used that fall on black bears in the Navajo country and on mule deer in the Kaibab Preserve. Jack had it restocked by R. D. Tait of Dunsmuir, California, and fitted with a Lyman receiver sight. It was sold at Flagstaff in about 1932 to pay doctor bills, as mentioned above.

Remington Model 30 in .25 Remington: This was Eleanor's first big-game rifle, bought for her by Jack in 1931, with which she shot her first deer that fall on the Kaibab, mentioned elsewhere in this book. It was equipped with a Lyman receiver sight and hooded front sight.

Remington Model 30-S in .257 Roberts: Acquired in 1934 or 1935 when the .257 Roberts first came out, this one replaced

Eleanor's .25 Remington. It was custom-stocked by Adolph Minar of Fountain, Colorado, and originally equipped with receiver sights, but later had a Noske scope mounted, bringing its weight up to 10½ pounds. Eleanor used this rifle to take her first Coues deer in Arizona and other deer and javelina in Sonora. It was replaced in 1942 by a lighter custom Mauser of the same caliber.

Sukalle-Minar Custom Springfield .30-06, #1273272: This was Jack's first made-to-order custom rifle, completed in 1934, and was his favorite for many years. It was built on a 1926 NRA Springfield Sporter action, with metalwork by William A. Sukalle, then of Tucson. The stock was by Adolph G. Minar of Fountain, Colorado, who was considered a master of classic stocks in his day. (His stocks are very rarely seen, for he died from appendicitis in 1936.) The bolt knob and pistol-grip cap were engraved by Rudolph Kornbrath. The rifle's sights were a Lyman 48 receiver and a 2.75X Hensoldt in a detachable side mount. Scopes being relatively new, that scope was usually carried by Jack in a leather case on his belt and put on the rifle when desired. Later a Noske scope was used and finally a Zeiss Zielklein 2.25X on a Stith mount.

By 1938 Jack had recorded taking seven mule deer, twenty-two Coues deer, five antelope, two sheep, and four javelina with this rifle. Two of the antelope were taken in 1936 under special permit for the Arizona State Museum.

The rifle went with Jack on his 1943 hunt to Alberta and was used on the first of many grizzlies he took with it. He shot his last desert bighorn ram with it in 1946. In *The Rifle Book* (Knopf, 1949) he wrote of it:

> In the rack is an old beaten-up Springfield sporter. It is scarred and battered and its third barrel is now so worn that it won't keep its bullets in a two foot circle at two hundred yards. Once down in Mexico the front saddle cinch broke, and the runaway horse battered its poor stock terribly.

Another time in the same country when I was hunting sheep a rotten granite ledge gave way with me and I had to drop the rifle to save myself. The stock is badly cracked and held together with a bolt, the checkering is smooth and the rifling is gone. But I'll always keep that rifle. I shot my first elk with it on the Mogollon Rim of northern Arizona, my first grizzly with it in Western Alberta. I have carried it in Sonora, Arizona, Wyoming, British Columbia, Alberta and the Yukon. It has five grizzlies to its credit, and I feel the same way about it as a horseman feels about an old but much loved mount.

In 1961, contrary to his word, Jack gave the rifle to John Jobson, then hunting editor of *Sports Afield*, whose writing Jack appreciated. Jobson and his father before him had searched for a Minar rifle for years to no avail, and John tells of Jack's rifle in "My Quest for the Minar" from *The Best of John Jobson* (Amwell Press, 1982). Another story about this rifle was published in the April 1982 issue of the *American Rifleman* titled "O'Connor's Other Rifle" by Bob Hills, who had photographed it at Jobson's home shortly before Jobson died in 1979.

In April 1999 I spoke with Jobson's widow, Anna, about the Minar Springfield. She was blind and in poor health but had a vivid memory of the rifle, the stock of which she had refinished. She said she was forced to sell it to a Salt Lake City businessman after John's death in order to survive. Mrs. Jobson is now deceased.

Winchester Model 52 Sporter in .22 Long Rifle: Jack purchased this rifle, used, in 1934 for $50 shortly after moving to Tucson. It came with a Winchester fiber case and a Fecker 3X scope. The O'Connor boys, Jerry and Brad, used this rifle as well as a Winchester 75 Sporter on jack-rabbit hunts in later years. This rifle also went along on some northern sheep hunts, where it was used to pot blue grouse for camp meat. Jack sold it in the 1970s through Lolo Sporting Goods in Lewiston, Idaho.

Mauser Sukalle-Minar Custom 7x57mm: Jack bought this rifle secondhand in 1934 at Bill Sukalle's shop in Tucson for $75. The stock was fitted with a German trap buttplate and a trap grip cap. It had a German Girard scope on claw mounts as well as a Lyman 1A peep on the cocking piece and a ramp-mounted gold-bead front sight. Due to poor mounts that wouldn't hold zero, Jack traded the scope off and used the iron sights, making a double on mule deer the first time he took it to Mexico. As the little rifle had a 21-inch barrel and weighed just 7 pounds, Jack thought it would make a handy sheep rifle, and it did. As told in the desert-sheep chapter in this book, it is believed Jack used the little 7x57 to kill his first three desert rams, the last one after he'd replaced the Lyman 1A peep sight with a Noske 4X scope on a Noske side mount.

Jack took several mule deer, including a nice Kaibab buck in 1937 that has appeared in many published photos, with this rifle, along with javelina, a couple of antelope, and a whitetail or two. He had Sukalle replace the barrel once but eventually traded the rifle to Al Ronstadt (Linda Ronstadt's uncle) about 1940 because it tended to change zero from time to time.

Winchester Model 71 Deluxe in .348 Winchester: The Model 71 was introduced in 1936, and Jack had one of the first Deluxe models with checkered stock and fore-arm and the nifty bolt-mounted peep sight that was fully adjustable. Although Jack was not a lever-action fan, he thought the newly designed stock on the Model 71 was one of the best that Winchester turned out and felt there was a place for the powerful .348 cartridge. Jack wrote of taking a couple deer and a desert bighorn with the rifle before trading it off. There is a photo of this rifle in camp with Charlie Ren on one of Jack's sheep hunts. Ren died the summer of 1938, but the year Jack killed the ram with the 71 is not known. The rifle was poorly suited for most southwestern hunting, so it is not a surprise that Jack had it for a relatively short time.

Mauser Sukalle-Linden Custom .270 Winchester, #8184: Built in 1937 by Arizona barrelmaker and gunsmith Bill Sukalle and stocked by Alvin Linden, this was Jack's second .270 and the rifle he claimed to have shot more game with than any other. It had a 24-inch barrel, a flat bolt handle, trap buttplate, and a Noske 2.5X scope with 4-minute dot reticle on a Noske side mount. It cost $170 back then. Jack's first Coues deer taken with a .270 was a three-antlered buck shot with this rifle in the Cucurpi Mountains of Sonora in 1939 while hunting with Carroll Lemon and Frank Siebold. He also used it on desert bighorns, his best desert mule deer buck (taken 31 December 1941 in Sonora), his last Rocky Mountain bighorn (Wyoming, 1944), and the first of many bull elk taken with the .270. He used it to make a long shot on a buck antelope when Arizona's first season opened in 1941, and shot his first Dall ram with it in the Yukon in 1945. It was used on countless jack rabbits, coyotes, and Mexican Coues deer and mule deer. Jack gave it to his friend Richard Harris in 1966.

Springfield Sukalle-Linden .35 Whelen: Jack intended this one, built in 1937, to be his elk rifle. He used it only on a couple of mule deer. In January 1938 he took it to Houserock Valley to observe the buffalo shoot, thinking someone might want to use it. No one did, most regarding it as a small cannon. Jack decided he really didn't need it for elk, and had it rebarreled to .257 Roberts. It was one of seven Linden-stocked rifles Jack owned at one time or another.

Sukalle-Minar Sharps-Borchardt R-2 Lovell, #19768: In 1940 Jack sold his Sukalle-Minar 7x57 to buy this custom single-shot varmint rifle. He first wrote about it in an article called "A Super-Duper Hornet" in the September 1941 issue of *Outdoor Life* and referred to it in a dozen more pieces over the years. Photos of Jack with this rifle appeared in his *Outdoor Life* column as well as in a couple of his books. The R-2 is a blown-out version of the .22-3000 Lovell, which itself is a long-obsolete wildcat made by necking down the old .25-20 single-shot case to .22 caliber. In its day, it filled the gap between the .22 Hornet and .220 Swift, as the .222 and .223 do today.

This rifle, built on a strong Sharps-Borchardt single-shot action, had a 28-inch Sukalle heavy barrel fitted with a ramp front sight and a Lyman 1A tang sight and weighed 10 pounds 4 ounces. Jack mounted a Weaver 440 scope on Weaver 29S mounts, and it became his jack-rabbit rifle. He soon added scope blocks so he could put a Lyman 8X target scope on it, which he would use on crows and prairie dogs during summers at Slade Ranch in the White Mountains.

I used to drool over the photo of Jack with his R-2 after first discovering it in *The Rifle Book* at the Tucson High School library in the 1950s. I loved to hunt jack rabbits and dreamed of having a custom single-shot varmint rifle like it someday.

In discussions with Jack twenty years later, he told me he sold or traded the rifle about 1947 for two reasons: Brass was no longer available, and the rifle was slow to reload for shots on running jacks. Although Jack never publicly promoted the use of .22 centerfires on deer, he confided to me that he shot several javelina, a few Coues deer, and one large desert mule deer buck with the R-2 in Sonora. He just made sure he had good, clear, broadside shots when he pulled the trigger.

In August 1971, Jack reviewed the new Sharps-Colt single-shot rifle in his "Shooting" department for *Outdoor Life*. It was an expensive, quality firearm based on a modernized Sharps-Borchardt action but didn't succeed. In his column, Jack also reminisced about his old R-2 Lovell, ending by saying, "I sold the beautiful 2-R (sob!). Just why I did so I do not remember. The probable reason was that I was coming down with another rifle and was trying to raise money."

In 1995 I saw an ad in the *Gun List* for a Sharps-Borchardt R-2 Lovell that sounded very similar to Jack's. After speaking with the dealer, who was selling the gun on consignment, I was even more encouraged when I learned it had a Weaver 440 scope, a 28-inch Sukalle barrel, and a Lyman 1A tang sight. As the rifle was in my home state of Oregon, it was easy to arrange to see it and speak with the owner. She had inherited the rifle years ago from her brother, who had inherited it from their father. The father had been a sporting-goods dealer and gun collector in Sumner, Iowa, and the daughter remembered her father being especially proud of this rifle for it had belonged to a famous outdoor writer. She believed that her father had traded his cousin out of the rifle when the family had made a trip to New Mexico in 1947.

It didn't take long to verify the Minar custom stock and the fact that the rifle was indeed the one Jack had owned. With the rifle were fired cases, old reloads stuffed with Jack's pet load, and a box of unfired brass. In addition, papers in a file I was given included a letter from Jack to the owner's husband, written in 1972, in which Jack opined that the rifle was his, judging by close-up photos he had seen.

The rifle was still in excellent condition inside and out, the only damage being to the operating lever, which had broken and been crudely welded back together. I bought the rifle, thus fulfilling a daydream of forty years earlier. Since that time, Jack's rifle has revisited its old haunts in Arizona. It nailed the first running jack rabbit I shot at near Robles Junction, and was photographed at the old Slade Ranch cabin in the White Mountains in the hands of Jack's son Bradford, who had used it there fifty years earlier. And yes, I have proved that it will still kill a deer with one shot!

Mauser Sukalle-Griffin & Howe Custom in .257 Roberts: This rifle was built for Eleanor O'Connor in 1942 as a lightweight replacement for her Remington 30-S .257 described earlier. The action was a Mauser Model 93, trimmed down and fitted with a 22-inch Sukalle barrel and mounted with a Weaver 330 scope on Weaver B mounts. Griffin & Howe stocked the rifle with Circassian walnut, checkered and fitted with a trap butt plate and metal grip cap. Length of pull for 5' 2" 115-pound Eleanor was 13¼ inches. Weight was 7½ pounds.

Eleanor used this rifle a great deal during her Arizona years to take Coues deer, mule deer, javelina, jack rabbits, and coyotes. Her sons Jerry and Bradford both took their first deer with it in the 1940s, and Jack shot some mule deer with it in Sonora as well. In the 1960s, the rifle was given to Jim Rikhoff's wife Janet, who was even shorter than Eleanor. In 1971 it was a birthday gift to eleven-year-old Jimmy Rikhoff, who soon shot his first deer with it in Texas.

Winchester-Linden Model 70 in .270 Winchester: Jack's third .270 was acquired in spring of 1943 while his custom Mauser was being rebarreled. It was purchased new in Tucson and restocked by Alvin Linden. It had folding-leaf rear sights and carried a Weaver 330 scope in Stith Streamline mounts. It was finished in time to go on Jack's first Canadian pack trip to Alberta and British Columbia in 1943 and was used to take his first Rocky Mountain bighorn ram (now part of the O'Connor collection at the University of Idaho) and his first mountain goat, caribou, and moose. The rifle was acquired by a friend, the late Jim Wilkinson of Prescott, Arizona, about the time the O'Connors moved to Idaho.

Mauser Bayer-Stegall Custom in .22-250: This was O'Connor's first rifle, built in 1944, for the then-wildcat .22-250, also known as the Varminter. Built on an M98 Mauser action altered by Albert Bayer of Walla Walla, Washington, it had a Buhmiller barrel and a checkered straight-comb stock by Keith Stegall, who was just getting started then. Jack used both a Lyman 8X Targetspot and a Weaver 440 scope on the rifle, which weighed 10½ pounds. He used it at Slade Ranch in the White Mountains for crows and prairie dogs, and around Tucson on jack rabbits. Jack detailed this rifle project in "A Varminter from Scratch" (*Outdoor Life*, December 1944).

Mauser Sukalle-Owen Custom in .270 Winchester: Jack's fourth .270, built in the spring of 1946 was planned to be a mountain rifle, lighter than his Linden Mauser. Based on a commercial Mauser flat-bolt action brought back from Germany by a GI, complete with engraving (heavy scroll and stag on the floor plate), it had a 22-inch Sukalle barrel. The French walnut stock by Bob Owen had extensive point-pattern checkering, an ebony fore-end cap, trap buttplate, and oval monogram plate between the toe and grip cap. It was equipped with a Stith scope in Streamline mounts and had a ramp front sight and receiver sight base as well. It weighed 8½ pounds.

This rifle was the main medicine used on Jack's 1946 pack trip to British Columbia, where he took three Stone rams and a big moose with it. He also had along his old Minar Springfield and a custom .270 Ackley Magnum stocked by Stegall, the latter only used by one of his partners to shoot a caribou. The Owen-stocked .270 was the rifle in Jack's classic sheep-hunting story "A Day in Ram Heaven."

Jack was not completely happy with the Owen stock and later replaced it with one by Biesen. He gave the rifle to his son Brad, who killed his first ram with it near Atlin, British Columbia, in 1951. Brad lost the rifle when it was stolen en route to Africa nearly twenty years later.

Mauser Sukalle-Biesen Custom in .30-06, #101: This rifle, built in 1947, replaced the Sukalle-Minar Springfield as Jack's favorite .30-06. It was the second rifle stocked for Jack by young Al Biesen, then living in Wisconsin.

It was based on an FN Mauser action with a Niedner buttplate, had a 22-inch Sukalle barrel with a 1:12 twist, and was equipped with a Lyman 48 receiver sight as well as a Lyman Alaskan 2.5X scope on a G&H side mount. The rifle weighed 8½ pounds—Jack's idea of a mountain rifle. The floor plate was engraved with scroll and a bear. The American walnut stock was checkered in a fleur-de-lis pattern and had an ebony fore-end tip.

Jack was delighted with the rifle and the way it grouped loads of different bullet weights to nearly the same point of impact. He wrote glowingly of it in his January 1949 "Getting the Range" column in *Outdoor Life*, saying ". . . it's the .30-06 I've been looking for since 1915!"

Jack used his Biesen '06 on a 1950 hunt in the Yukon, where he collected his best North American ram, a 43⅝-inch Dall that scored 177⅛ and ranked No. 12 in the 1952 Boone and Crockett record book. Several years later, in 1959, he used the same rifle to bag a 60-inch kudu in Tanganyika. In the mid-1970s Jack sold his pet .30-06 to a friend, Henry Kaufman of Lewiston. Henry used it on a Kenyan safari in 1977 just before hunting ceased in that country.

Springfield-Biesen Custom in .22-250, #3127703: Al Biesen moved to Spokane, Washington, in 1948 and worked briefly with Frank Twitchell's Columbia Gun Company before establishing his own custom gun business. This rifle, made in 1948 while Al worked with Twitchell, was the third one he built for O'Connor. It is based on a much-shortened Springfield action with a medium-weight 24-inch barrel attached to the stock with a bedding band at the front swivel. The stock of dark walnut has an ebony fore-end tip, is checkered in a fleur-de-lis pattern, and is fitted with a Niedner steel buttplate. The barrel is inscribed "Columbia Gun Co. Spokane, Washington Custom Built for Jack O'Conner." It is still an embarrassment to Al Biesen that he misspelled Jack's name.

Jack used this rifle along with a Model 70 in .220 Swift to shoot rock chucks in the Snake River canyons near Lewiston. Photos of this rifle appeared seven times in *Outdoor Life* between 1950 and 1969, and it is pictured in the book *Complete Book of Rifles and Shotguns*. Although Jack had various target/varmint scopes such as a 15X Unertl mounted on it at times, he ultimately settled on the now-obsolete Leupold 7.5X model.

Jack sold the rifle to Richard Harris in 1972, when he began to thin out his rifles. The Harrises both died tragically in 1973. I saw the rifle advertised in 1995 and bought it. I found a Leupold 7.5X scope to put on it and had Al Biesen replace the missing sling-swivel bases. Although it no longer possesses gilt-edge accuracy, it still shoots well enough that I made my longest shot on a ground squirrel with it—423 steps!

Mauser-Sukalle in .300 Weatherby Magnum: Jack's first rifle for the .300 Weatherby Magnum was a rebarreled German square-bridge .280 Halger that weighed 10½ pounds. Details of this rifle can be found in the "Jack and Roy" chapter. He used it to make his only one-shot kill on a mountain goat, while hunting with Roy Weatherby, Art Popham, and several others in southwestern British Columbia in 1947. He also killed a grizzly with it a couple years later in the Yukon. Jack sold the rifle because of its weight and had Weatherby make a custom .300 to his specifications, which is described next.

Weatherby Custom in .300 Weatherby Magnum, #846: The new rifle was built in 1952 on a modified FN Mauser action with a lightweight 24-inch barrel. The stock of California walnut had a conservative Monte Carlo comb, a slanted fore-end tip of rosewood, a la Weatherby, but had a slender Minar-style grip and weighed only 8½ pounds with a Stith 4X scope in Buehler mounts. Jack used this rifle on his first safari in 1953 and made some impressive kills with it on both greater and lesser kudu, sable, and other large antelope. Jack gave the rifle to Dick Gray in early 1972.

Weatherby Presentation in .300 Weatherby Magnum: Jack also owned a more typical Weatherby .300. It was presented to him in about 1957, possibly in conjunction with his winning the Weatherby Award that year. It was a typical Weatherby with fancy fiddleback walnut inlaid with a diamond of lighter-colored wood in the butt and with basket-weave carving. It had an engraved floor plate and a gold nameplate in the fore-arm. A Weatherby Imperial variable scope topped it off. I spoke with the Weatherby collector who advertised the rifle for sale in May 2000. He had a factory letter to document that the rifle had been presented to Jack. He wasn't sure why the inscription plate had someone else's name on it. The answer lies in a letter Jack wrote to Bill English of Seattle in 1964. English did stock work and had arranged for a well-known sporting-goods dealer to sell Jack's rifle on consignment. Jack wrote, "I will pack up the .300 Weatherby and send it to you, but remember to take the gold nameplate off the fore-end and substitute another one." Jack never pretended that the racy Weatherby Magnums were his cup of tea!

Winchester Model 70-Pachmayer Custom in .257 Roberts, #796: Jack's favorite .257, made in 1950, was built by Pachmayer Gun Works of Los Angeles and was inscribed "Custom Made by Pachmayer Gun Works for Jack O'Connor" on the barrel, which was 22 inches long. A floor-plate release button was built into the trigger guard, and the figured walnut stock was fitted with a trap buttplate. The stock was checkered in a fleur-de-lis pattern with a modest carved border on the fore-arm. The rifle was originally equipped with a Weaver K4 scope in a Pachmayer Lo-Swing mount.

Before his death in 1978, Jack had negotiated the sale of this rifle, which was concluded by Eleanor afterward. A photo of this rifle can be found in the original edition of *The Big Game Rifle* (Knopf, 1952).

Mauser Burgess-Leonard Custom in 7x57mm, #50569: In 1951 crack metalsmith Tom Burgess modified a Czech VZ24 Mauser action for O'Connor, fitting a hinged floor plate and a 22-inch barrel chambered for the 7x57mm cartridge. Spokane stock maker Russell Leonard then fitted a stock with fleur-de-lis checkering to the barreled action, and Jack had his first 7mm since he'd traded off the Minar in 1940. Or did he? Eleanor O'Connor tried the little rifle, fell in love with it, and, after the stock had been shortened a bit, claimed it as her own. She proceeded to use it to bag everything from elk to eland for the rest of her hunting career. One of her most impressive trophies taken with the rifle was a 44¼-inch Dall ram shot in the Yukon in 1963 that won a Boone and Crockett medal. Dr. Sib West, who accompanied the O'Connors on a long safari in Mozambique in 1962, recently said to me, "Jack was a good shot, but Eleanor was a little better. She took seventeen animals with nineteen shots with that little 7mm." This rifle, with its Leupold 3X scope, is still owned by the O'Connor family today.

Burgess-Anderson-Oslin Custom in .450 Watts: This was Jack's first real big-bore rifle, made especially for his 1953 safari to Kenya and Tanganyika. Tom Burgess did the necessary metalwork on an M98 Mauser action and fitted a Holland & Holland floor plate, magazine, and trigger guard. Harvey Anderson of Yakima, Washington, installed the barrel and slotted it as an integral muzzle brake. Alvin Oslin of Clarkston, Washington, stocked the rifle, which was equipped with iron sights only. The floor plate was decorated with some scroll engraving and Jack's monogram. The Watts wildcat predated the .458 Winchester factory round, so Jack had to handload ammunition: 82 grains of No. 4895 behind 480-grain .450 Nitro Express bullets in the long, necked-up .375 H&H cases.

Jack used the rifle to take his first Cape buffalo (a 43½-inch bull), his only black rhino (19-inch horn), and a zebra. Jack's story "Buffaloes Shoot Back!" in the January 1954 *Outdoor Life* told of the rifle and of being charged by the bull. What happened to this rifle? Who knows?

Winchester Model 70 Griffin & Howe Custom in .375 H&H Magnum, #13242. During his life Jack owned several .375 Magnum rifles, but this one, a prewar model acquired about 1950, was the one he used most. It had a 25-inch barrel with the factory ramp front sight, a Lyman 48 rear sight, and a 2.75X Kollmorgen scope in a G&H side mount. It was stocked by G&H and, unlike many of their stocks, had the front sling swivel attached to the stock instead of the barrel. With this rifle Jack took his first three lions (1953, 1958, 1959), his first tiger (1955), his first and only leopard (1959), and two Alaska brown bears (1956), as well as kudu, sable, and eland. Jack made one of his best shots with this rifle—a heart shot on a running lion at 150 yards while hunting with John Kingsley-Heath in Tanganyika (Tanzania) in 1959. At the conclusion of the hunt, he gave the rifle to Kingsley-Heath, whose future clients used it on an estimated fifty lions. After semi-retirement to England with its strict gun laws, Kingsley-Heath sold the rifle at auction in the 1990s. It was resold in 2000 for $3,000 and in late 2001 for $4200.

Winchester Model 70-Biesen Custom in .270 Winchester, #287566: This rifle, made about 1953, replaced the Linden-stocked Mauser as Jack's favorite .270. Gunmaker Al Biesen turned down the standard barrel and shortened it to 22 inches. He stocked it in French walnut with an ebony fore-end tip, fleur-de-lis checkering, and a trap buttplate and grip cap of his own design. The rifle weighed 8 pounds complete with a Stith Kollmorgen 4X scope on Tilden mounts. Jack bagged a big six-point bull elk with this rifle the fall of 1954 while hunting with Fred Huntington out of Les Bowman's ranch near Cody, Wyoming. The very next year he used it in India on blackbuck and in Iran on red sheep and ibex. In 1956 he took a 40-inch Dall ram from Prospector Mountain in the Yukon with it, and another bull elk in Idaho. In 1958 it went on safari to the Sahara and was used on addax and scimitar-horned oryx, dama gazelle, and aoudad sheep.

This was one of Jack's fabled pair of favorite .270s, referred to as his Number 1 rifle. In the 1970s, Jack sold it to his friend Henry Kaufman, who has used the rifle in Africa as well as Scotland.

Enfield Apex-Biesen Custom in .416 Rigby: Jack's first .416 was built a couple of years after his first safari in 1953. Apex Rifle Company of Sun Valley, California, reworked the Enfield action and installed a 24-inch Apex barrel. Al Biesen stocked the rifle, which carried a Weaver K2.5 on a G&H side mount and weighed 10½ pounds. Factory ammo was not readily available then, as it is now, so Jack made brass by turning the belts off .378 Weatherby cases and then sizing them in a full-length die. He used this rifle to work up .416 Rigby handloads by trial and error.

In 1962 the Enfield went on its first and only safari, to Mozambique. Jack used two 400-grain solids to kill a Cape buffalo that had a spread of 40½ inches. Harry Manners was the PH with Jack at the time.

I remember looking at this rifle at Jack's home in 1973 but do not know what happened to it. A good photo of it can be found in the second and third editions of *The Rifle Book*.

Winchester Model 70 Biesen Custom in 7x57mm, #361582: In January 1957, Jack was badly injured in an auto accident. He later claimed that his recovery began the day this rifle was delivered to his hospital bed by his friend Al Biesen. The rifle was based on the last barreled action the Winchester factory had assembled in this caliber. Biesen shortened the barrel to 22 inches and stocked it in French walnut in what was becoming recognized as the "O'Connor Classic" design— straight-combed stocks with fleur-de-lis checkering, black fore-end tips, steel buttplate and grip cap, detachable sling swivels. In this case, a mountain goat is engraved on the buttplate and an antelope on the grip cap. The rifle wears a Weaver K4 in Redfield two-piece mounts and weighs 8 pounds. It was Jack's idea of an ideal mountain rifle. In September 1958, Jack tried it out on antelope near Rawlins, Wyoming. His son Brad, Al Biesen, and friend Doc Wygant of Lewiston were along when he shot a 15¼-inch buck.

The rifle was used most by Jack during the fall of 1972 when he and Eleanor went on safari to Southwest Africa (Namibia) and Rhodesia (Zimbabwe). Jack took sable, kudu, gemsbok, and Hartmann zebra with it, using 140-grain Nosler handloads. Jack later sold the rifle to Lewiston wheat farmer Henry Kaufman. It traveled to Sonora, Mexico, with Henry and me in 1988 on a Coues deer hunt memorializing the tenth anniversary of Jack's passing. Henry took an old Coues buck and a javelina with it. Jack would have been proud.

Winchester Model 70 Biesen Custom in .270 Winchester, #423509: This new Featherweight Model 70 was purchased in 1959 from Erb Hardware in Lewiston by Jack and sent to Al Biesen for some refinements and restocking. His purpose was to use it for everyday shooting and testing in order to conserve his favorite Model 70 .270 already mentioned. He was somewhat surprised when this rifle shot even better than the other. The French walnut stock is checkered in Biesen's classic pattern and fitted with a trap buttplate engraved with a ram, and a grip cap engraved with a moose head. Equipped with a Leupold Mountaineer 4X scope in Buehler mounts, the rifle weighed 8 pounds. It became Jack's favorite .270 and was used on gemsbok and other antelope on his 1966 Botswana safari. It went to Spain, Iran, and Scotland soon after that. In British Columbia Jack shot his last three Stone sheep with it, the last ram killed in the Cassiars in 1973. Jack's only northern whitetail was shot with this rifle as it ran from a brushy Idaho canyon in 1971. In 1977 Jack took the rifle on what was his last big-game hunt, to Wyoming and Montana for antelope and whitetails. Jack's health and eyesight were failing, and he fired not a shot, although his friend Henry Kaufman and son Bradford both bagged game. Jack's favorite .270 is still an O'Connor family possession today, as he wished.

Mauser Biesen Custom in .244 Remington (no serial number): Al Biesen built this rifle for Jack in 1958 on a

Mexican Mauser action. It had a 24-inch Buhmiller barrel with a 1:10 twist and was mounted with a Leupold 8X scope. The stock was French walnut, classic Biesen design, and the rifle weighed 8 pounds. Jack used it only on rock chucks, writing a story about such a hunt in southern Idaho that he made with Eleanor and his friend Dr. James Flanagan. The story ran in the March 1972 issue of *Outdoor Life*. This rifle is still owned by the O'Connor family.

Jeffery .450-400, 3-inch double rifle, #24358: Jack bought this rifle, used, in Nairobi in 1959 while on his third safari, to Tanganyika. It is the only double rifle Jack owned, and was purchased mostly out of romantic sentiment. As Jack wrote in *The Last Book*:

> I once had a pretty little Jeffery double rifle for the .450-400, 3-inch cartridge. I bought it almost entirely for the cosmetic effect. Put me in my bush jacket, my Terai hat with pugaree, my Nairobi safari boots, and let me carry my nifty little double and you could just about hear the lions roaring over by the water hole in the donga.

Several years ago, I bought the fitted canvas-covered trunk case that Jack had Holland & Holland make for this rifle in 1962 at a cost of $85. The label in the lid has Jack's name on it as well as the rifle's serial number. Where Jack's Jeffery went after he sold it in the late 1960s is a mystery, but possibly some reader of these words will come forth and help reunite the case with the rifle.

Winchester Model 70-Biesen Custom in .375 H&H Magnum, #433357: Al Biesen stocked this rifle in 1960 from a piece of Iranian walnut Jack received as a gift from Prince Abdorreza Pahlavi. The rifle was a replacement for Jack's G&H Model 70 given to John Kingsley-Heath in 1959. It had the front sling swivel attached to the barrel, which had a ramp front and express rear sights as well as a Weaver K3 scope on G&H side mounts. This rifle was used by Jack on his 1962 Angola and Mozambique safaris arranged by Bob Lee. Jack shot his best lion to that date with this .375 and wrote of it in "Big Lion of Mucusso," an *Outdoor Life* story. In 1965 he used it to take his second tiger. It featured in a Cape buffalo adventure the following year in Bechuanaland (Botswana), where Jack and John Kingsley-Heath had to team up to put down "The Indestructible Buffalo" (*Outdoor Life*, April 1967). In the early 1970s, Jack sold the rifle to Alex Schimek, a Canadian O'Connor fan who in turn sold the rifle to Jack's old friend Bob Lee about 1993.

Ruger No. 1 Presentation in .375 H&H Magnum: Jack and Bill Ruger were close friends who had respect for each other. Jack received this single-shot presentation rifle from Bill Ruger, about 1970. This rifle was similar to others that were known as "21 Club" rifles, presented to noted gunwriters. It had a game scene on one side of the receiver and Jack's monogram inlaid in gold on the other side. Jack valued this rifle but never hunted with it. It was in Jack's estate but has been sold outside the family.

Mauser Burgess-Milliron Custom in .375 H&H Magnum, #57260: Jack's last custom .375 was completed late in 1971. It was on a prewar square-bridge Magnum Mauser action with a 24-inch barrel and Weaver K3 scope. Tom Burgess did the extensive metalwork, and Earl Milliron stocked it in French walnut. Jack offered the rifle to me in 1973 for $1,400 as consolation for missing out on another of his rifles that I'd wanted. Money was scarce, and I declined. He sold the rifle that September to Henry Kaufman at a higher price.

Winchester Model 70-Biesen Custom in .338 Winchester Magnum, #25235: Jack's first custom .338 was built in 1962 in anticipation of a brown bear hunt in Alaska the next spring. It had a 22-inch barrel, Leupold 4X scope on Tilden mounts, and was stocked in French walnut by Al Biesen. The bear hunt was made with the same guide Jack had used in 1956—Ralph Young of Petersburg, Alaska—and they used a boat as a base camp. The other hunters were Eleanor and Robert Chatfield-Taylor, an old friend from Arizona days. Taylor got a nine-foot bear on Admiralty Island, and Eleanor got a large black bear, but Jack never connected.

In 1969 Jack took the same .338 to Zambia and used it on sable and kudu but was disappointed with the performance of its bullets in the brush. He gave the rifle to the late Peter Alport of Portland, Oregon.

Winchester Model 70, Burgess-Milliron Custom in .338 Winchester Magnum, #520190: Jack had another Model 70 custom .338 built before the end of 1968. Tom Burgess did the metalwork and Earl Milliron stocked it. This rifle, with 24-inch barrel, was given to Victor O'Farrill, a wealthy Mexican sportsman and businessman, about 1970.

Winchester Model 70-Biesen Custom in 7mm Remington Magnum, #65085: O'Connor used a factory Remington Model 700 in the brand-new 7mm Remington Magnum caliber on safari in Mozambique and Rhodesia in 1962, the year the cartridge was introduced. Upon his return he had Biesen build the custom Model 70, which was completed in 1963. The rifle was a typical Biesen classic with French walnut stock, 24-inch Buhmiller barrel, and Leupold 4X scope on Redfield mounts. Jack shot his best Idaho bull elk with the rifle in November of 1964 while hunting from Moose Creek Lodge on the Selway with Eleanor and Ray Speer. The story of that hunt appeared in the October 1965 *Outdoor Life* as "Bull Elk in the Brush." Jack hunted little with this rifle, believing that his .270 performed nearly as well with less noise and recoil. He sold the rifle in the early 1970s to Alex Schimek, who resold it in 1993.

Winchester Model 70-Brownell Custom in .30-06, #569788: This rifle was planned during a Yukon hunt in

1963 in which Jack, Eleanor, Bill Ruger, Lenard Brownell, and Bob Chatfield-Taylor all took part. The rifle was made for Eleanor in anticipation of an Indian shikar in 1965, on which the hunted game would include tiger and the large nilgai or blue bull. The rifle was finished in 1964 and became Eleanor's "heavy" rifle. Its factory barrel was shortened to 22 inches and turned down. It is marked "Lenard M. Brownell Sheridan, Wyo. No. 27" on the barrel. The stock is French walnut, ebony fore-end, with recessed, borderless checkering in a fleur-de-lis pattern, fitted with an engraved trap grip cap and leather-faced recoil pad. For the Indian hunt, the rifle had the then-new Redfield 2–7X variable scope in Redfield mounts. On subsequent hunts it wore a Weaver K3. It weighed 7¾ pounds with the K3 scope.

With her .30-06 Eleanor proved that well-placed bullets do not have to be cigar-sized to get the job done. In India she killed two tigers, two nilgai, chinkara gazelle, and chital or axis deer. The next year she shot gemsbok, zebra, and red lechwe in Botswana. In Zambia in 1969, she killed a lion, a sable, a bull elephant with a single brain shot, and other game. For elephant she used a Winchester 220-grain full-metal-jacket handload. Most of the other game was killed with 180-grain Remington softpoints. Eleanor's rifle was sold to Alex Schimek about 1972. I've owned it since 1996.

Sako-Brownell Custom .222 Remington, #51330: In 1964 Lenard Brownell stocked a Sako lightweight barreled action for Jack. With a Weaver K6 on Sako mounts, it weighed 7¼ pounds and would still shoot under minute-of-angle groups. It was Jack's pet rifle for carrying up canyons in search of rock chucks. He sold the rifle to the late Fred Huntington, his friend and RCBS founder, in early 1973. When I last talked to Fred in the late 1980s, he still had the rifle.

Mannlicher-Schoenauer Model 1903 Carbine in 6.5x54mm, #15531: This rifle is included here simply to demonstrate Jack's love for classic rifles of the world, for he never hunted with it. He is believed to have bought it in the 1960s, then had a Leupold 4X scope mounted on a G&H side mount. In his chapter "Costumes for the Job" from *The Last Book* (Amwell Press, 1984), Jack explains:

> There is much self dramatization in rifles and other equipment for hunting. I have always fancied myself a striking figure when I was outfitted as a northern sheep hunter wearing down jacket, Italian cowboy hat, wool pants, hobnail boots, carrying a light Biesen-stocked .270 and wearing around my neck my Bausch & Lomb 9X35 binocular. I also think I would present a fetching picture if I had a Tyrolean chamois hunter's costume on—6.5x54 Mannlicher-Schoenauer, long, tubular 8X56 Hensoldt Dialyt binocular suspended by a neck strap, shorts, hobnail boots.

At age 71, Jack probably figured his chamois-hunting opportunities were past and sold his cute little Mannlicher to Henry Kaufman. Someday Henry and I plan to use our 6.5mm Mannlichers (yes, I have one too!) on a hunt.

Mauser Burgess-Milliron Custom in .280 Remington, #114070: Tom Burgess of Spokane did the metalwork on this rifle, which included installing a 23-inch Sharon barrel on the Mauser-Werke square-bridge action Jack had bought from a London gunmaker, and building special Burgess mounts for the Browning 4X scope. He billed Jack $139.75 for the work in August 1965. The rifle was stocked by Earl Milliron of Portland and weighed 8 pounds when finished in 1966. Jack never actually hunted with the rifle and in about 1974 sold it to Alex Schimek, who sold it more than twenty years later to another O'Connor fan, John Iacopi, a CPA of Stockton, California.

Mauser Milliron Custom in .280 Remington, #H700: Another custom .280—built somewhat later on a Czech Brno Mauser-type action with integral scope bases on the receiver bridge, hinged floor plate, and adjustable single-stage trigger—was also stocked by Milliron for Jack. The barrel is marked "Bliss Titus" (a Heber City, Utah, barrelmaker bought out by David Huntington about then) and is ribbed and 24 inches long. The Claro walnut stock is fitted with a trap buttplate. The rifle was sold to Henry Kaufman about 1975.

Brevex Mauser Burgess-Johnson Custom in .416 Rigby, #66179: Made in 1966 on a Brevex Magnum Mauser action, this was Jack's second .416 Rigby. It had a 24-inch barrel fitted with gold-faced post ramp front sight, open-vee rear sight on a permanent base, and a Weaver K2.5 on special Burgess bases marked "Thos. Burgess, Riflemaker, Spokane, Wash." and "Caliber .416 Rigby." It has a jeweled bolt and magazine follower, Burgess-hinged floor plate with trigger-guard release, magazine to hold three rounds, and a front sling swivel attached to the barrel. The Bob Johnson stock has an ebony fore-end tip, simple arrowhead-checkered pattern on fore-arm and grip, checkered-steel grip cap, and solid red rubber recoil pad. The wood is modestly figured, straight-grain walnut. The gun weighs 10¼ pounds empty. This rifle was used on the 1969 Zambian safari to take Jack's best African lion, his only bull elephant, and a Cape buffalo.

When Jack began selling his rifles, a Canadian told him in 1972 that he would buy the .416. When spring of 1973 came and Jack had heard no more, he offered the rifle to me for $1,400, including all his dies, brass, and bullets. I had finally scrounged together the money, and Jack and I had set a date to get together and shoot the rifle, when the Canadian showed up with cash in hand. Jack, as usual, honored the deal and then offered me the .375 mentioned earlier at the same price. Long story short, I had another opportunity to buy the rifle a few years ago and got the job done. Jack's .416 may see Africa again!

Mauser Burgess-Johnson Custom in .338 Winchester Magnum, #114809: The December 1966 issue of *Outdoor Life* carried O'Connor's shooting column titled "The Elegant Sporter." His words tell part of this rifle's story:

> The Mauser Werke action, in the photograph accompanying this article, is one I obtained by buying an old 9.3x62mm Mauser Sporter with a rusted out barrel and a battered stock. I threw barrel and stock away, had Tom Burgess fit, chamber to .338 Winchester Magnum and contour a Sharon .338 blank. Burgess altered the bolt handle for low scope mounting, hand checkered the bolt knob by filing, fitted a one-stage trigger and a safety of his own manufacture, made and fitted two piece bases for Redfield rings. Action, barrel, and Weaver K4 scope weigh 6½ lbs. With stock, the rifle will weigh 9¼ lbs.

Jack's estimate was close. The completed rifle, after being stocked by Bob Johnson, weighed 8½ pounds. It is not surprising that this rifle, except for its darker-colored stock and fleur-de-lis checkering, appears to be just a slimmer twin to the .416 above. Jack's initials, JOC, are stamped on the action but are hidden by the stock.

Jack never mentioned using this rifle, but twenty years later I bought it from dealer George Douglass, and it has been used since. It is extremely accurate, usually putting three shots in a one-inch group at 100 yards. In 1996 my daughter, hatched the same year the rifle was built, used it in Zimbabwe to take her first game animal, a zebra stud, with a single frontal shot. I made one-shot kills on sable and waterbuck with it. Recently, one shot nailed a big Utah bull elk for me.

Mauser Biesen Custom .458 Winchester Magnum, #A0046: It didn't take Jack O'Connor long to begin planning another safari after his return from Zambia in 1969. He had taken his first elephant there and began thinking of a safari primarily for a big elephant. At the time, Jack did not have a .458, though he had owned a custom Model 70 for a while right after the cartridge was introduced in 1955. Early in 1970 he ordered a new Interarms Mark X Mauser action, made in Yugoslavia, as a basis for a new .458. "I am getting this .458 to weigh 11 lbs.," he wrote to a friend in June. The rifle, built by Al Biesen and so stamped on the barrel, has a 24-inch heavy barrel without iron sights. The stock is straight-grained walnut with a multipoint checkering pattern fitted with a checkered-steel grip cap, solid red recoil pad, and silver initial plate. With the Weaver 3X scope in Redfield mounts, it weighs exactly 11 pounds.

During 1971 Jack wrote to several friends of his intention to go to Kenya for elephant in 1972, possibly with Brad and Eleanor. He mentioned that Brad would use a .458. For whatever reasons, most likely the expense, the O'Connors did not go to Kenya in 1972, but did go to Southwest Africa and Rhodesia, as mentioned elsewhere. The .458, which Jack had given to Brad, did not go along.

In 1986 Brad sold the .458 to me, and the next year, I took it to Botswana, where it worked just fine on a cantankerous old lone buffalo in the Okavango.

Mauser Pachmayer Custom in .270 Winchester, #73: This rifle was sent to Eleanor as a gift from Frank Pachmayer about 1972. It has a 23-inch barrel on a Model 98 action, which is engraved. The floor plate features a gold moose with floral and scroll engraving. A gold grip cap is inscribed "Custom Made for Eleanor O'Connor by F. Pachmayer, L.A. Calif, USA." The stock is highly figured Circassian walnut checkered 28 lines per inch, with a solid red recoil pad. It has a 4X Leupold scope on a Redfield one-piece mount.

When I was shown the rifle shortly after it was received, Jack said Eleanor hefted it, pronounced it too heavy, and never used it. The O'Connors sold it to Henry Kaufman a few years later.

Springfield Griffin & Howe Custom in .30-06, #1308: Jack and Eleanor traveled to New York City in February 1973 to attend a retirement party for *Outdoor Life*'s editor, Bill Rae. Jack checked out Abercrombie & Fitch while he was there and discovered this prewar sporter and bought it. It had a good French walnut stock with a trap buttplate, Lyman 48 rear and ramp front sight on a 20-inch barrel with a Lyman Alaskan scope on a G&H side mount. A toe plate had the initials HMS on it.

Jack showed me this rifle about a month after getting it. He was thrilled with it, and had refinished the stock with oil. He'd gotten it at a good price—$450. Later he had Al Biesen put a Model 70-style safety on it. It seemed to me Cactus Jack had come full circle—back to a G&H Springfield Sporter like he'd had in 1925. He sold the rifle to Henry Kaufman that fall for $800.

Fred Wells-Clayton Nelson Custom in .458 Winchester Magnum, #1: Jack, still as enthusiastic over a new rifle or a planned hunt at age seventy-one as he ever was, ordered one of Fred Wells's superb double square-bridge Magnum Mauser actions with a 25-inch .458 full-ribbed octagon barrel and sent it to Clayton Nelson to be stocked. Nelson delivered the rifle to Jack at the Game Coin convention in May 1973 at San Antonio, Texas. Jack mounted the usual Weaver K2.5 scope on the integral G&H-style side mount. Engraved on the rib is "No. 1 Custom Built for Jack O'Connor by Fred F. and R. F. Wells."

Shortly before picking up this rifle, Jack wrote Truman Fowler expressing his dismay at the political upheaval that was going on in Africa: "I think African hunting is about over. Just for the Hell of it, would have liked to have shot a BIG elephant, but I don't suppose I ever will."

Jack's plan for the Wells .458 was to at least use it on buffalo in Botswana, which was planned for 1974 and then canceled, as was a safari to Zambia with the Dick Grays. In July of

1974, another letter to Fowler closed with a wistful line: "I would really like to hunt elephant in Kenya but probably never will. Things are really getting loused up over there."

Before his death, Jack sold the .458 to his good friend Henry Kaufman. It still has never seen Africa.

Jack's Last Rifle: Ruger Model 77-Biesen Custom in .280 Remington, #72-8463: At the time of Jack's death in January 1978, Al Biesen was working on another of Jack's projects. At the funeral, with all present, the family instructed Al to complete the rifle. The finished product had a 22-inch recontoured Ruger barrel with custom bases for a 4X Leupold scope. The stock, with fleur-de-lis checkering, is fitted with a skeleton grip cap and buttplate.

It was the O'Connor family's decision to allow Jack's friend Henry Kaufman, who had been with Jack on his last hunt the previous fall, to keep the custom Ruger at the cost of Biesen's work.

Jack's last rifle had been designed by Bill Ruger, an American firearms designer without peer, whom Jack greatly admired and considered a good friend. The custom work was done by another close friend, Al Biesen, whose work Jack preferred over nearly all others. Lastly, its custodian would be another friend who shared Jack's appreciation for fine rifles and would see that it was well kept. What more could a rifle lover ask for?

PART II: SHOTGUNS

Jack's interest in shotguns developed later than his first love—rifles. However, in his last years it was the shotgun that gave him most of his enjoyable days afield.

When Jack was a boy, most hunters believed that a gun needed a long barrel and a tight choke to shoot "hard," as they called it, and his first shotguns were that style. One might say that Jack's real education in shotgunning began in Texas in the late 1920s when he decided to take his new bride's little Ithaca 20-gauge double after blue quail. He did so well with its open-choked 26-inch barrels that he was amazed.

Jack's early wingshooting was on whitewing and mourning doves and Gambel quail in Arizona. He became a fan of the light, short-barreled side-by-side double for upland shooting and remained so all his life. He abhorred double triggers and automatic safeties.

During the 1940s, Jack thought the best upland gun was a 16-gauge double. By 1960 he had lived in Idaho for more than twenty years; had hunted pheasants, mountain quail, chukars, and Hungarian partridge in rough country; and was fifty-eight years old. His preference by this time had shifted to the 20-gauge, which he thought could be made in a lighter, livelier gun that, with modern shells, could be plenty effective up to the 40-yard range of most upland shooting.

During their years in the Southwest, Jack and Eleanor's favorite wingshooting was for quail. After moving to Idaho in 1948 and shooting his first pheasant that fall on an island in the Boise River near Caldwell, the big, gaudy, and wily ringneck became his favorite gamebird. In his last years Jack maintained a membership at Fay Weidemann's Pheasant Valley Preserve near LaCrosse, Washington, where he could still enjoy a private day of shooting pheasants with friends when he was no longer up to ten-mile jaunts through Palouse stubble fields.

A lifelong admirer of the Winchester Model 21, Jack also recognized early on, in the 1950s, that the better-made Spanish doubles were a good bargain, and he owned several during his lifetime made by Ugartechea, AYA, and Arizaga. He also admired Italian guns and used several high-grade Berettas. He considered his Model 450 EL sidelock the highest-quality gun he ever owned.

Although Jack figured that anyone could satisfy his various bird-hunting needs with two shotguns, he usually owned many more. Typical was his inventory of nine in 1963, consisting of three in 12-gauge, one 16-gauge, two 20-gauges, two 28-gauges, and one .410. He had little use for the .410 but frequently took a Model 42 Winchester on sheep hunts to pot grouse with.

Jack's taste in shotguns was similar to that in women: He preferred them small and trim. In 1967 he wrote that he considered a 20-gauge sidelock side-by-side double with straight stock and 26-inch barrels the handsomest of all shotguns, followed by the 20-gauge boxlock side-by-side and 20-gauge over/under designs, in that order. He also thought beavertail fore-ends were more practical and useful than the traditional English splinter-style ones.

Twenty O'Connor shotguns are listed below:

Iver Johnson single-shot in 20-gauge: This was Jack's first shotgun, given to him in 1910 at age eight by his maternal grandfather, James Wiley Woolf. He used it near Tempe on doves, quail, and ducks along the Salt River, which then flowed year-round. He traded this one for the gun below.

Winchester Model 1897 in 12-gauge: Depending on which of Jack's accounts of this old pump gun you read, it had either a 30- or a 32-inch full-choke barrel. He used it during his teen years at Tempe, most successfully for pass-shooting doves and ground-sluicing ducks and quail, which were always welcomed at his mother's table.

Remington Model 1894 Double in 12-gauge: Jack didn't speak of this old double much, except to say it had 30-inch barrels choked modified and full and that he'd traded his Model 97 for it.

Winchester Model 12 in 12-gauge: This was the only shotgun Jack owned when he married Eleanor in 1927. It had a 30-inch full-choke barrel, and he used it effectively in Texas on ducks but did poorly on the running scaled or blue quail as they are called there. This gun moved to Flagstaff, Arizona, with the O'Connors in 1931 but had to be sold to pay doctor bills soon afterward.

Ithaca Grade 2 Double in 20-gauge: Jack bought this little double, with its minimal engraving, automatic ejectors, and 26-inch improved-cylinder/modified barrels, as a Christmas gift for Eleanor in 1928. It cost a little less than $100—about two weeks' salary at the rate Jack was paid then. The gun was the right size for Jack's 5' 2", 115-pound bride, who, with his coaching, managed to drop some ducks with it but became much more enthusiastic about quail hunting. It was this light, fast little 20-gauge, which Jack borrowed to hunt Texas blues one day, that kick-started his life-long love of short-barreled doubles.

In Arizona Eleanor used her Ithaca to shoot ducks and quail when they lived at Flagstaff, and after their 1934 move to Tucson she shot quail and doves with it. Later, after she switched to a 16-gauge Model 21 as her main shotgun, the Ithaca was used by her teenage sons in Idaho. Its ultimate fate is not known.

L. C. Smith Field Grade in 20-gauge: Jack bought this gun in Flagstaff from a widow in 1932 for $17.50. It had 30-inch barrels choked modified and full, auto ejectors, and came with a mutton-leg case. Jack used it on ducks in northern Arizona and later thought it as good a gun as he ever used on Gambel quail when he lived at Tucson. It was also used to shoot both whitewing and mourning doves in Arizona and Sonora. Jack traded it for a Grade 4 Ithaca about 1941.

Winchester Model 21 Double in 16-gauge, #12390: Bought in 1940 for $115, this was Jack's first Model 21. The 26-inch barrels were bored skeet 1 and skeet 2 (choked cylinder and modified), and the stock had a straight grip and red rubber recoil pad. It wasn't long until Eleanor tried the gun and claimed it from then on, using it in Arizona, Idaho, Washington, Alberta, Tanganyika, and Spain. Jack did manage to sneak it away on his 1953 safari to Kenya, where he shot sand grouse with it. Eleanor was deadly with the gun, for she didn't use any other and became thoroughly familiar with it.

On a 1966 hunt in Alberta, she made doubles on pheasant, sharp-tailed grouse, and Hungarian partridge in a single day!

Ithaca Grade 4 Double in 12-gauge, #467671: Jack acquired this high-grade double with two sets of 26-inch barrels about the time he lost his 16-gauge Model 21 to Eleanor. In fact, there is a photo of Eleanor with this gun in the October 1941 issue of *Outdoor Life*.

The Ithaca had a highly figured black-walnut stock and beavertail fore-arm with Ithaca's fancy checkering pattern and engraving typical of a Grade 4. It also had Ithaca's selective single trigger. One set of barrels was choked improved cylinder/ quarter choke and the other modified/full. Jack used this gun in Arizona on doves and quail. After moving to Lewiston, Idaho, in 1948, he was invited on a pheasant hunt with Vernon Speer, the bullet maker, and shot his first pheasant with this gun on a small island in the Boise River near Caldwell. Thus he immediately became enamored with pheasant hunting. He proclaimed this fact to the world in a July 1950 *Outdoor Life* story called "Pheasants I Love You," written under one of his pen names—Bill Ryan.

Jack explored the country on both sides of the Snake River that first fall of 1948. With Eleanor and their hunting cocker spaniel, Pat, he located valley-quail hotspots and Hungarian-partridge hangouts. The next fall, Idaho opened the season on sage grouse for the first time in many years. Vernon Speer, who owned a light plane, flew Jack, sixteen-year-old Brad, and Doc Braddock to Caldwell, where they met a couple of local hunters and drove south to hunt grouse. On this hunt, described in a March 1950 story, "Sagehen Hunters Need Alibis," Jack used the 8-pound Ithaca, and Brad shot his mother's Model 21.

Vernon Speer, who frequently hunted pheasants with Jack, eventually traded Jack out of the Ithaca in the 1950s. Vernon's son Ray remembers the gun well, for he, too, enjoyed using it. Upon Vernon's death, the gun was sold through a Spokane dealer about 1981, then resurfaced in 1998 with Texas dealer Herschel Chadick. I bought the gun from Herschel and used it on Kansas prairie chickens and Oregon ring-necks that same year. The gun is in great condition and comfortable to shoot.

Winchester Model 21 Double in 12-gauge: Jack bought this Custom Grade gun new from the factory with two sets of barrels and used it first during the 1950 season. One set of 26-inch barrels was choked skeet 1 and 2, the other modified and improved modified. It had a beavertail fore-arm and pistol-grip stock and became Jack's most widely used gun. In addition to local pheasants, quail, and Huns, he shot driven grouse with it in Scotland in 1959 and driven red-leg partridge in Spain in 1967. This gun weighed 7¾ pounds and replaced the Ithaca as Jack's pheasant gun. It is believed Jack sold this gun about 1970.

Winchester Model 21 Custom in 16-gauge: Jack got this gun on a trade in the 1950s. It had two sets of 26-inch barrels choked skeet 1 and 2 and modified/full. It had a beavertail fore-arm, straight grip, and the only skeleton buttplate I've seen on an original Model 21. Jack's son Bradford won this shotgun from his father in a skeet match, which he suspects was "fixed," when he was a young man. He still uses it today.

Arizaga Sidelock Double in 28-gauge, #34525: This was the first Spanish shotgun Jack bought, in 1953. It has scroll-engraved sidelocks, 25½-inch barrels choked modified and full, and weighs 6 pounds. The stock, which Jack had recheckered by Al Biesen, has a straight grip, beavertail fore-arm, and checkered butt. When Jack had trouble with it doubling, he had a G&H nonselective single trigger installed. Jack began using it occasionally on pheasant hunts in 1958 when Federal brought out its 1-ounce load for the 28-gauge. He wrote of it often and reported making a double on roosters in 1969 with the older ⅞-ounce No. 6 load. The gun is owned today by Henry Kaufman.

Winchester Model 21 Double in 20-gauge, #27396: Jack ordered this gun from Winchester in 1954 with 26-inch barrels chambered for the 3-inch shell and choked modified and full. When hunting pheasants, he loaded the more-open barrel with a 2¾-inch shell with the standard 1-ounce load of No. 6 and the tighter-choked tube with the 1¼-ounce magnum load. About 1960 Jack had this gun restocked by Al Biesen with a piece of Iranian Circassian walnut. He sold this gun a few years before his death for $3,000.

Arizaga Sidelock Double in 20-gauge, #49401: With two sets of barrels choked improved cylinder/modified and modified/full, this gun, purchased in 1956, became one of Jack's favorites for birds in later years. He had Biesen recut the checkering and had a Miller single trigger installed. Jack shot his first sharp-tailed grouse with this gun in 1966 on a hunt he made with Eleanor to Alva Bair's ranch in southern Alberta. This cased gun is still in the O'Connor family's possession today.

Remington Model 11-48 Skeet in 28-gauge #P-403243: In the March 1952 issue of *Outdoor Life*, Jack reviewed the new 11-48 semiauto skeet gun. The DeLuxe Model, with nice checkering and ventilated rib, was and still is a nice-looking gun. Jack shot skeet with his and used it to introduce his daughter Caroline to shotgun shooting. The O'Connor family still has this gun.

Beretta ASEELL Over/Under in 20-gauge, #28672: When Jack made his 1959 safari to Tanganyika, he stopped en route in Italy and bought this lovely 20-gauge for $660. A model no longer made, it was the highest-grade boxlock, with sideplates engraved in full-coverage floral scroll and a filigreed top lever. With 26½-inch modified/full barrels, it weighed just under 6 pounds. The straight-grip stock was beautifully figured and fitted with a Mershon red rubber pad and a gold toe plate engraved with Jack's initials. It had a nonselective, gold-plated single trigger. In later years Jack sold this gun to friend Peter Alport, whose son sold it after his father's death. I added it to my collection of O'Connor guns a couple of years ago.

Jack had another ASEELL 20-gauge, #31210, acquired in 1966, which he sold in the 1970s for $2,000.

Winchester Model 101 Skeet Set in 20-gauge, 28-gauge, .410 #232764: In 1963 Winchester introduced its Model 101 over/under made in Japan to its specifications. Initially in 12-gauge, the model's smaller gauges soon followed. Jack couldn't resist the small-gauge skeet set with three sets of barrels and matching fore-ends in a factory luggage case. This skeet set has remained in the family.

AYA Model 53 Sidelock Double in 20-gauge, #283933: Number 1 of a matched pair Jack purchased in the early 1960s, this gun has 26-inch improved cylinder/modified barrels, hand-detachable side locks, and a Miller single trigger. Jack showed me this gun in early 1973 after admiring the stock on a similar AYA I'd bought. He had his gun restocked by Earl Milliron the previous year because he thought the wood was too plain. The Milliron stock had a checkered butt like the original AYA furnished. If Jack mentioned the whereabouts of the Number 2 gun of the pair, I've forgotten. He sold the cased AYA to his good friend Henry Kaufman a couple of years later.

Beretta S03EL Over/Under in 12-gauge, #30691: Purchased in July 1966, this gun replaced Jack's Model 21 as his favorite pheasant gun for a few years, primarily because it weighed just 7 pounds. It had a 26-inch barrel choked quarter choke/modified, auto ejectors, single selective trigger, and a straight grip and was cased in an oak-and-leather fitted case. This was a handsome gun, just one grade beneath Beretta's top sidelock models at the time. In the United States this would have been called an S04 grade. I had an S05 about this time, and Jack and I, being of similar height and build, suffered bruised cheeks from the sharp continental-style combs on these guns. After we rounded the combs somewhat, they were more comfortable to shoot. But I still could not shoot skeet with mine satisfactorily, so I sold it. Jack eventually gave his to Bradford, who still has it.

Beretta Model 450 EL Sidelock Double in 12-gauge, #C71741: In 1968 Jack bought this top-grade Beretta with two sets of barrels (28-inch modified/full and 26-inch improved cylinder/modified), cased in oak and leather with an overcase. He considered it the highest-quality shotgun he ever owned. About 1975, Jack broke the buttstock and had it replaced with a duplicate by Boise master gunmaker George Hoenig. Henry Kaufman accompanied Jack on his last pheasant hunt, at Pheasant Valley Preserve in late 1977, and remembers Jack using this gun that afternoon. In October 1992, Henry Kaufman hosted the last of the traditional O'Connor memorial hunts at Pheasant Valley Preserve. Brad used his father's Beretta on the hunt and made some nice shots, which we caught on film.

AYA Model XXVSL Sidelock in 12-gauge, No. 1: #279729; No. 2: #279730: Jack received this cased matched pair of sidelock guns in August 1968. Being Churchill copies, they had 25-inch barrels choked improved cylinder/modified and modified/full with the narrow Churchill-style rib. Jack was very fond of these guns and probably used them on a Winchester dove shoot in Arizona and possibly in Mexico. They are still owned by the family.

Winchester Model 21 in 20-gauge, #W31512: In 1971 Jack was selected by over 5,000 outdoor writers as Outdoorsman of the Year and was presented this shotgun by Winchester to mark his achievement. It had 26-inch barrels choked improved cylinder/modified, a straight-grip stock with checkered butt, and Jack's initials on a gold toe plate. The gun came with a leather trunk case. Jack was very proud of this gun but did not use it much. It was part of his estate, but was sold out of the family later on.

PART III: HANDGUNS

It will come as a surprise to some younger O'Connor fans to learn that Jack owned and used several handguns during his life. What's more, he wrote about them, however sparingly. His first "Arms & Ammunition" departmental piece for *Outdoor Life* devoted to the handgun was entitled "Dope on the Mysterious 38's and What Fodder To Use in Them" and appeared in August 1947. His last handgun writing was a short review of the then-new Browning Medalist International competition .22 pistol in October 1970 for his column "Getting the Range." In between were reviews on eleven new handguns, from the S&W K-22 model in 1948 to the Colt Gold Cup .38 Special in 1966.

Major handgun articles started in 1948 with an excellent one on the basics of pistol shooting. In it Jack recommended .22 handgun practice as an inexpensive way of learning good centerfire rifle technique. As a certified pistol instructor for many years, I can vouch for the quality of advice given in this article. Later, in 1954, Jack did a similar piece called "Beginning with a Handgun." Perhaps his best handgun writing was in a 1952 "Arms & Ammunition" piece called "The Handgun's a Barrel of Fun."

The first handgun Jack fired was a Colt Single Action .45 when he was a kid. The next was a Model 1911 .45 Auto when he was in military service. Jack considered the handgun fun to take on family picnics to plink with, handy to pot small game with on big-game hunts, but not a primary arm for taking big game. Of course, times were different then; scope-sighted handguns were barely on the scene when Jack passed away, and very few states allowed big-game handgun hunting, much less provided special seasons for it, as is the case today.

One of Jack's early accounts of the handgun's utility had to do with a hunt he and a friend made in Arizona's White Mountains in 1925. They had brought meat for the first night and the next day but planned to live off the land after that. Their quest for mule deer, turkeys, and bears was eventually successful, but not before they'd subsisted for the first ten days on Abert's squirrels plinked with a Colt Police Positive Target Model .22 Jack had brought along.

Handguns Jack owned and enjoyed using included two Colt Officer Models in .22 and .38 Special, an S&W Military & Police .38 Special, an S&W Model 1950 .44 Special, an S&W K-38 and a K-22, and a Colt Officers Model Match .38 Special He spoke of potting blue grouse from trees with his K22 and shooting jack rabbits and cottontails in Arizona with his Colt Officers Model .22. He also admitted to using his Officers Model Colts to entertain and babysit the kids at the old Slade Ranch in Arizona to allow Eleanor a little private fly fishing for trout in nearby streams.

Based on reader mail, Jack perceived *Outdoor Life* readers of his day as being only marginally interested in handguns, so his neglect of the short arms was not entirely due to his preference for rifles. Also, for those *pistolero* fans, there was another writer of the day, one Elmer Keith, who more than made up for Jack's reticence on the subject of the six-gun. Jack was happy to have Elmer hold forth as the king of handgun writers.

Jack's personal preference was for revolvers rather than semiautos because he felt he could shoot better with them. Three of Jack's handguns are described below:

Smith & Wesson K-22, #K19303: After World War II, S&W introduced its new K-Series of match competition revolvers, which were similar to earlier versions with adjustable sights but featured a ribbed barrel. They were made in .22 L.R., .32 S&W Long, and .38 Special calibers. The first of these, all K-22 models, were available 3 December 1946 and began with number K101. According to S&W records, this revolver was shipped to Jack in Tucson 6 May 1948. He had reviewed the revolver the month before in *Outdoor Life*'s "Getting the Range" column.

Upon Jack's death, this revolver and his K-38 were sold from the estate to a family friend. Within a few years, Idaho dealer George Douglass, a friend of mine, had them for sale. I bought them from him in 1985, and in 1991 had Marvin Huey make a case for the pair, which I thought would help keep the guns together in future years.

Smith & Wesson K-38, #K79386: The first K-38 revolvers were for sale 9 June 1947, beginning at serial number K1161. In 1950, beginning with number K75000, a wider-ribbed barrel was available in the .32 and .38 revolvers, which brought all three K models closer together in total weight—a real plus in conventional three-gun bull's-eye pistol competition of the day. This K-38 was one of the wide-ribbed models with a wide target-style hammer spur and experimental factory oversize grips. It was shipped from the factory 20 January 1950 to Jack at Lewiston, Idaho. He reviewed the gun in the May issue of *Outdoor Life*.

After purchasing this gun, as mentioned earlier, I found it to be exceptionally accurate. I used it in the spring of 1986 to take a big Utah cougar, which claimed an award from the North American Hunting Club for the largest taken with a handgun that year.

Colt National Match .38 Special, #4874-MR: Jack reviewed this semiauto match pistol, designed as a mate for Colt's renowned Gold Cup .45 auto, in February 1966. Jack's friend Henry Kaufman, who later purchased the gun, thinks Jack bought it with intentions of doing some local indoor shooting with it. That never happened. When I acquired the gun a few years ago, it was still like new and a very accurate shooter.

The whereabouts of any of Jack's other handguns are not known.

12

Eleanor

"Her dreams had all returned the same,
Swinging along the homebound track,
Just empties coming back."

Angelo De Poinciano

On the first day of October in 1927, a young woman stepped from a Southern Pacific passenger train to a dusty depot platform. As she stood there, she felt herself being buffeted by a hot west wind. She could literally feel her skin drying out. Behind her a young man cursed as he wrestled with their luggage. Back in her home state of Missouri, fall was already in the air with crystal days and crisp nights. Here there were only yellow sun-baked hills with an occasional juniper tree and the unceasing wind. She glanced up at the words on the weathered sign on the depot roof: Alpine, Texas. What had she done?

The young woman was the former Miss Eleanor Barry. Back in Missouri, her family was a prosperous one. But she had turned her back on a life of ease and privilege and the prospect of marriage into another well-to-do family to elope with a young, smart-aleck, soon-to-be English professor. Her family had resented this audacious young man from the hick state of Arizona almost from the beginning. His proposal had consisted of a telegram to Eleanor in July of 1927 at a Colorado dude ranch where she was spending part of the summer. It had read: "Got job. Alpine, Texas. $3,600 a year. Why wait? Love, J.O'C." A short two months later, the vivacious young woman had become the new Mrs. Jack O'Connor. Their honeymoon had consisted of a jolting, crematorium-hot, three-day ride in the upper berth of a train from Missouri to Alpine. There had been no traditional wedding ceremony, few gifts, and no encouragement from family and friends. Now there was no turning back.

The newlyweds settled into a rented small frame house on Holland Avenue. By the time they had arrived in Alpine, the fall semester at Sul Ross State Teachers College where Jack was to teach was already under way. Therefore, the next day after hitting town, Jack was off to his duties as associate professor of English at the school.

Eleanor's husband Jack was a cauldron of energy and natural curiosity. During that first fall in Alpine, he came home each day with new stories about his classes, students, other activities at the college, and various new people he had met about town. Jack enjoyed life greatly. Soon he was full of plans for hiking, camping, hunts for quail and deer, and even plans for an antelope hunt far to the south across the border in Chihuahua, Mexico. By nature a very hard worker, he was also confident to the point of arrogance. Since Alpine was not unlike much of his native Arizona, Jack was quickly very much at home.

Eleanor, on the other hand, was in a state of cultural and geographic shock. She was hundreds of miles from her native Missouri. Five years younger than Jack, she lacked his inherent buoyancy and confidence. She was by nature not gregarious or a "joiner." With no car, little money, and no friends, the long fall days of 1927 weighed heavily on her. She began to shrink from life.

It marked the beginnings of emotional, psychological, and behavioral patterns that would follow her for the rest of her life. And she had one other very dark secret. Eleanor was an alcoholic.

216

Eleanor also had a relatively fragile emotional make-up and probably suffered significantly from mental depression for her entire life. So, even considering the fact that she was very much in love with Jack (and remained so for the rest of her life), it is not too difficult to see that, for the young Eleanor, in a strange place, away from family and friends, and alone for a great part of the time, the long road that lay ahead in 1927 may not have looked too bright.

The O'Connors lived in Alpine from October of 1927 until the spring of 1931. Jack then accepted a job with Arizona State Teachers College in Flagstaff where they lived from 1931 until the fall of 1934.

It was during these periods that Jack began to acquaint Eleanor with his world of guns and hunting. Jack had a wonderful habit of wanting to share his own enjoyable experiences with those he loved and cared about. To teach Eleanor to shoot and hunt was as natural to him as breathing. There is no way of knowing just how agreeably Eleanor may have taken to these avocations in the very beginning. She may well have thought that, if she was going to be truly a part of her husband's life, she had damned well better take up his hobbies.

Of course, as would become very evident in Jack's writings in later years, Eleanor indeed became a very good rifle shot and an even better wing shot, despite the fact that as Jack commented on several occasions that "She can hardly tell one gun from another!"

However grudging it may have been at the onset, Eleanor's willingness to learn her husband's passionate pastimes was a very wise decision, for it would give the couple some of their best times and happiest moments, from Arizona quail to African elephants.

The years in Flagstaff were the hardest ones for the O'Connors from an economic standpoint. Their first son, Jerry, had been born in Texas in 1930. A second son, Bradford, followed in 1933. Although Eleanor never worked outside the home, her roles as homemaker and mother kept her very busy during those years. It was during this period that it began to be evident that the burdens of everyday life rested heavily on Eleanor's shoulders.

In the fall of 1934, Jack accepted a position at the University of Arizona in Tucson. By this time, Jack's freelance writing career was really beginning to blossom. He was always in motion, teaching, writing, planning hunts, his head filled with projects and ideas. Eleanor began increasingly to feel that she was on the sidelines watching Jack as he lived his own exciting and interesting life.

For reasons that need not be mentioned, 1937 and 1938 were years of sadness, anger, and marital strife for Jack and Eleanor, so much so that they considered divorce. For Eleanor's part in this, she would never forgive herself. It proved to be yet another burden that she would carry forever.

The couple's first daughter, Cathy, was born in 1938. It has been stated that the baby was a result of the O'Connors' decision to reconcile. In 1939, their second daughter and last child, Caroline, was born. The fact that five years separated Jerry and Brad from Cathy and Caroline created its own set of parenting burdens that would also wear heavily on Eleanor. Also, in the early 1940s, the strange behavior and personality of her eldest son, Jerry, brought still another emotional strain to bear on her.

Because Eleanor was such a private person and bore her anger and hurt silently and sought solace from it increasingly in bouts of drinking, there is little in the way of reliable information about her from a diagnostic sense. Therefore, a certain amount of subjectivity is necessary to comment on her life at all. What is apparent is that, through the 1940s and 1950s, Jack's growing fame and notoriety became increasingly difficult for Eleanor to cope with mentally and emotionally.

It was mentioned earlier that Eleanor apparently had a tendency to be depressed, lacked focus and discipline, and was emotionally fragile as well. For her to be juxtaposed to a life partner in Jack who was ultra-focused, very disciplined, mentally tough, and upbeat must have made her plight seem all the more futile.

In her defense, Eleanor never had the benefits of the diagnostic skills, counseling, and treatment expertise of today's medical field. She apparently had a chemical disposition toward alcohol. This would mean that, in a medical sense, she was an alcoholic whether she ever had a drink or not.

Eleanor's anger and resentment over Jack's success reached perhaps its zenith when Jack embarked on his second African safari in January of 1958. It triggered a bout of depression and drinking on her part that was the most serious to that time. From then on and for various reasons, Eleanor accompanied Jack on almost all of his significant hunts.

In conclusion, it is perhaps most correct to say that Eleanor was a talented, creative, beautiful woman who, in other circumstances, *might* have done much with her own life had this life not been spent in the long and sometimes oppressive shadow of Jack. Of course, there is no way of knowing for sure how her life might have developed had she indeed had the opportunity of playing her own hand. With her apparent problems of depression and lack of discipline and focus, coupled with her drinking, there is no guarantee that a life of her own crafting would have necessarily been a successful one.

On the other hand, it was not Jack's fault that his personality was so forceful and dynamic. Almost certainly he had no intention of stifling Eleanor in any manner. No blame should attach itself to Jack because of his personality, drive, and talents. That Jack was very aware of Eleanor's plight is evident in the fact that his praise of her grew even more profuse and glowing in his writings after 1959 when Eleanor accompanied him on her first safari to Africa.

Perhaps the most gentle and yet the most correct thing that could be said is that she simply had a hard time with life.

13

Thoughts on Jack

> *"I wanted to do things I was interested in.*
> *I wanted to hunt and travel in faraway places.*
> *I wanted to wear good clothes and rise above the mob."*

Jack O'Connor—private letter to family member in March 1964

I commented in the introduction to this book that I hoped readers would emerge from it with a better understanding of and a newfound or enhanced respect for the man who was Jack O'Connor. Now, at the conclusion of the book's writing, I feel that my wish for its readers has come to pass to a great degree for me as well.

I have essentially refrained from making any "leaps of faith" about O'Connor in terms of his personality, inner thoughts, dreams, ambitions, frustrations, or failures.

Hundreds of hours of reading, crosschecking, researching, and plain digging have gone into this work. To that can be added many dozens of interviews and telephone conversations with O'Connor family members, old friends, and other fans. I might also say that I have talked in depth with O'Connor supporters and detractors alike.

I am somewhat sad to say that Jack O'Connor has remained an enigma to the end. And it is only after what I feel has been an honest and sincere effort to learn everything possible about this talented man and a great deal of thought on my part that I will venture a few subjective comments.

By the time Jack was a precocious fourth-grader at age ten, he was well on his way to being a snob. He read brilliantly well and was an excellent student, although he was smaller and younger than almost everyone else in his classes. He also began at a very early age to look down on other students around him and to see them more or less as bumpkins. His somewhat superior attitude cost him many a cut lip and bloody nose. But let it here be said that little Jack never shrank from a fight.

Between his maternal grandfather, James Wiley Woolf, and his paternal uncle, Jim O'Connor, the fatherless boy had two very loving and strong surrogate father figures. Both were of an agnostic persuasion, although each was the kindest and most benevolent of men. It was doubtlessly from them that Jack gained his earliest agnostic leanings.

His Uncle Jim was perhaps the most demonstrative of the two and probably had the most influence on young Jack. Jim O'Connor was a keen student of human nature and passed this trait on to the boy. Both his Grandfather Woolf and Uncle Jim were also cynics by nature, albeit good-naturedly so. Taking his boyhood cues from the two men who meant so much to him, Jack began rather early to have a rather low opinion of mankind in general. However, unlike his grandfather and uncle, Jack's opinion about John Q. Public would develop, especially in his later years, into one of near-disgust. This opinion would remain more or less unchanged for the rest of his life.

By the time of World War I, Jack had become an avid reader and follower of the writings of H. L. Mencken. Mencken was a brilliant young newspaper writer, political essayist, and columnist who at the tender age of twenty-six had become the editor of an East Coast newspaper, the *Baltimore Sun*.

Mencken redefined the word cynicism. In his columns he attacked almost every American tradition from preachers to presidents, from the Elks Club to the entertainment industry. Mencken's critiques of the American social and political scenes crackled with bitter wit and dripped biting cynicism. From 1920 until 1930, there was hardly a single American tradition that did not feel the sting of Mencken's bloody literary whip. Most of his venom was directed at what he perceived to be the sorry intellectual state of the average American citizen and the depraved state of the U.S. version of the English language. At first, Mencken was alternately worshipped and reviled. But later he grew wildly popular. Readers couldn't get enough, and Mencken loved giving it to them.

For language-lover and budding cynic O'Connor, H. L. Mencken became the Pied Piper. In Mencken Jack found all the corroboration he would ever need for his own low opinions of the average American working stiff. Increasingly throughout his life, Jack viewed humankind (or at least the U.S. version) as lazy, shortsighted, greedy, and lacking in restraint and dignity. Other events later in his life would galvanize even further Jack's thoughts along these lines. He never changed his mind.

The beginning of the Great Depression in 1930 popped H. L. Mencken like a toy balloon with the American public. Mencken's harpoon that had been so sharp in the giddy 1920s was suddenly out of favor. Americans needed some good news in their lives. They turned in droves to a man who was the journalistic antithesis of Mencken: Will Rogers. But Jack never forgot Mencken and remained a follower all his life (Mencken died in 1956).

Yet another event that hardened Jack's ideas about the public was what he saw as a pseudo-naive, hypocritical reaction to the few words of profanity contained in his first novel, *Conquest*. This criticism hurt O'Connor much more than he ever revealed, and it may have been a part of his reasoning in the decision never to pursue publication of perhaps as many as five other novel manuscripts that he completed between 1927 and 1934.

However, we must fast-forward to the mid-1940s for the final blows that soured Jack on the average citizen. After the war, O'Connor began to receive vast amounts of fan mail as home-from-the-war servicemen began to buy guns and go hunting. At Editor Ray Brown's insistence, *Outdoor Life* ran a monthly advice column on guns and hunting. Every month, Jack answered certain sample questions from readers in this column. *Outdoor Life* expected him to answer them all. As fan mail increased to as many as 3,000 letters per month, this became a backbreaking task. O'Connor later wrote that it required three secretaries and another man to answer them, and then the load simply became impossible. O'Connor grew to resent the hell out of readers' mailed-in questions and his required response, principally because he found a great many of the letters simplistic, dull, and boring. But more than anything, he resented the fact that the great majority of the questions could have been answered with a small amount of research by the letter writers themselves. Although most of them were adoring fans, this was nonetheless further proof to O'Connor (in his mind anyway) that humankind in general was self-serving, lazy, and stupid.

This bitterness reached its zenith in 1971, when he wrote a piece for the 1971 *Gun Digest* titled "Letters to Jim Hack." Jack loosely disguised himself as "Hack," a mythical gun editor. The article contained a large sampling of actual fan letters that he had received over the years. O'Connor claimed that the letters were reprinted just "as he had received them, other than minor editing." Many of the letters were hilarious; others were maddeningly stupid and presumptuous. In truth, if the letters were a proper sample of Jack's fan mail during his career as *Outdoor Life*'s shooting editor (and there's no reason to believe otherwise), it's easy see why he was often exasperated to the point of tearing his hair out by the roots. For anyone wanting to read O'Connor at his most hilarious, the article is well worth the trouble of digging up. It also appeared in Jack's 1977 book, *The Best of Jack O'Connor*.

Was Jack an elitist?

Oh, yeah.

He also hated being patronized. I found this out to my dismay in the early 1970s at a Game Conservation International convention in San Antonio. I asked him a rather mundane question to which I already knew the answer, hoping merely to draw him into a more in-depth conversation. He saw through me like I was cellophane, snorting: "You know the Goddamned answer to that as well as I do!" However, on other occasions, when I asked him questions that intrigued him and to which there were no ready answers, he seemed to appreciate the questions for their own merit and me for broaching them. He was ingratiating and thoughtful, and these questions invariably led to fascinating subsequent conversations. A similar thing happened in my letters to him (I'm afraid I fell into the "Letters to Jim Hack" category myself a time or two). His reply to one particularly numbing letter I wrote him in 1970 cut me off at the shoe tops! I got what I deserved.

Though O'Connor kept his finger on the pulse of his readers and fans extremely well throughout his *Outdoor Life* career, correctly seeing them as a barometer for forecasting trends in the hunting and shooting sports, it is ironic that he often found fans difficult to cope with on an individual basis.

There can be no doubt that O'Connor was an intellectual bully. I have read many hundreds of his private letters in the course of work on this book. In correspondence with individuals whom he deemed beneath him, he occasionally ripped them to shreds. This was almost always done very subtly. In fact, one often has to read between the lines to see these put-downs, but they're there. On the other hand, in correspondence with friends or others whom he considered his intellectual equal, O'Connor was the best of pen pals—engaging, witty, and obviously very sincere. Some of those with whom O'Connor maintained long-running correspondence were H.I.H. Prince Abdorreza Pahlavi, Les Bowman, Oscar Brooks, Angus Cameron, Herb Klein, Jay Mellon, George W. Parker, Colonel Harry M. Snyder, Robert Chatfield-Taylor, Bill Ruger, and Jack's great long-time pal and perhaps the letter-writing champ of all time, fellow sheep hunter John H. Batten.

Jack was always absorbed with money. He had great admiration for families or individuals who had "old money." He watched these people with a great deal of interest to see how they lived and how, where, and on what they spent their money. As Jack's reputation grew, he made more and more wealthy friends. He relished these friendships.

He had a similar fascination with self-made men. He envied those who had the nerve to put their dreams into action, pouring all their energy and hopes into their plans. He looked with equal wonder at men with the courage to put their money—all of it, as well as all they could borrow—on the line for something they believed in completely. And although Jack certainly trusted himself completely, this trust never really manifested itself in a manner that would have given him the courage to take significant calculated business risks. Given O'Connor's intelligence and foresight, such risks in all likelihood would have paid off handsomely. Jack inherently was just too frugal and conservative for such risks (he would have called them "gambles"), no matter how well they might have been thought out. It is my belief that in a way he despised himself for this.

Several of Jack's best and oldest friends were self-made men. Herb Klein, the Texas oil tycoon (as Jack called him), drilled dry wells right and left and was down to his last marble before he hit a big strike. Scope maker Bill Weaver and arms manufacturer Bill Ruger were men who seemingly flew by the seat of their pants. But their thinking and planning were sound. Ditto for Roy Weatherby, whom Jack admired greatly despite occasional spats. Jack stood by and watched such men and their successes with open-mouthed wonder and something of a "why can't I do that?" attitude.

Another Jack trait was his habit of flat-out asking certain people how much money they made. This was, of course, a ridiculously rude question. In O'Connor's case, it would appear that he asked the question merely to see how his earnings and overall financial situation stacked up against those of others (which was still no excuse).

My limited commentary about Eleanor O'Connor in this book is out of respect for Nancy J. Lewis's excellent profile of Eleanor that appears in the 2000 edition of *Arizona Wildlife Trophies*. I should say further that Jack and Eleanor loved each other with a rare passion all their lives. As difficult as this is to picture for a hardened Jack fan, Ol' Mr. .270 and the trim, vivacious Eleanor would frequently move the furniture aside in their living room on Saturday nights and dance to the music of "The Lawrence Welk Show" on television.

Jack O'Connor worked very, very hard all his life. He was a dedicated college professor who tried hard to stimulate and motivate his students. He was always involved in all manner of college activities and committees and was an impeccable citizen.

Outdoor Life could never have paid O'Connor what he was worth to the magazine. He was honest to a fault, adhering steadily to the truth as he saw it in his writings. He never misrepresented any product and couldn't be compromised. It's a pretty safe bet that Jack never had a guilty conscience in his entire professional life.

He was devoted to his family and tried hard to relate to each of them in a special way, although he could be eccentric and ornery as hell about a lot of things. But aren't we all?

He never lost his unwavering vitality and curiosity about life, remaining until the very end an incurable romantic filled with grumpy energy and plans for future adventures.

We'll not see his like again.

Epilogue

I spent some time in Lewiston, Idaho, in the fall of 1999. I wanted to soak up some of the atmosphere of the town that was Jack's home from the summer of 1948 until his death in 1978. One of the places I particularly wanted to visit was Lolo Sporting Goods in downtown Lewiston. Because Jack had no federal firearms license, guns sent to him for testing arrived at Lolo Sporting Goods. Jack would pick them up, test them, and report the results, as well as his thoughts on the new products, in the pages of *Outdoor Life*. Then, because he refused to be obliged to anyone, he would periodically rebox such guns and bring then down to Lolo to be sent back to the makers. Jack also bought loading components at Lolo and occasionally held court there.

I ventured there with two of Jack's old friends, Eldon Buckner and Henry Kaufman, on a dreary morning during the first week of November. Despite the ultra-modern rifles, bullets, powders, and loading equipment, it still seemed that time had stopped in the old, high-ceilinged store—almost as if everything was in suspense awaiting Jack's return. From a framed 8x10 photograph on the wall behind the counter, a somber, raingear-clad Jack stared out at any customer who dared make eye contact.

But Jack wasn't coming back. The reverie of several moments was broken when the front door clanged open. A

6' 3" college-aged kid on in-line skates rolled into the old store—headphones in his ears, tape player on his belt, stubbly beard, and earrings. He made a quick, disinterested pass around the shelves holding the primers, brass, and reloading presses and was gone as quickly as he had come. Maybe it was better that Jack had not lived to see such irreverence for the world he had known so well.

I thought about it for a moment. If Jack were here today, what would he think of this computer-mouse, internet, on-line-trading, warp-speed world of ours? Would he still be clacking angrily away on his old manual Underwood, bemoaning the sorry state of humanity and cussing the world in general? What would he think of the Rollerblade kid?

But Jack himself had been a hell-raiser in his college days, with a strong sense of irreverence all his own. Even so, his sense of style, restraint, and a certain crusty dignity had been ever with him.

As the in-line kid rolled out the front door, I took a peek at Jack in the picture and found myself wondering what he would have thought.

JACK O'CONNOR: A CHRONOLOGY

by Eldon "Buck" Buckner

1902 January 22   John Woolf O'Connor born at Nogales, Arizona Territory, to Andrew John and Ida Florence O'Connor.

1905 December 23   Jack's sister, Helen Virginia O'Connor, born.

1907   Parents divorce. Jack, Helen, and Ida O'Connor initially live in two tents on a large lot in Tempe, owned and occupied by Ida's father, James Wiley Woolf, and her mother.

1911   Receives first gun—Iver Johnson single-shot 20-gauge—from Grandfather Woolf.

1912   Bags first big game (javelina) on Uncle Jim O'Connor's ranch southeast of Florence, Arizona. Arizona Territory achieves statehood.

1913   Spends summer with Uncle Jim O'Connor in Florence, Arizona.

1914   Shoots first deer on Uncle Jim's desert ranch at age 12.

1915   Enters academic department of Tempe Normal and takes military drill (Arizona National Guard). Pancho Villa poses with Jack for photographs at Nogales, Sonora. Grandfather James Wiley Woolf dies at age 68.

1916   Buys his first Savage Model 99 in .250-3000; Pancho Villa raids Columbus, New Mexico.

1917 December 3   Enlists at age 15 in U.S. Army, 150th Infantry Regiment, Camp Kearney, California. Uncle Jim O'Connor dies.

1918 January 18   Receives discharge from army on medical disability, due to chronic pulmonary tuberculosis.

1919 Spring   Graduates from Tempe Normal academics (high school).

Summer   Works in Sinaloa, Mexico, for an uncle as a meat hunter instead of the truck driver he was hired to be.

Fall   Enlists in U.S. Navy, serves as hospital corpsman on U.S.S. *Arkansas.*

1920   Sails on naval cruise to Hawaiian Islands.

1921 January   Crosses equator on naval cruise to Chile.

July   Receives discharge from U.S. Navy.

1921	September	Enrolls at Tempe Normal using funds earned from financing shipboard gamblers in navy.
1922		Attends Tempe Normal; is member of tennis team and participates in school drama productions; is president of "N Club."
1923	Spring	Completes two-year course at Tempe Normal.
	Fall	Enrolls at University of Arizona, Tucson. Shoots his first Arizona Coues deer in Catalina Mountains.
1924	Spring	Completes his junior year at University of Arizona.
	Summer	Works at Ray Consolidated Mines.
	Fall	Enrolls at University of Arkansas and pledges Sigma Chi Fraternity.
1925	June 15	Receives B.A. degree in banking & finance from University of Arkansas and returns to Tempe; receives G&H Springfield Sporter as graduation gift from a well-to-do uncle.
	Summer &Fall	Buys a Winchester Model 54 in brand-new .270 Winchester caliber and uses it in the White Mountains and Kaibab Reserve that fall on mule deer and black bear; goes to work for *Chicago Tribune* as cub reporter.
1926	September	Enrolls in graduate school at University of Missouri, Columbia, in English after becoming disillusioned with newspaper work.
	September 16	Meets Eleanor Bradford Barry, an 18-year-old sophomore and his future wife, at a mixer dance.
1927	June	Receives M.A. in journalism from University of Missouri.
	July	Accepts position as associate professor of English at Sul Ross State Teachers College, Alpine, Texas.
	September 10	Elopes with Eleanor and moves to Alpine, Texas. In addition to teaching, works as an Associated Press correspondent on the side.
1928	Spring	Buys Eleanor a Winchester Model 57 in .22 caliber and teaches her to shoot.
	Summer	Travels to Arizona, where Eleanor meets Jack's family and sees natural wonders such as the Grand Canyon.
	September	Eleanor diagnosed with tuberculosis and enters sanatorium at El Paso, Texas.

1928	Fall	Hunts in Chihuahua, Mexico, and takes a black bear and deer on one trip and antelope on another.
1929	Summer	Completes his first novel, *Conquest*, and sells it to Harper & Brothers Publishers.
	December	Eleanor is released from sanatorium at El Paso.
1930		*Conquest* is published just in time for the Great Depression and becomes one of the controversial novels of the day, banned by the El Paso library.
	November 23	First son, Gerald Barry, is born in Alpine, Texas.
1931	Spring	Resigns from Sul Ross faculty and accepts position with Arizona State Teachers College at Flagstaff (now Northern Arizona University) as professor of English and public-relations agent.
	September	Moves to 210 E. Dale Street in Flagstaff. Sells his first outdoor article, "Rifles and Cartridges for Southwestern Game," to *Sports Afield* for $12.50.
	November	Eleanor kills her first deer, a large buck, in the Kaibab Forest.
1932	Fall	Kills a big buck in the Kaibab, hunting from Jack Butler's Moquitch Camp; salary is cut from $2,500 per annum to $2,250 as the Depression worsens.
1933		Salary is again reduced, to $2,000 per year.
	June 3	Second son, Bradford Clare O'Connor, is born in Flagstaff.
1934	May	*Outdoor Life* publishes its first O'Connor article, titled "Arizona's Antelope Problem."
	August	Moves his family to Tucson after accepting position at University of Arizona as associate professor of journalism at $2,400 per year.
	October	Has short story "With Bells On" published in *Redbook*; has his first custom rifle built, a Sukalle-Minar Springfield .30-06.
	Fall	Shoots a record Coues deer on his first hunt in Sonora, Mexico, on Sierra Azul, 40 miles east of Imuris; with student Arthur C. Popham, kills bucks in the Kaibab Forest at Thanksgiving.
	December	Makes his first desert-sheep hunt at El Union Mine in Sierra del Viejo, Sonora, Mexico, and is unsuccessful; Grandmother Woolf dies in Tempe.

1935	August	With Arthur Popham, hunts desert sheep in western Sonora, guided by Charlie Ren. Art Popham is successful.
	September	Takes his first desert bighorn ram in western Sonora while hunting with José del Rosario.
	November	The O'Connors and Arthur Popham hunt elk on the Mogollon Rim during Arizona's first season.
	December	Hunts Coues deer at southern end of the Cucurpi Mountains in Sonora with Eleanor and her father and other friends,.
1936	Summer	Travels to New York City with Eleanor; meets with editors of the major outdoor magazines.
	October	Collects buck and doe antelope specimens from Anderson Mesa for Arizona State Museum at Tucson.
	December 7	Contracts with Ray Brown, *Outdoor Life* editor, for 18 articles over next 12 months for $2,700, which enables Jack to take a one-year sabbatical from teaching.
1937	Fall	Moves into the house formerly owned by his Grandmother Woolf in Tempe for the sabbatical year. Writes, finishing his second novel, *Boom Town*. In Arizona, Jack and Eleanor successfully hunt the Kaibab Forest for mule deer, and do a lot of quail hunting on the lower Verde River. In Sonora the O'Connors hunt Rancho El Datil, owned by the Aguirre family, for white-tailed deer.
	December	Bags a desert bighorn ram on a windy day near the Sea of Cortez with his 7x57.
1938	January	Bags two mule deer and a Coues whitetail in Sonora and observes the Arizona buffalo shoot in Houserock Valley.
	Spring	Makes his last hunt with Charlie Ren, taking a ram in the San Francisco Mountains of Sonora with his Minar Springfield. Charlie Ren dies shortly afterward.
	June	Moves to a cabin in Oak Creek Canyon to escape Tempe's summer heat.
	August 17	First daughter, Catherine Clare, is born in Flagstaff while the family is staying at Oak Creek.
	August 30	Writes the Coues-deer chapter for the Boone and Crockett Club's 1939 book.

1938	September	*Boom Town* is published by Alfred A. Knopf. Finishes work on his first hunting book, *Game in the Desert*. The O'Connors return to Tucson, where Jack resumes teaching at University of Arizona.
1939	Summer	Injures right hand when a broken firing pin in his old G&H Springfield causes an accidental discharge, demolishing the rifle.
	October 4	Second daughter, Caroline Ann, is born in Tucson. Serves as toastmaster at the annual Arizona Game Protective Association convention at Prescott. *Game in the Desert* is published by Derrydale Press in a limited edition of 950 copies.
	November	Column "Getting the Range" first appears in *Outdoor Life*.
	December	Hunts Coues deer in the Cucurpi Mountains of Sonora with friends Carroll Lemon and Frank Seibold and takes a three-antlered buck—the first Coues deer he ever shot with a .270.
1940	September	University of Arizona salary is raised to $2,500 per year.
	December	Andy O'Connor, Jack's father, dies at age 67 in Hawaii, where he worked as a customs agent.
1941	June	Chosen to replace Major Charles Askins as arms & ammunition editor of *Outdoor Life* at a salary of $200 per month.
	December 31	Takes the best desert mule deer trophy of his life while hunting with Eleanor near the Sonora coast.
1942	Summer	The O'Connor family spends the first of several summer vacations at the Slade Ranch cabin, a secluded cow camp in the White Mountains of Arizona near Greer.
	September	Annual salary as University of Arizona professor is increased to $2,600.
1943	Summer	*Outdoor Life* sends Jack on his first hunting trip to the Canadian Rockies of Alberta and British Columbia for new story material. Shoots his first and second Rocky Mountain bighorn sheep. Outfitter-guide is Roy Hargreaves.
	Fall	Salary at University of Arizona is raised to $2,730.

1944	September	Takes his third (and last) Rocky Mountain bighorn ram while on a mixed-bag hunt with outfitter Ernie Miller in Wyoming.
1945	March 3	Resigns from University of Arizona in favor of full-time gun-editor position with *Outdoor Life*.
1945	Summer	Takes his second pack trip for *Outdoor Life* and shoots three Dall rams and other game in the Yukon Territory, outfitted by the Jacquot Bros. *Hunting in the Southwest* is published by Alfred A. Knopf.
1946	Fall	With Dr. Wilson DuComb, makes a long pack trip in northern British Columbia for Stone sheep, outfitted by Frank Golata. Jack takes three rams, thus completing three Grand Slams of sheep on this trip.
	November	Shoots his last desert bighorn ram in the Los Mochos range of Sonora.
	December	Hunts Sonora for white-tailed and mule deer with his sons, Jerry and Brad.
1947	Spring	Shoots his last javelina while hunting with son Brad north of Sasabe.
	Fall	Hunts goats and deer in southwestern British Columbia with Roy Weatherby, Art Popham, and several others.
	December	Arranges hunt for N. Myles Brown in Sonora for desert sheep and helps guide for a week. Fourth book, *Hunting in the Rockies*, is published by Alfred A. Knopf.
1948	July	The O'Connors move from Tucson to Lewiston, Idaho, to escape Arizona's postwar population boom.
	Fall	Goes on his first pheasant hunt with Vernon Speer near Caldwell, Idaho.
1949	Fall	With son Brad and Vernon Speer, goes on Idaho's first sage-grouse hunt south of Caldwell. Takes a grizzly on his second trip to the Yukon. Fifth book, *The Rifle Book*, is published by Alfred A. Knopf.
1950	August	Takes his largest-ever Dall ram on Pilot Mountain, Yukon Territory.
	September	Makes a long shot of 485 steps while hunting antelope near Gillette, Wyoming.

1950	Fall	Bags a bull elk in Idaho's Selway area.
1951	January 29	*Outdoor Life* raises salary to $12,500 per year plus $55 per week for secretarial help.
	September	With Brad, Vernon Speer, and Doc Braddock, Jack hunts the Atlin, British Columbia, area; Brad gets a medal-winning caribou and a Stone ram.
1952	Fall	With Vernon Speer and Doc Braddock, hunts antelope near Gillette, Wyoming. Sixth book, *The Big Game Rifle*, is published by Alfred A. Knopf.
1953	February	Accompanies Herb Klein on an exotic game hunt on Frank Moss Ranch near Llano, Texas.
	Summer	Goes on his first African safari to Kenya and Tanganyika, with Herb Klein and Red Early, for 90 days and takes many great trophies.
1954	Fall	Goes on successful elk hunt, accompanied by Fred Huntington, founder of RCBS, with outfitter Les Bowman near Cody, Wyoming.
1955	May	Goes on a three-week shikar to India with Lee Sproul; bags a 9' 9" tiger and blackbuck antelope. They then hunt for red sheep and Persian ibex in Iran as guests of Prince Abdorreza Pahlavi.
	Fall	Hunts antelope near Cody, Wyoming, with Lee Sproul, Fred Huntington, and Les Bowman.
1956	May	Takes two Alaskan brown bears and two black bears on Admiralty Island, tipping outfitter Ralph Young with a custom .25-06 rifle.
	August	Goes on a Yukon pack trip, outfitted by Alex Davis, with *Outdoor Life* editor Bill Rae, Red Cole, and Fred Huntington. Shoots a 40¼-inch Dall ram near Prospector Mountain.
	Fall	Shoots bull elk on a hunt from Idaho's Moose Creek Ranch on the Clearwater River, and is accompanied by Fred Huntington.
1957	January 14	Jack and Eleanor are both seriously injured when their 1954 Dodge is struck head-on on an icy road near Rosalia, Washington.
	November 30	Becomes the second recipient of the Weatherby Award, presented by WWII marine fighter ace and South Dakota governor, Joe Foss.

1958	January	Makes his second African safari, to French Equatorial Africa, with Elgin Gates to hunt Sahara game and collects addax, scimitar-horned oryx, dama gazelle, and Barbary sheep trophies.
	July 14	Is issued a desert bighorn permit for Baja, California, good for 90 days, but never goes on the hunt.
	September	Hunts antelope with Brad, Al Biesen, and Doc Wygant near Rawlins, Wyoming. Shoots a 15¼-inch buck.
1959	September & October	Goes on his third safari to Tanganyika with Eleanor (her first safari). John Kingsley-Heath is their professional hunter. On the way, stops in Scotland for driven grouse shooting. On the return trip he is joined in Iran by Herb Klein. They shoot Urial sheep and ibex as Prince Abdorreza's guests.
	November	Meets Elmer Keith for the first time at Winchester's first promotional party and shoot at East Alton, Illinois.
1960	March	Initiates friendly correspondence with Elmer Keith following their meeting the fall before.
	September	Helps arrange part of Prince Abdorreza Pahlavi's marathon hunt in the American West and accompanies him in Wyoming.
	November	With Eleanor, attends the Weatherby Award dinner in California and hunts pheasants in the Sacramento Valley afterward with Fred Huntington.
1961	Summer	Takes Eleanor, daughter Caroline, and Fred Huntington Jr., on a pack trip to the Alberta Rockies and finds little game. Eleanor shoots a goat, and young Huntington bags a record-book elk.
	Winter	Attends the Winchester gunwriters' bash in Illinois and shoots ducks and pheasants. *The Complete Book of Rifles and Shotguns* and *The Big Game Animals of North America* are published by *Outdoor Life*.
1962		Gunwriter Townsend Whelen, admired by O'Connor, dies at 84.
	Summer	With Eleanor, visits the Scandinavian countries, then joins Fred Huntington and Dr. Sib West for a 30-day safari in Mozambique, followed by a 14-day

safari in Angola. Safari was arranged by Bob Lee; Harry Manners and Count Werner von Alvensleben were two of the professional hunters.

1962	August 1	Ida Woolf O'Connor, Jack's mother, dies at age 88.
1963	Spring	With Eleanor and Robert Chatfield-Taylor, hunts for bears off southeast Alaska from outfitter Ralph Young's boat. Chatfield-Taylor gets a brown bear, Eleanor a black, but Jack doesn't connect.
	July	Addition to Jack's trophy room is completed.
	August	Eleanor shoots a huge Dall ram (44¼ inches) while on a mixed-bag pack trip in the western Yukon with Jack, Bill Ruger, Lenard Brownell, and Bob Chatfield-Taylor.
	November	Shoots quail with his friend Jim Rikhoff during Winchester's annual party at Riverview Plantation near Camella, Georgia.
	December 23	Boone and Crockett Club invites Jack to serve on Judges Panel for 1963 Awards. *Outdoor Life* publishes *Jack O'Connor's Big Game Hunts*.
1964	Spring	Eleanor appears on TV show *To Tell The Truth*.
	Summer	The O'Connors visit friends in Mexico City, where Jack observes Mexicans shooting moving targets at 300 meters.
	September	Eleanor gets her first bull elk near Cody, Wyoming.
	November	Shoots his best Idaho elk while hunting at Dave Christensen's Moose Creek Ranch in the Selway with Eleanor and Ray Speer.
1965	February	On a 30-day shikar in India with John and Katy Batten, Eleanor bags two tigers, nilgai, and axis deer with her .30-06 while Jack collects a tiger with his .375 magnum. They also visit Iran and London on this trip.
	Fall	The O'Connors hunt elk at Moose Creek Ranch in Idaho with Bob Chatfield-Taylor; travel to New York in November; shoot geese in Maryland; then fly to San Francisco to meet Prince Abdorreza and attend the Weatherby Awards party. They also visit Florence, Arizona, while doing some quail hunting. *The Shotgun Book* is published by Alfred A. Knopf, while *Outdoor Life* brings out *The Complete Book of Shooting*, co-authored by Dunlap, Kerr, and Cooper.

1966	July & August	After traveling in Ireland, Belgium, and Germany, takes Eleanor on his sixth safari, to Bechuanaland (Botswana) with Mr. & Mrs. Richard Harris; John Kingsley-Heath is their professional hunter. They spend time in Madrid, Spain, on their way home.
	October	With Eleanor, makes a trip to Alberta to hunt pheasants, Hungarian partridge, and sharp-tailed grouse on Alva Bair's ranch.
	November	The O'Connors travel to Patagonia, Arizona, to hunt Mearns quail with Wendell Swank, director of Arizona Game and Fish Dept., and Jack Mantle, a game commissioner.
1967	August	With Eleanor, Brad, and their friend Frank Baker, hunts British Columbia's Cassiars with John Creyke-Dennis; all collect Stone sheep.
	October	With Eleanor, spends a week in southern Alberta bird hunting, then hunts pheasants near Twin Falls, Idaho.
	November & December	The O'Connors attend Winchester's annual bash in Italy, then travel to Spain to visit Spanish gunmakers and shoot driven red-leg partridge as guests of Nicholas Franco. *The Art of Hunting Big Game in North America* is published by Alfred A. Knopf.
1968	August	With Eleanor, goes on a poorly outfitted pack trip in British Columbia, where Eleanor catches grayling to eat and shoots the only game—a caribou.
	September	The O'Connors travel to London, spend a day at the Holland & Holland shooting school, meet up with *Gun Digest* editor John Amber and Winchester's Jim Rikhoff, and travel to northern Scotland for red stag stalking and rough-shooting for red grouse.
	December 21	With Eleanor, travels to Monaco, where they meet Prince Rainier and Princess Grace and take Werner von Alvensleben to an expensive luncheon. Jerry O'Connor dies in Las Cruces, New Mexico.
1969	Summer	With Eleanor and Bradford, goes on safari to Zambia, where they all shoot elephant and Jack takes his best lion.

1969	Fall	The O'Connors visit Dale Prior's ranch near Ingram, Texas, where Eleanor shoots a blackbuck and a Corsican ram and Jack takes a Corsican ram. At Remington's gunwriters' party at the YO Ranch, Jack shoots his first turkey since leaving Arizona. *Horse and Buggy West* is published by Knopf and later considered one of his best efforts.
1970	February	With Eleanor, travels to Mexico City, attends bull-fights, and visits Oscar Brooks, who hosts a duck hunt at Cuernavaca.
	March	Has surgery for severe gallstones and, after recuperating, attends the NRA convention in New Orleans.
	August	With Eleanor, travels to Jasper Park to play golf and enjoy the scenery.
	September	Goes to Phoenix for a Winchester-sponsored dove shoot.
	October & November	The O'Connors and Mr. & Mrs. Richard Harris travel to Italy, then to Iran to hunt ibex and Urial. Afterward the O'Connors go to Spain; Jack shoots a fallow deer on the Pardo Estate.
	December	The O'Connors attend the Weatherby Awards dinner and afterward shoot pheasants on two preserves with Fred Huntington. *The Hunting Rifle* is published by Winchester Press.
1971	January	With Eleanor, travels to Yucatan, Mexico, to hunt for jaguar, oscillated turkey, and curassow.
	May	Travels to New York for a dinner at the 21 Club honoring Prince Abdorreza.
	June	Dr. Jim Flanagan of Ontario, Oregon, hosts the O'Connors on a rock chuck shoot near the Weiser River.
	August	Goes on a successful Stone sheep hunt in British Columbia with Jim Rikhoff and Dick Gray, outfitted by Frank Cook.
	September	Participates in the Arizona dove shoot with Winchester.
	October 1	Takes his first northern whitetail on the Salmon River while hunting with Eleanor and Bradford.
1972	January	Attends Mzuri Safari Club meeting in Reno, Nevada.

1972	February 9	Pete Kuhloff, outdoor writer and Jack's University of Missouri classmate, dies.
		Attends NRA Annual Meeting in Portland, Oregon.
	Spring	Receives 1971 Outdoorsman of the Year Award at a special dinner at the 21 Club in New York City and is presented a Model 21 in 20-gauge double by Jim Rikhoff of Winchester. This party also celebrates his retirement from *Outdoor Life*.
	July	Last column as shooting editor appears in *Outdoor Life*.
	August	With Jim Rikhoff, goes on a 14-day pack trip in the Yukon with Teslin Outfitters. Rikhoff gets a ram, but Jack doesn't.
	September	With Eleanor and Volker Grellman, goes on safari in Southwest Africa (Namibia); Eleanor shoots a 60-inch kudu. Afterward they travel to IWABA in Rhodesia (Zimbabwe) and join Bradford for another safari; PH is Peter Seymour-Smith. They rest up in Rome, Italy.
	November	The O'Connors hunt elk unsuccessfully from Moose Creek Ranch. Attends Weatherby Awards dinner in California.
1973	February	Attends retirement party for Bill Rae, *Outdoor Life* editor, in New York City.
	April 15	Signs initial contract as executive editor of the new *Petersen's Hunting* magazine for three years at $500/month for one story per month plus $9,000-per-year expense account.
	May	Attends Game Conservation International (Game Coin) convention in San Antonio and picks up his Wells-Nelson .458 rifle.
	August	Makes his last sheep hunt, in northern British Columbia with Frank Cook, and shoots his last ram with his favorite Model 70 in .270 caliber.
1974	Spring	Is inducted into the Hunting Hall of Fame during ceremonies held in Memphis, Tennessee, receiving a bronze sculpture from John Batten.
	July	With Eleanor, goes on a European cruise, visits Paris, Vienna, Prague, and the Rhine River, and spends a week in Ireland.

1974	October	*Sheep and Sheep Hunting* is published by Winchester Press and is widely acclaimed.
	November	Goes on a disappointing elk hunt in Colorado.
	December	Undergoes prostate surgery.
1975	May	The O'Connors go on a cruise to Norway, Sweden, Finland, Poland, Denmark, and Scotland.
	September	With Brad, hunts moose out of Watson Lake, Yukon Territory. Last Canadian hunt.
1976	Spring	The O'Connors go on another cruise, after which Eleanor becomes ill with severe pneumonia and is placed on supplemental oxygen at home.
	April 11	Hunts at Pheasant Valley Preserve near LaCrosse, Washington, and shoots eight pheasants.
		Works on his last book, which he tentatively titles "Confessions of a Gun Editor." Two books, *The Best of Jack O'Connor* and *Game in the Desert Revisited,* are published in limited editions by Jim Rikhoff's Amwell Press.
1977	Fall	With his Lewiston friend Henry Kaufman, goes on a combination antelope and white-tailed deer hunt in Montana, guided by Jack Atcheson. Due to arthritis and failing vision caused by cataracts, does not shoot anything but still enjoys the hunt.
1978	January 20	Dies from heart failure aboard the ship *Mariposa* as he and Eleanor return from a cruise to Hawaii.
	July 25	Eleanor dies of emphysema at home in Lewiston.
1984		Sixteenth original book, *The Last Book—Confessions of a Gun Editor*, is published posthumously by Amwell Press.

Selected Bibliography

Jack O'Connor Published Short Stories

"Bucolic Wedding." *Midland,* undisclosed date.
"Easy Mark." *Fiction Parade,* undisclosed date.
"Homecoming." *Mademoiselle,* undisclosed date.
"With Bells On." *Redbook,* October, 1934.

Jack O'Connor Reference Bibliography

O'Connor Collection. Reference Library, Washington State University, Pullman, WA.

O'Connor Family Archives. Bradford O'Connor, Cathy O'Connor, and Caroline O'Connor, Olympia, WA, and Seattle, WA.

Robert M. Anderson Collection. Rockwall, TX.

Eldon "Buck" Buckner Collection. Baker City, OR.

Personal Correspondence. Jack O'Connor to Robert M. Anderson, 1970–1977.

Personal Correspondence. Jack O'Connor to Bob Housholder, executive director, Grand Slam Club, 1956–1977.

Record Books

Alberts, Robert C., ed. *North American Big Game.* Pittsburgh: Boone and Crockett Club, 1971.

Baker, Milford, ed. *Records of North American Big Game.* New York: Holt, Rhinehart and Winston, 1964.

Ely, Alfred, Harold E. Anthony, and R. R. M. Carpenter, eds. *North American Big Game.* New York: Scribners, 1939.

Webb, Samuel B., Grancel Fitz, and Milford Baker, eds. *Records of North American Big Game.* New York: Scribners, 1952.

Webb, Samuel B., Grancel Fitz, and Milford Baker, eds. *Records of North American Big Game.* New York: Henry Holt and Company, 1958.

Rowland Ward Publications. *Rowland Ward's African Records of Big Game,* XIX Edition. San Antonio: Game Conservation International, 1984.

Lewis, Nancy L., ed. *Arizona Wildlife Trophies.* Mesa: Arizona Wildlife Federation, 2000.

Periodicals

Outdoor Life (1934–1972, inclusive). Raymond J. Brown and William Rae, eds. New York: Popular Science Publishing Co. (Contains the entire body of O'Connor's work for *Outdoor Life,* including feature pieces, monthly columns, departmentals, "Getting the Range," and advice columns.)

Petersen's Hunting (1972–1978, inclusive). Ken Elliott, ed. Los Angeles: Petersen's Publishing Company.

"Grand Slam Club Newsletter," Nos. 1–74 (1967–1989). Bob Housholder, ed. Phoenix: Grand Slam Club.

General

Anderson, Robert M. *Great Rams and Great Ram Hunters.* Dallas: Collectors Covey, 1974.

————. *Wind, Dust, and Snow.* Dallas: Collectors Covey, 1998.

Babala, Jim. *The Arizona Desert King and I.* Whitehorse, Yukon: Jim Babala, 1989.

Batten, John H. *Skyline Pursuits.* Clinton: Amwell Press, 1981.

Biscotti, Matthew L. *The Borzoi Books for Sportsmen*. Madison, OH: Sunrise Publishing, 1992.

Casey, Clifford B. *Brewster County*. Seagraves, TX: Pioneer Book Publishers, Inc., 1974 (regarding O'Connor's time in Alpine, Texas).

Clark, James L. *The Great Arc of the Wild Sheep*. Norman: University of Oklahoma Press, 1964.

Garraty, John A. and Mark C. Carver, eds. *American National Biography*, Vol. 15. New York: Oxford University Press, 1999 (biographical material concerning H. L. Mencken).

Gresham, Grits and Tom Gresham. *Weatherby: The Man. The Gun. The Legend*. Natchitoches, LA: Cane River Publishing, 1992.

Housholder, Bob. *Hunting and Guiding for Desert Bighorn Sheep*. Phoenix: Bob Housholder, 1973.

Housholder, Bob, ed. *Grand Slam of North American Wild Sheep*. Phoenix: Imperial Lithographers, Inc. and Roswell Bookbinding, 1974.

Jamsheed, Rashid. *Memories of a Sheep Hunter*. Long Beach: Safari Press, Inc., 1996.

Keith, Elmer. *Hell! I Was There!* New York: Winchester Press, 1974.

Klein, Herbert W. *Lucky Bwana*. Dallas: Herbert K. Klein, 1953.

Neuweiler, Phillip L. *Big Game Trails in the Far North*. Anchorage: Great Northwest Publishing and Distributing Company, 1989.

Russell, Andy. *Horns in the High Country*. New York: Alfred A. Knopf, 1973.

Snyder, Harry M. *Snyder's Book of Big Game Hunting*. New York: Greenberg, 1950.

A Bibliographical Essay
on books by Jack O'Connor

by Henry van der Broecke

When I first promised Robert Anderson that I would create a thorough bibliography of Jack O'Connor's books, I thought that the project could be completed in one afternoon. After all, I had handled all of O'Connor's hardcover books at one time or another, so I was quite familiar with his titles. I have, furthermore, a sporting-book database that contains extensive notes and information I have gathered over the past ten years or so, and this database includes many O'Connor entries. How wrong I was. I quickly found myself immersed in a project that would take a lot longer than one afternoon.

I have attempted to compile all information as carefully as possible. Even so, when gathering the information for this essay, I found that my own sporting-book database contained numerous errors in regard to O'Connor books. While I corrected all the mistakes I found, I make no claims to being perfect, so it's likely that some errors will remain.

In presenting this list of books to you, I want to alert the reader to the "small print," as the lawyers say. First of all, I have only listed, with a few notable exceptions, first editions by O'Connor or books for which he was the coauthor. One exception is *Hunting in the South West,* and it is included because a number of people mistake it for an original title. *Game in the Desert Revisited* and *The Rifle Omnibus,* the two other exceptions, are included because they were issued as limited editions signed by O'Connor. Otherwise, I have confined myself to first editions.

The reason for this is that the volume of reprints and revised editions of North America's most prolific gunwriter is simply staggering. I am not saying it cannot be done, but to compile a complete bibliography of every edition and printing of all JOC's books would take almost a book by itself. With a total of nineteen hardcover books that were written solely by O'Connor, not counting the softcover pamphlets and the works to which O'Connor was a contributing author, there was enough to keep me working for many long hours.

Second, my bibliographical remarks are random. In some cases I comment on the contents of the book, in others on the artwork. I have included small items such as initial print runs and other interesting bits that I have collected over the years. I have not written a blow-by-blow account of what the content is of each book since I feel that most titles are fairly well known.

My third and last caveat concerns the O'Connor softcover booklets. For reasons that are obvious, very few of the early softcover booklets have survived. In fact I am fairly certain O'Connor wrote a booklet on how to choose binoculars and scopes, but neither Richard Beagle, who ably assisted me with this work, nor I could unearth any hard data on it. Since many of these booklets have not survived the test of time, I will make apologies right here and now for the incompleteness of this section. I have done my best, and I acknowledge up front that perhaps it is not good enough. Hail and farewell to those who take my initial feeble attempt and make it complete, or nearly so. As John "Pondoro" Taylor would say, "There you have it!"

Hardcover Publications

O'Connor, J. *Conquest: A Novel of the Old West*. New York: Harper & Brothers Publishers, 1930. 1st edn., 293pp.
   Binding—Brown cloth with yellow letters on spine and front cover.
   Bibliographical Notes—JOC's very first book, dedicated to Eleanor. The first edition has a brown cloth binding, a second printing has an orange cloth binding; it was also

reprinted by Grosset & Dunlap in 1930. All this would indicate that quite a few copies should be around. Nothing could be farther from the truth; this title is much harder to find than any of his hunting books. Although it is almost certain that at one time more copies of this book were in existence than the first edition of *Game in the Desert* by the Derrydale Press, the survival rate of *Conquest* was probably pretty low. A first edition in dust jacket is a rarity.

O'Connor, J. *Boom Town: A Novel of the Southwestern Silver Boom.* New York: Alfred A. Knopf, 1938. 1st edn., 331pp.
Binding—Green cloth with silver lettering and decorations on spine and front cover.
Bibliographical Notes—O'Connor's second book. A promotional passage from the later softcover edition reads ". . . the West to which men came to find gold and silver, and where merchants and ladies of low moral standards followed them to relieve them of their gains." One can almost imagine O'Connor penning these words to promote his book, and who knows, maybe he did. Appears to have gone through but one printing in hardcover. Later Dell Publishing Co. did a softcover. Again, a first edition in dust jacket is very rare, although less so than for *Conquest.*

O'Connor, J. *Game in the Desert.* New York: Derrydale Press, 1939. 1st edn., 298pp., illus., color frontis, limited edn. of 950 numbered copies.
Binding—Green simulated snakeskin cloth with gilt letters on spine and front cover.
Bibliographical Notes—Jack's hardest-to-obtain hunting book and most costly of all his books. Written when he was still relatively unknown on the big-game hunting scene. A superb account of the desert and Rocky Mountain bighorns, elk, mule deer, antelope, etc. Of all his books,

this is the best produced in terms of paper, layout, and binding. It was originally issued in a presentation box with a white label that had a number corresponding to the book written on it. These boxes are now very scarce indeed. It is illustrated with drawings by T. J. Harter. This book was reissued in a new format in 1945 as *Hunting in the South West*. In 1977 Amwell Press issued yet another somewhat revised edition of this book entitled *Game in the Desert Revisited*, which was limited to 950 copies and signed by O'Connor. Both revised editions have text virtually identical to the Derrydale Press edition. In the 1980s and 1990s both Amwell and Derrydale reprinted their respective editions of this book.

O'Connor, J. *Hunting in the South West.* New York: Alfred A. Knopf, 1945. 277pp., illus.
Binding—Red cloth with gilt letters on spine and a blind embossed "Borzoi Books" emblem on the front cover.
Bibliographical Notes—This book was printed only once by Alfred Knopf; it was in print from 1945 till 1951, by which time 3,604 copies had been sold. The original price was $4.00. It was simultaneously printed by the Ryerson Press in Canada. Knopf publicized this book as a revised and updated title, but in reality the text was virtually verbatim from *Game in the Desert*. Whereas the Derrydale edition had drawings of game by T. J. Harter, this edition replaced the artwork with photographs. Because of its title, it is often erroneously assumed that this book is not only a first edition but also completely different from *Game in the Desert*. This is not the case.

O'Connor, J. *Game in the Desert Revisited.* Clinton, NJ: Amwell Press, 1977. 306pp., drawings, ltd. edn. of 950, numbered, signed, slipcased copies.

Binding—Green cloth with gilt letters on spine and National Sporting Fraternity emblem on front cover.

Bibliographical Notes—Contains a new foreword by JOC. The drawings in this edition are by Rich Hauser, but otherwise this book's text is virtually identical to *Game in the Desert*. Entered here because this edition was signed by JOC and is, therefore, much sought after by collectors. Amwell issued several trade editions of this book also.

O'Connor, J. *Hunting in the Rockies*. New York: Alfred A. Knopf, 1947. 1st edn., 297pp., photos, maps.

Binding—Red cloth with gilt letters on spine and a blind embossed "Borzoi Books" emblem on the front cover.

Bibliographical Notes—This book was printed only once by Alfred Knopf, and a total of 3,346 copies were sold. It stayed in print from 1947 till 1957. The original price was $5.00. It was simultaneously printed by the Ryerson Press in Canada. Only one other printing of this book was done, in 1988 by Safari Press, and it contained a new photographic section.

O'Connor, J. *The Rifle Book*. New York: Alfred A. Knopf, 1949. 1st edn., 332pp., illus.

Binding—Gray cloth with brown letters on spine and a blind embossed "Borzoi Books" emblem on the front cover.

Bibliographical Notes—This book was remarkably more successful sales-wise than *South West* and *Rockies*. It was first published by Knopf in 1949 and retailed for $5.95. It was reprinted twice in 1950 and again in 1953. These first four printings sold 14,175 copies by the time the first edition went out of print in 1963. However, copies with "first edition" on the title page (presumably this means first printing) are quite scarce, indicating a small initial print run. Possibly the publisher underestimated the demand because of the modest successes of *South West* and *Rockies*, thus ordering a limited number of copies printed for the first printing. Subsequently, a second revised edition was published in 1964 and a third revised in 1979. The first edition was printed simultaneously by McClelland and Stewart, Ltd., in Canada.

O'Connor, J. *The Big-Game Rifle.* New York: Alfred A. Knopf, 1952. 1st edn., 370pp., illus.
   Binding—White cloth, green letters on spine and a blind embossed "Borzoi Books" emblem on the front cover.
   Bibliographical Notes—First published by Knopf in 1952 and at the same time by McClelland and Stewart, Ltd., in Canada. It sold for $7.50. It was in print from 1952 till 1961 but only saw one printing. A total of 3,607 copies were sold. A possible reason for this book being far less successful than *The Rifle Book* was that it dealt more with large-caliber rifles. Also the market may have perceived a duplication of content, although this is by and large not true. Reprinted in 1994 by Safari Press.

O'Connor, J. *Sportsman's Arms and Ammo Manual.* New York: Outdoor Life/Popular Science Publishing Co., Inc., 1952. 1st edn., 252pp., photos.
   Binding—Brown pebbled cloth with white letters on spine and cover; hunter aiming shotgun on front cover.
   Bibliographical Notes—All about the selection, care, and handling of sporting firearms and their accessories. A rather dull production that pales compared with all previous O'Connor books. It was reissued in the same year in softcover as *Outdoor Life Arms and Ammunition Annual*, to which it is identical except for the title and binding. It was also issued with dark green pebbled boards. Some 1952

books do not have "First edition" printed on the copyright page, so presumably this book was reprinted at least once.

O'Connor, J. *Complete Book of Rifles and Shotguns with a Seven-Lesson Rifle Shooting Course.* New York: Outdoor Life/Harper Brothers, 1961. 1st edn., 477pp., illus.
Binding—Dark gray cloth with silver and red letters on spine.
Bibliographical Notes—The first printing is marked as 1965 on the copyright page and has a price of $6.50 on the jacket. It is, quite likely, JOC's most popular book ever. I have not been able to substantiate hard figures on it, but I have heard it claimed several times and read once that this title sold over 100,000 copies. It was a main selection of the Outdoor Life Book Club and was widely popular. It went through numerous printings; one copy I saw stated "sixteenth printing," and there may have been more.

O'Connor, J. *The Big Game Animals of North America.* New York: Outdoor Life/E. P. Dutton & Co. Inc., 1961. 1st edn., 264pp., 20 color plates, drawings, folio.
Binding—White cloth with gilt and blue letters on spine and cover and a whitetail stamped in gilt on the front cover.
Bibliographical Notes—O'Connor's most eye-catching book in that it is illustrated with large color drawings. Physically it is large to the extent of being almost unwieldy. It covers all North American big-game species. Entirely illustrated by images in black and white and color by Douglas Allen. O'Connor stated in *The Last Book* that he was unhappy with the artistic rendition of the desert bighorn. The first edition apparently went through only one printing. In 1977 a smaller, revised and updated edition was produced, and it had a new desert sheep painting!

O'Connor, J. *Jack O'Connor's Big Game Hunts*. New York: E.P. Dutton & Co./Outdoor Life, 1963. 1st edn., 415pp., illus.
Binding—Green/blue cloth with gilt letters on spine.
Bibliographical Notes—Many people feel this is JOC's best adventure book to read. It certainly contains O'Connor's best writings. Curiously, this book appears to have gone to only one printing. It contains JOC's hunting adventures from Africa to Mexico and tells well-crafted stories about deer, lion, buffalo, and sheep alike. This book was translated into Spanish as *Caza Mayor por Jack O'Connor*.

O'Connor, J. *The Shotgun Book*. New York: Alfred A. Knopf, 1965. 1st edn., 332pp., illus.
Binding—Red cloth with gilt letters on spine and a blind-stamped "Borzoi Books" emblem on the front cover.
Bibliographical Notes—This is the first and only book O'Connor did exclusively about shotguns. Like so many of his other books, it was published by Alfred Knopf. Primarily known as a rifle man, O'Connor was very knowledgeable on shotguns and quite a good shot as well. All first editions state "First Edition" on the copyright page. The book was revised in 1978, and both editions went through numerous printings.

O'Connor, J. *The Art of Hunting Big Game in North America*. New York: Alfred A. Knopf, 1967. 1st edn., 404pp., illus., maps.
Binding—Light tan cloth with green and black letters on the spine and a blind-stamped sheep on the cover.
Bibliographical Notes—A popular title that appealed to a diverse segment of hunters and contained information on how to hunt anything from a white-tailed deer to an Alaskan brown bear. The drawings showing the difference among small, average, and great trophies of the various North American game animals add great value to this

book. The first edition lists Alfred A. Knopf as the publisher on the title page and the spine. An identical second printing, issued in 1967 also, indicates only Outdoor Life as the publisher. In 1971 a smaller issue was printed in what appears to be Taiwan and may very well have been a bootleg edition. In 1977 a slightly revised edition was published.

O'Connor, J. *Horse and Buggy West: A Boyhood on the Last Frontier.* New York: Alfred A. Knopf, 1969. 1st edn., 302pp., illus.
Binding—Green cloth with gilt and red letters on spine and a red desert landscape on the front cover.
Bibliographical Notes—Gives a great deal of insight into how Jack grew up in the Southwest from very humble beginnings. Contains some of the finest non-hunting text he ever wrote. The original issue price was $5.95. Strangely enough, the title page of the first edition of this book states "1969" while the copyright page states "First Edition" and "1968." Probably the book was scheduled for release in 1968, and, when it appeared in 1969, this was updated on the title page and not the copyright page. As best as I know, it went through two printings and is now rather scarce.

O'Connor, J. *The Hunting Rifle.* New York: Winchester Press, 1970. 1st edn., 314pp., illus.
Binding—Brown cloth binding, gilt letters on spine, blind-stamped Winchester model 70 on front cover.
Bibliographical Notes—Essentially an update of the previous rifle books Jack had published in the 1940s and 1950s. Quite interesting to read, especially since he refers to his rival Elmer Keith repeatedly (without mentioning his name) and takes issue with Keith's caliber recommendations for big game. The first edition, first printing, retail price on the jacket states $8.95, and it has a

brown cloth binding. Later printings have paper boards with a cloth spine rather than a complete cloth binding.

O'Connor, J. *Sheep and Sheep Hunting*. New York: Winchester Press, 1974. 1st edn., 308pp., illus, photo endpapers. **Binding**—Blue cloth with gilt lettering on spine. **Bibliographical Notes**—Generally regarded as JOC's magnum opus, and well it should be. No modern book has ever covered North American wild sheep as thoroughly as this book, and it still remains the standard-bearer today—after more than 25 years since the first edition saw the light of day. It went through numerous printings and could still be bought in the late 1990s.

O'Connor, J. *The Best of Jack O'Connor*. Clinton, NJ: Amwell Press, 1977. 1st edn., 192pp., photos, limited to 1,000 slipcased copies signed by the author. **Binding**—Red cloth with gilt letters and decorations on spine; National Sporting Fraternity emblem on front cover. **Bibliographical Notes**—Accumulation of magazine stories written by O'Connor during his years at *Outdoor Life*. This was one of the earliest books published by Amwell Press, which was headed by O'Connor's friend James Rikhoff who had left Winchester Press to start his own publishing company. It contains some delightful JOC stories such as "Letters to Jim Hack" and "How K. R. Balz Won the Krautbauer Trophy." It also has a reprint of the last column he wrote for *Outdoor Life* entitled "Hail and Farewell." The first edition was limited to 1,000 copies signed by JOC. Now quite scarce. Amwell has reprinted this title off and on since 1977.

O'Connor, J. *The Last Book*: *Confessions of an Outdoor Writer*. Clinton, NJ: Amwell Press, 1984. 1st edn., 247pp., illus., limited edition of 1,000 slipcased copies signed by Bradford O'Connor.

Binding—Red cloth with gilt letters and decorations on spine; National Sporting Fraternity emblem on front cover.

Bibliographical Notes—Published posthumously, for some strange reason years after JOC died. Together with *Horse and Buggy West*, it gives the best biographical insight into the man who was Jack O'Connor. This is the last book JOC wrote and intended to be a book.

O'Connor, J. *Hunting on Three Continents with Jack O'Connor.* Long Beach: Safari Press Inc., 1987. 1st edn., 303pp., photos, ltd. to 500 numbered copies, signed by Bradford O'Connor.

Binding—Light blue cloth with gilt letters on spine.

Bibliographical Notes—After retiring from *Outdoor Life*, JOC reemerged in a magazine during the years 1973 to 1977 when he wrote for *Petersen's Hunting* magazine. The best material from these stories was made into a book. It contains an interesting sketch on Walter Bell, the elephant hunter; JOC's views on the .375; and hunting stories in North America and Africa. Surprisingly scarce to find in first edition and quite costly. Subsequently reprinted once by Safari Press, also in 1987.

Softcover Publications

O'Connor, J. *Sporting Guns*: *How to Choose and How to Use Them.* New York: Franklin Watts Inc., 1947. 94pp., photos.

Binding—Softcover.

Bibliographical Notes—A rather obscure booklet that was intended to do exactly what the title says: help the hunter and shooter select and use a rifle. Divided into 15 sections that deal with different rifles and shotguns as well as handguns.

O'Connor, J., *Outdoor Life Shooting Book*. New York: Outdoor Life/Popular Science Publishing Co., Inc., 1957. 1st edn., 1st printing, 80pp., illus.
Binding—Softcover.
Bibliographical Notes—A large-format softcover that features JOC on the front cover pointing a target rifle. It contains hints on how to shoot your rifle, shotgun, and handgun. Information is intended mostly for hunters. Contains two chapters on the ubiquitous .30-06 and the .270. This title was completely revised and issued in a smaller format in 1978 as *The Hunter's Shooting Guide*.

O'Connor, J. *How to Buy a Rifle*. Handbook No. 1. New York: Outdoor Life, 1960 (circa, not dated). 13pp.
Binding—Softcover.
Bibliographical Notes—Another obscure O'Connor publication. Since it has a serrated edge on the outside cover, it seems likely it was bound in another publication. Quite possibly it was bound into and distributed with an issue *of Outdoor Life* magazine.

Coauthored by O'Connor

O'Connor, J., et al. *Complete Book of Shooting*. New York: Outdoor Life/Harper & Row, 1965. 1st edn., 385pp., illus.
Binding—Light gray cloth with green and black letters on spine.
Bibliographical Notes—Title page of this book states: "*Complete Book of Shooting* by Jack O'Connor with Roy Dunlap, Alex Kerr, Jeff Cooper." JOC is clearly indicated as the main author. It was first issued in 1965 and went through several printings and was later revised. First editions

state "copyright 1965 by Outdoor Life" on the copyright page and were published by Outdoor Life/Harper Row.

O'Connor, J., et al. *Outdoor Life's Deer Hunting Book.* New York: Outdoor Life/Harper Row, 1974. 1st edn., 275pp., line drawings and photos.
Binding—Brown cloth, gilt letters on spine, blind-stamped deer on front cover.
Bibliographical Notes—There are seventeen total contributors, including Archibald Rutledge, Charles Elliott, Ben East, Erwin A. Bauer, Clyde Ormond, and others. Went through several printings and editions. Contains 30 illustrated chapters that cover every aspect of deer hunting. The chapter "Deer and Deer Rifles" was written by Jack O'Connor.

O'Connor, J., et al. *The Rifle Omnibus.* Highbridge, NJ: Amwell Press, 1976. 342pp., 314pp., & 238pp., many illus., limited to 750 numbered, slipcased copies, signed by all three authors.
Binding—Red cloth with slipcase.
Bibliographical Notes—In the 1970s, newly formed Amwell Press reprinted three previously published books and them in one cover. The books are *The Hunting Rifle* by O'Connor, *The Accurate Rifle* by Warren Page, and *The Modern Rifle* by Jim Carmichel. This is now quite scarce. The exact date Amwell Press issued this book is unclear. All three individual books retain their copyright pages in this volume, and all three show different dates! However, the foreword is dated 4 July 1976, so it seems likely that it was issued in 1976 or possibly in 1977. The book went through only one printing of about 750 copies.